W9-AFR-951

Inventing
the People

BY EDMUND S. MORGAN

The Puritan Family: Religion and Domestic Relations in
Seventeenth-Century New England

Virginians at Home; Family Life in the Eighteenth Century

The Stamp Act Crisis: Prologue to Revolution *(with Helen M. Morgan)*

The Birth of the Republic

The Puritan Dilemma: The Story of John Winthrop

The Gentle Puritan: A Life of Ezra Stiles

Visible Saints: The History of a Puritan Idea

Roger Williams: The Church and the State

So What about History?

American Slavery—American Freedom: The Ordeal of Colonial Virginia

The Genius of George Washington

The Challenge of the American Revolution

The Meaning of Independence: John Adams, George Washington,
and Thomas Jefferson

EDITED WORKS

Prologue to Revolution: Sources and Documents on the Stamp Act Crisis

The Diary of Michael Wigglesworth: The Conscience of a Puritan

The Founding of Massachusetts: Historians and the Sources

The American Revolution: Two Centuries of Interpretation

EDMUND S. MORGAN

Inventing the People

The Rise of Popular Sovereignty in England and America

———◆———

W · W · NORTON & COMPANY

NEW YORK · LONDON

Copyright © 1988 by Edmund S. Morgan. *All rights reserved.* Published simultaneously in Canada by Penguin Books Canada Ltd., 2801 John Street, Markham, Ontario L3R 1B4. Printed in the United States of America.

FIRST EDITION

The text of this book is composed in Janson, with display type set in Garamond Oldstyle. Composition and manufacturing by the Maple-Vail Book Manufacturing Group. Book design by Marjorie J. Flock.

Library of Congress Cataloging-in-Publication Data

Morgan, Edmund Sears.
  Inventing the people.

  Includes index.
  1. Representative government and representation—
Great Britain—History.   2. Representative government
and representation—United States—History.
3. Sovereignty—History.   I. Title.
JF1059.G7M67   1988   320.2'0973   87–23986

ISBN 0-393-02505-5

W. W. Norton & Company, Inc., 500 Fifth Avenue, New York, N. Y. 10110
W. W. Norton & Company Ltd., 37 Great Russell Street, London WC1B 3NU

1 2 3 4 5 6 7 8 9 0

For Marie

Contents

Acknowledgments

T

HIS BOOK has been long in the making. Parts of it in earlier versions were presented and discussed at Cornell University (as the Carl Becker Lectures), at the Lionel Trilling Seminar of Columbia University, and at the Davis Center of Princeton University. I have tried to profit from the discussions on those occasions and also from readings by friends better informed than I. Linda Colley read the entire manuscript in a late draft and saved me from numerous blunders. And a number of scholars gave me good advice, not always heeded, about the first chapter: Paul Christianson, Jack Hexter, the late Joel Hurstfield, Barbara Malament, Conrad Russell, Lawrence Stone, and David Underdown. Probably no one of them would agree with the interpretation offered in it. Marie Caskey Morgan and James L. Mairs also read the entire manuscript and helped me to give it whatever clarity it possesses. Avery Hudson has been the kind of copy editor that every author hopes for. Finally I wish to thank the many librarians who have smoothed my way at the British Library, the Bodleian, the Virginia Historical Society and especially the Yale University Library and the Henry E. Huntington Library.

Parts of the second chapter were published in the *Yale Review* for April 1983 and are here reprinted with permission.

PART ONE

Origins

—◆—

NOTHING IS MORE SURPRISING *to those, who consider human affairs with a philosophical eye, than to see the easiness with which the many are governed by the few; and to observe the implicite submission with which men resign their own sentiments and passions to those of their rulers. When we enquire by what means this wonder is brought about, we shall find, that as Force is always on the side of the governed, the governors have nothing to support them but opinion. 'Tis therefore, on opinion only that government is founded; and this maxim extends to the most despotic and most military governments, as well as to the most free and most popular.*

David Hume, "Of the First Principles of Government," *Essays and Treatises on Several Subjects,* 1758 edition

WE MAY PERHAPS QUESTION today whether force is *always* on the side of the governed or even whether it always has been, but by and large Hume's observation commands assent. Put it another way, all government rests on the consent, however obtained, of the governed. And over the long run mere force, even if entirely at the disposal of the governing few, is not a sufficient basis for inducing consent. Human beings, if only to maintain a semblance of self-respect, have to be persuaded. Their consent must be sustained by opinions.

The few who govern take care to nourish those opinions. No easy task, for the opinions needed to make the many submit to the few are often at variance with observable fact. The success of government thus requires the acceptance of fictions, requires the willing suspension of disbelief, requires us to believe that the emperor is clothed even though we can see that he is not. And, to reorder Hume's dictum, the maxim extends to the most free and most popular governments as well as to the most despotic and most military. The popular governments of Britain and the United States rest on fictions as much as the governments of Russia and China.

Government requires make-believe. Make believe that the king is divine, make believe that he can do no wrong or make believe that the voice of the people is the voice of God. Make believe that the people *have* a voice or make believe that the representatives of the people *are* the people. Make believe that governors are the servants of the people. Make believe that all men are equal or make believe that they are not.

The political world of make-believe mingles with the real world in strange ways, for the make-believe world may often mold the real one. In order to be viable, in order to serve its purpose, whatever that purpose may be, a fiction must bear some resemblance to fact. If it strays too far from fact, the willing suspension of disbelief collapses. And conversely it may collapse if facts stray too far from the fiction that we want them to resemble. Because fictions are necessary, because we cannot live without them, we often take pains to prevent their collapse by moving the facts to fit the fiction, by making our world conform more closely to what we want it to be. We sometimes call it, quite appropriately, reform or reformation, when the fiction takes command and reshapes reality.

Although fictions enable the few to govern the many, it is not only the many who are constrained by them. In the strange commingling of political make-believe and reality the governing few no less than the governed many may find themselves limited—we may even say reformed—by the fictions on which their authority depends. Not only authority but liberty too may depend on fictions. Indeed liberty may depend, however deviously, on the very fictions that support authority. That, at least, has been the case in the Anglo-American world; and modern liberty, for better or for worse, was born, or perhaps we should say invented, in that world and continues to be nourished there.

Because it is a little uncomfortable to acknowledge that we rely so heavily on fictions, we generally call them by some more exalted name. We may proclaim them as self-evident truths, and that designation is not inappropriate, for it implies our commitment to them and at the same time protects them from challenge. Among the fictions we accept today as self-evident are those that Thomas Jefferson enshrined in the Declaration of Independence, that all men are created equal and that they owe obedience to government only if it is their own agent, deriving its authority from their consent. It would be difficult, if not impossible, to demonstrate these propositions by factual evidence. It might be somewhat easier, by the kind of evidence we usually require for the proof of any debatable proposition, to demonstrate that men are not created equal and that they have not delegated authority to any government. But self-evident propositions are not debatable, and to challenge these would rend the fabric of our society.

It is not the purpose of this book to challenge them, and my use of the word fiction has no such intention. I have been troubled by the pejorative connotations attached to the word, but I have been unable to find a better one to describe the different phenomena to which I have applied it. I can only hope that readers who persevere to the end of the book will recognize that the fictional qualities of popular sovereignty sustain rather than threaten the human values associated with it. I hope they will also recognize that I do not imply deception or delusion on the part of those who employed or subscribed to the fictions examined here, fictions in which they *willingly* suspended disbelief. My purpose is not to debunk, but to explore the wonder that Hume points to, the fact that most of us submit willingly to be governed by a few of us. The opinions to which Hume attributes this wonder are doubtless of many kinds, but I am concerned with those that seem to defy demonstration. I prefer to call them fictions rather than self-evident truths, because what we accept as self-evident today did not seem so three or four centuries ago.

At the time when England's American colonies were founded, the fictions that sustained government—and liberty—were almost the reverse of those we accept today. Englishmen of the sixteenth and early seventeenth century affirmed that men were created unequal and that they owed obedience to government because the Creator had endowed their king with his own sacred authority. These propositions too were fictional, requiring suspension of disbelief, defying demonstration as much as those that took their place. How then did the one give way to the other? How did the divine right of kings give way to the sovereignty of the people? And how did the new fictions both sustain government by the few and restrain the few for the benefit of the many? In other words, how did the exercise and authentication of power in the Anglo-American world as we know it come into being? These are the questions for which I have sought answers.

The search begins with the old fiction, the divine right of kings. Since we have long since given up suspending our disbelief in this one, we should have no difficulty in perceiving its fictional qualities. It enjoyed, nevertheless, a longer duration than the sovereignty of the people has yet attained. In examining its operation in the years just before its collapse, we may gain some initial insights into the way political fictions can both sustain and limit the authority of government.

CHAPTER *1*

The Divine Right of Kings

MONARCHY has always required close ties with divinity, and, in the Western world at least, politics have mingled promiscuously with theology. If Christian and Jewish theology created for us an anthropomorphic deity, Christian politics, and English politics not least, created a theomorphic king. At some times, as Ernst Kantorowicz has shown, kings were conceived in the figure of Christ the son, at others in the figure of God the father. And in England the legal fictions that accompanied the everyday workings of the king's government endowed him with all the attributes of divinity. He was, for example, immortal: it could not be admitted that the king ever died. And like God he was perfect: he could do no wrong, so no action at law could ever lie against him. Indeed, like God he was the giver of laws, but also like God he acted according to the laws he gave. Like God he was omnipresent, for in himself he constituted the "body politic" over which he ruled. But like the son whom God sent to redeem mankind, he was man as well as God; he had a "body natural" as well as his body politic, and the two were inseparable like the persons of the Trinity.[1]

The ratiocination necessary to sustain these absurdities was as complex as that required to explain the existence of evil in a world created by a beneficent and omnipotent God. Sustained they were, at first to justify the authority of one man rather than another, a king

[1] Ernst H. Kantorowicz, *The King's Two Bodies: A Study in Mediaeval Political Theology* (Princeton, N.J., 1957).

rather than an emperor, an emperor or a king rather than a pope, and to reconcile the many to the government of that man. But finally and perhaps less obviously, the fiction was sustained in England as an instrument that gave to the many a measure of control over the man to whom the fiction seemed to subject them so absolutely.

In England in the first half of the seventeenth century the doctrine of the divine right of kings, as expounded by James I and acted out by his son Charles I, reached a culmination. At that time, when England's first American colonies were settling, the Counter-Reformation was in full swing, and the divine right of kings had become a necessary fiction in Protestant countries. The pope claimed to be the vicar of God on earth, with sole powers to legitimate secular authority, either directly or by controlling the allegiance of subjects. And the pope was not in the habit of legitimating the authority of Protestant kings. The way to fight divinity was with divinity. And James I, who ruled England from 1603 to 1625, had sallied forth as the champion of Protestantism by demonstrating, to the satisfaction of Englishmen at least, that God had no truck with the pope (who was no other than Antichrist). God conferred authority with his own hand on rightful rulers, including James I, especially James I. Anyone, including the pope, especially the pope, who challenged the authority of a true king was challenging God himself.[2]

Englishmen applauded their God-given monarch and made an extravagant hostility to Rome the test not only of true religion but of patriotism. The divine right of the king became a declaration of independence, the basis for England's freedom from a foreign potentate. And to paraphrase a famous dictum of the historian Carl Becker in another context, if the king's divinity was so vital to home rule, it could scarcely be ignored at home. James had no intention that it should be. In defending his title against the pope he took pains to inform his subjects of the awesome authority that God's commission gave him over them. Since he was God's lieutenant, he could do no wrong, and within his realm his righteousness and the authority that went with it were not to be questioned.[3] He might seek advice and

[2]C. H. McIlwain, ed., *The Political Works of James I* (Cambridge, Mass., 1918), esp. xv–xciv; J. N. Figgis, *The Divine Right of Kings*, 2nd ed. (Cambridge, England, 1914; New York, 1965), esp. 66–106, 137–76.

[3]The doctrine that the king could do no wrong had already become an accepted and essential legal fiction, serving technical legal as well as political functions, by the sixteenth century. W. S. Holdsworth, *A History of English Law*, 7th ed. (London 1956), III, 465–66.

information from his subjects in Parliament, but his was the God-given authority.

James never missed an opportunity to lecture his Parliaments on this topic, and the Commons generally took the lectures in good part. Indeed they often echoed his claims so eagerly as to make us already a little suspicious of what they were up to. At the opening of a session the Speaker would repeat the platitude "that kings were visible gods and God an invisible king."[4] When the king rebuked the Commons for anything, they would respond with seemingly abashed reverence: "because the King is a God upon earth I would answer him as we should answer God in heaven, that is with a prayer."[5] John Pym (who for his later political behavior was tagged "king" himself), when proposing a measure in the 1620s, went a step beyond the usual attributions of omnipotence and righteousness and endowed the king with omniscience: "though I know we can propound nothing to his Majesty but that which he already knows, yet it is good sometimes to shew a man's own thought to himself."[6] Even when Charles I dissolved Parliament in 1629 (not to call another until 1640) because the Commons were insisting on rights that he did not recognize, they responded that they "professed in all things to obey him as the highest under God."[7]

Since the king was God's lieutenant it followed that he was supreme among men, or at least among Englishmen. The government was his government, the people, including the members of Parliament, were his subjects. The members of the House of Lords, though they sat in their own right, were subjects; and the Commons, who represented the rest of the people, were subjects, both individually and as representatives. As subjects they did not share in the king's authority. But subjects did have rights, and English subjects had more rights than the subjects of other kings. It was over these rights that king and Commons sometimes contended, the king insisting that rights were favors granted by him or his predecessors (and thus conceivably revocable), the Commons contending, in effect, that rights were simply right, insured by laws which might derive their authority from

[4] Wallace Notestein, Frances H. Relf, and Hartley Simpson, eds., *Commons Debates 1621* (New Haven, Conn., 1935), II, 15.

[5] Elizabeth R. Foster, ed., *Proceedings in Parliament 1610* (New Haven, Conn., 1966), II, 89.

[6] *Commons Debates 1621*, II, 464.

[7] Wallace Notestein and Frances H. Relf, eds., *Commons Debates for 1629*. Research Publication of the University of Minnesota. Studies in the Social Sciences, No. 10 (Minneapolis, 1921), 253.

God's lieutenant but which nevertheless bound him because they were right, because they embodied his godly will, even if he might momentarily think otherwise.

The contests between king and Commons in the first three decades of the seventeenth century were formerly the centerpiece in historical accounts of that period. More recent investigations have shown that the contests were not quite what they seemed to be. Many of them were reflections of divisions in the king's own court or within the ranks of local oligarchies, not expressions of opposition to the king. The leaders in the Commons' disputes, it turns out, were often clients of noble lords. And the House of Commons as an institutional force in government with a mind and will of its own now appears considerably diminished. We have been shown that it did not use the power of the purse effectively. We have been shown that its winning of the initiative in legislation meant little because during these decades no significant legislation passed.[8]

Yet when all is said and done, genuine contests between king and Commons do figure largely in the records of debates, and they evince a strong institutional consciousness among the members that their House stood apart from the king and his court. The House may have been, as in the sixteenth century, an agency employed by the king in governing his people, but it was also, and not merely nominally, an agency of the people he governed. Representatives, as we shall try to show in the next chapter, have always been both governed and governing, and while acting as a branch of government they neither could, nor did they try to, shake off their character as subjects. As subjects, they were obliged to regard government as something other, something

[8] A classic statement of the older view was Wallace Notestein, *The Winning of the Initiative by the House of Commons* (London, 1924). The most comprehensive—and most compelling—statement of the new views is Conrad Russell, *Parliaments and English Politics 1621–1629* (Oxford, 1979). Earlier adumbrations may be found in Conrad Russell, "Parliamentary History in Perspective, 1604–1629," *History* 61 (1976), 1–27; Geoffrey Elton, "Studying the History of Parliament," "The Stuart Century," and "A High Road to Civil War?" *Studies in Tudor and Stuart Politics and Government* (Cambridge, England, 1974), II, 3–18, 155–82; A. M. Everitt, *The Community of Kent and the Great Rebellion, 1640–60* (Leicester, England, 1966); J. S. Morrill, *The Revolt of the Provinces* (London, 1976); Kevin Sharpe, ed., *Faction and Parliament* (Oxford, 1978); Paul Christianson, "The Causes of the English Revolution: a Reappraisal," *Journal of British Studies* 15 (1976), 40–75; and the articles by Christianson, Clayton Roberts, Mark Kishlansky and James E. Farnell in *Journal of Modern History* 49 (1977), 575–660. Compare the powerful responses by J. H. Hexter and Derek Hirst in ibid., vol. 50 (1978), 1–71, and by Hirst, Theodore Rabb, and Christopher Hill in *Past and Present*, no. 92 (1981), 55–124.

with which it was possible, however respectfully, to disagree and contend. Whatever external divisions may be reflected in their contests, those outsiders, including courtiers and noble lords, who extended their disputes into this arena, had to accept the rules of the game; to seek support in the Commons was to seek support from representatives of the governed and to seek it because they were representatives of the governed. There is still, I think, something to be learned about the government of the many by the few, from those contests, from the way the House of Commons exalted the king and diminished his subjects in the very act of contending for the rights of subjects within a government which they formed a part of and yet stood apart from.

The rules of the game, if we may call it that, were simple: the first was that God's lieutenant could do no wrong; the second was that everyone else (including everyone who sat in Parliament), was a mere subject. Acknowledged subjection to a faultless authority would seem to leave little room for political maneuvering. But divinity, when assumed by mortals (or imposed upon them) can prove more constricting than subjection. Indeed, the attribution of divinity to the king had probably always been motivated in some measure by the desire to limit him to actions becoming a god. In the 1620s the Commons exalted him to a height where he could scarcely move without fracturing his divinity, and out of subjection to him they fashioned maneuvers to direct his government.

Before looking more closely at the way they did it, we should remind ourselves that both were acting out a fiction, that neither king nor Commons was what each pretended to be. It is obvious enough that the first two Stuart kings fell somewhat short of the character they attributed to themselves. James I, who made the most extravagant claims to divinity, was about as ungodlike a man as anyone could hope to find; and his son Charles I, who succeeded to the throne in 1625 and who created a fine facade of majesty, turned out to be a habitual liar. He eventually got himself beheaded because he simply could not be trusted to keep any agreement he made. There is no need to belabor either the human depravity of these two or their extravagant pretensions to authority. That the fiction of divine right should have reached a high point in the reigns of two such improbable monarchs is perhaps a measure of the need that Englishmen felt for it in a world under the shadow of the Counter-Reformation.

But if neither James nor Charles looked or acted much like a god, neither did the Commons look or act much like mere subjects, despite their ritual repetition of the claim to be no more than that. They were in fact the top echelon of an order of men who ranked just short of the peerage, namely the gentry, whom the Tudor kings and queens of the sixteenth century had used to give the monarchy power and authority throughout the country. Many of those who sat in the Commons were younger sons or relatives of peers or elder sons who had not yet succeeded to the title. We need not consider whether the gentry in general were rising or falling economically, a matter about which historians disagree. What seems indisputable is that they were rising or had risen politically. The growth of royal power in England at the local level had come in large part by extending the numbers and functions of royally appointed justices of the peace in every county at the expense of local institutions. The royal appointees were all gentlemen, often the same gentlemen who sat in the House of Commons. At Westminster they might proclaim their subjection to the best of kings; at home they proclaimed the subjection of everyone else and wielded the king's authority as their own.

But the justices were not bureaucrats. They were amateurs, gentlemen who lent their own weight in their communities to support the law and order on which their prosperity and the king's authority depended. To be sure, not all gentlemen were justices and not all justices were members of Parliament; but all justices were gentlemen, and a large proportion of the House of Commons were or had been justices. During the preceding two centuries, with the assistance (often at the behest) of their noble connections, the gentry had pretty much taken over the House of Commons, nudging out local burghers from the borough seats. England's monarchs had smiled on the process, expanding the number of seats in the Commons, just as they expanded the number of justices in every county, so as to enlist the support of the gentry for drastic reforms in the religious and political organization of the whole nation. But political support can never be bought for nothing. The men exalted as justices in the king's county courts looked still less like mere subjects when summoned to Westminster to assist in making the laws they enforced. While the king proclaimed himself as the source of all law and the giver of all good things, he knew and the Commons knew (and knew that he knew) that they and their kind were an essential part of his government, that without them, short of the development of a huge new royal bureaucracy, the government could not operate. If government is the rule of the few over the many, the members of the House of Commons, whether at home or at Westminster, must be numbered among the few.[9]

It would be wrong, then, to accept at face value the identification of the Commons with the subject. But it would be equally wrong to dismiss it as meaningless. The members of the House of Commons did not sit there in their own right, as the members of the House of Lords did. The Commons were representatives, or as they more often expressed it "representers." They claimed indeed to represent all other subjects. The full implications of that claim must be reserved for succeeding chapters. Here it must suffice to notice the restraints that representation imposed on the Commons.

Representation is itself a fiction, and like other fictions it could restrict the actions of those who espoused it. Because they claimed to represent all subjects, the gentlemen who sat at Westminster had to act not merely for their own kind but for everyone else. If they gave money to the king, they gave for everyone, and by the same token if they contended for the rights of subjects, they were under some constraint to contend for all subjects. They need not have done so out of altruism. The people of England did not all enjoy the same rights, in or out of Parliament. Gentlemen had rights that did not belong to ordinary men. Early in his reign King James had urged the Commons to make laws that hunting "be used by none but gentlemen, and that in a gentlemen-like fashion. For it is not fit that clowns should have these sports."[10] And the Commons, gentlemen all, had responded with strict penalties to protect pheasants from peasants. But when it came to freedom from arrest, when it came to security of property, when it came to trial by jury, the Commons did not think these too good for clowns. They were doubtless more worried about protecting their own property then they were about that of lesser men, but when they spoke of the rights of subjects, they did not say, nor did they mean, the rights of gentlemen or even the rights merely of property-holders.

[9] On the political role of the gentry as justices of the peace and members of the House of Commons, see in general J. E. Neale, *The Elizabethan House of Commons* (London, 1949); May McKisack, *The Parliamentary Representation of the English Boroughs during the Middle Ages* (Oxford, 1932); Kenneth Pickthorn, *Early Tudor Government: Henry VII* (Cambridge, England, 1934), 51–88; Holdsworth, *History of English Law*, I, 285–98; and Geoffrey Elton, "The Body of the Whole Realm: Parliament and Representation in Mediaeval and Tudor England," in *Studies in Tudor and Stuart Politics and Government*, II, 19–61.

[10] *Proceedings in Parliament 1610*, I, 51.

As representatives of subjects, they made the most of their position, recognizing perhaps that there was a certain majesty in humanity itself that could be placed in the scales against the divinity of the king.

That they claimed to be subjects, mere men, dealing with God's lieutenant spurred the Commons, as it may even have spurred the barons in 1215, to state their rights in universal terms. When they confronted King John at Runnymede, we have been told, the barons were actually claiming rights only for barons, but that is not what they said. In their Magna Carta they made the king, already in the process of deification, promise that he would not do various unpleasant things to any free man. Similarly the seventeenth-century Commons, in their remonstrances and protestations and petitions, and particularly the Petition of Right of 1628, affirmed the rights of all the king's subjects, not to be taxed or confined without "common consent by act of parliament" and "due process of law."[11] To have limited their claim would have been to weaken it: the king was God's lieutenant, and God was said to be no respecter of persons. The Bible, which the members were fond of quoting, did not have much to say about the rights of gentlemen.

The Commons' assertions of universal rights were thus in a manner dictated by the premises from which they started. The fiction of their own status as representatives and the fiction of the king's status as God's lieutenant required them to speak in universals if they were to speak at all. Even when claiming a privilege exclusive to Parliament, like freedom from arrest during sessions, the Commons were careful to affirm it as essential to the rights of all subjects. "The heart-blood of the Commonwealth," said Sir John Eliot, "receiveth life from the privilege of this House."[12] "The freedom of this House," said Sir Edward Coke, "is the freedom of the whole land."[13] To have said less would have been to reduce their eloquence to impertinence.

The members may not quite have intended themselves to be taken literally, any more than the barons in 1215, or any more than the American Continental Congress would in 1776 when proclaiming all men to be created equal. Nevertheless, if we may judge from what they said in debates among themselves, and what they said in their

---

[11] R. C. Johnson, M. F. Keeler, M. J. Cole, and W. B. Bidwell, eds., *Commons Debates 1628* (New Haven, Conn., 1977–78), III, 339–41.

[12] *Commons Debates for 1629*, 85.

[13] *Commons Debates 1621*, II, 56.

Petition of Right in 1628, the Commons accepted the implications of their position. They considered themselves the representatives not merely of their own class nor even of the qualified voters, but of the rest of the population too. Their insistence that they were mere subjects, however unrealistic, resulted in a definition of rights that extended to all Englishmen. The Commons not only phrased the Petition of Right in absolute terms and fought off every move to soften those terms, but they obliged the king to accept it in a manner that eventually put it on the statute books, along with Magna Carta, where all men could lay claim to its benefits.[14]

It is, perhaps, not surprising that the Commons, in acting out their chosen role, should have felt obliged to insist on rights for all subjects. What is more remarkable is that they were able to turn the subjection of subjects and the exaltation of the king into a means of limiting his authority. By placing the king's rectitude, wisdom, and authority on the plane of divinity the Commons denied the possibility of any other mortal sharing in these royal attributes: in particular they denied the possibility of the king's transferring them to any subject. Divine authority must be inalienable authority, and the Commons made themselves the guardians of it against any subject who might arrogate a part of it. Those who did things in the king's name did so at their own peril, for it would be a kind of lèse majesté to take action on his behalf that he might not approve. Nothing could be more presumptuous than to do wrong in the name of him who could do no wrong.

This is not to say that the king could not delegate authority to enforce his laws. Thomas Egerton, who was to become the king's lord chancellor and who was already a champion of the royal prerogative, explained in 1604 that the king could be present in his law courts through his judges, because the judges as well as those they judged had the laws to inform them of the king's "known will." What the king could not transfer was his "participation with God," which endowed him with an absolute power "onelie proper to himselfe, and

---

[14] The manner of presenting the Petition of Right and of the king's response to it were subjects of intense discussion in the Commons. The consensus seems to have been against presenting the petition as a bill but insisting on the king's answering it in Parliament, in such a way that the courts would be obliged to honor it. *Commons Debates 1628*, III, 627–34; IV, 1–186 *passim*, esp. 181–86. See also Elizabeth R. Foster, "Petitions and the Petition of Right," *Journal of British Studies* 14 (1974), 21–45; J. A. Guy, "The Origin of the Petition of Right Reconsidered," *The Historical Journal* 25 (1982), 289–312; and Michael B. Young, "The Origins of the Petition of Right Reconsidered Further," ibid., vol. 27 (1984), 449–52.

his place and person." It was impossible for him to "infuse" into others "the wisdome, power, and guifts which God in respect of his place and Charge hath enabled him withall."[15] It was this superhuman, nonnegotiable, inalienable wisdom and power that the Commons, taking the king at his word, attributed to him and denied to anyone who claimed to be acting in his name.

At the simplest level we can see the strategy at work in the indignation of the Commons in 1628 over a parliamentary election in Cornwall, in which a group of local magnates tried to prevent the reelection of two former members, Sir John Eliot and William Coryton, who had been prominent in Parliament's insistence on the rights of subjects. Both men had refused to pay the forced loan of 1626, which the king had demanded of leading citizens after Parliament had failed to supply him with needed funds. Eliot and Coryton, like many other Englishmen, had regarded this as a mode of taking their property without consent. They had been imprisoned until the king, having decided to summon a new and, with luck, less recalcitrant Parliament, reluctantly released the pair as a peace offering. At the time of the election Cornwall was petitioning the king for a number of privileges, and several of the county squires were eager to make their own peace offering by not returning these two to Westminster. They told Eliot and Coryton that they had heard "how many ways his Majesty hath expressed his displeasure against you. And his Majesty will conceive your election to be an affront to his service; and so we shall draw the displeasure of the King on us." If Eliot and Coryton persisted in standing for election, their big neighbors would "oppose you all we can." Eliot and Coryton, who were no small men themselves, were nevertheless elected; and since they were old hands in Parliament, it is not surprising that their opponents were brought to the bar, sent to the Tower for a spell, and required to make public confession of their fault at the county court in the county in which they were justices.[16]

What is significant is not that the Commons punished an attempt to influence an election but the grounds on which they did it. Sir Robert Phelips, perhaps the most astute member of the Commons in

---

[15] Discourse concerning the Royall Prerogative," in L. A. Knafla, ed., *Law and Politics in Jacobean England: The Tracts of Lord Chancellor Ellesmere* (Cambridge, England, 1977), 197–98.

[16] *Commons Debates 1628*, II, 33–34; III, 386–89. This case seems to have left a lasting impression on later Parliamentarians. See *The Plain Case of the Common-Weal* (London, 1658), 6; *Freedom of Elections to Parliament a Fundamental Law and Liberty of the English Subjects* (London, 1690), 21–22.

every contest with the king, explained the need for proceeding with particular severity against the Cornwall magnates: "If my reason fail not," he said, in the first speech after the disclosure of the Cornwall affair, "we ought to be sensible of this injury that any subject should presume to arrogate to himself his Majesty's judgment."[17] The Cornwall men had tried to second-guess the king; and though they were great men in their county, they must be reminded that they were mere subjects. As Sir Edward Coke put it, in demanding that they make public and local acknowledgment of their fault, "That that moves me is that they have entered into the King's breast as [if] to say: His Majesty will be justly provoked, and suppose that we countenance you [Eliot and Coryton] against him. Thus they climb up to the King's heart."[18] No subject should be allowed to climb so high as to speak or act for the king. They must be made to climb down and eat humble pie, and they must do it in Cornwall, so that ordinary subjects there might witness their humiliation.

The Cornwall magnates were easily put down, because they could claim no authorization from the king for what they had done.[19] But what if the king had come to their rescue and affirmed that they had a place in his heart and had done what he in his wisdom and righteousness had wanted them to do or approved of their doing? Something of the sort had already occurred in the case of Richard Montagu in 1625. Montagu was a clergyman who had argued that the Church of Rome and the Church of England were less far apart than Christ and Antichrist and might one day be reconciled. The Commons took him into custody, censured him for his doctrines, which, they were careful to point out, ran contrary to King James's demonstration that the pope was Antichrist. For this tenuous dishonor to the king, the Commons were preparing to present Montagu to the House of Lords for more severe punishment than they dared impose themselves, when Charles I, who had just succeeded to the throne, warned them off with a message informing them that he had made Montagu his chaplain.[20] What more pointed way could there be of saying that he approved Monta-

---

[17] *Commons Debates 1628*, II, 34.

[18] Ibid., III, 389.

[19] But when the session was over, the king immediately ordered their release from the Tower and himself paid the charges of their imprisonment. (Ibid., IV, 404n) In 1629 he put Eliot and Coryton back in prison, where Eliot died.

[20] S. R. Gardiner, ed., *Debates in the House of Commons in 1625*, Camden Society, new series, VI (1873), 47–53, 62, 69–70, 179–86; John Rushworth, *Historical Collections* (London, 1682–1700), I, 173–76, 209–212.

gu's doctrines? Nevertheless, though the Commons were uncertain how to take the case from there, they did not jump to the conclusion that they must let Montagu go because the king seemed to have scooped him up into the protected sphere of his own unassailable divinity. Whatever the king might say, however high the king might seek to raise him, Montagu was only a subject. Although it was not constitutionally clear that religion fell within the purview of the Commons, Edward Alford, one of the most experienced Parliamentarians in the House, said it would destroy Parliament if they failed to proceed against Montagu simply because the king had told them not to.[21] The Commons continued to press charges against him in succeeding sessions and petitioned the king to punish him and have his book burned. The king had the book burned but punished Montagu by making him bishop of Chichester.[22]

Although the Commons evidently came off second best in the Montagu case, the fact that they proceeded at all shows their determination to keep the king from sharing any aspect of his divinity with a subject. Another example of this determination occurred in 1629, when, at the opening of the session, a member made it known that he had had some goods seized by the customs officers for refusing to pay tonnage and poundage. Parliament ordinarily had voted these duties on imports to a monarch for the duration of his reign but had explicitly declined to vote them to Charles, and Charles had now summoned them to ask for other grants of taxes. The members were quick to perceive that unless the seized goods were returned, a grant of other taxes would imply that the seizure had been valid and that the king could collect tonnage and poundage without their consent.[23] For him to do so, in their view, would clearly be wrong, but the king could do no wrong. It was therefore the customs officers who must be wrong, not to mention the judges of the Court of Exchequer, who had approved the seizure. They were all subjects and had done bad things in the king's name. It required some stretch of the imagination to dissociate these officers from the king, particularly as the king had farmed the custom to them, that is, he had given them a charter (or lease) to collect tonnage and poundage. But to extol the king's righteousness

---

[21] *Debates in the House of Commons in 1625*, 70.

[22] *Commons Debates 1628*, III, 131–32; IV, 283–41, 260–62, 273–74; Rushworth, *Collections*, I, 633.

[23] *Commons Debates for 1629*, 62.

while condemning the officers' culpability was a way to confine the king within his divinity and keep subjects out of it. The learned John Selden was certain that "What we doe in a right way and justly will not displease his Majesty,"[24] and he framed the accusation against one of the officers, "that he when there was noe [grant of] tonnage and poundage by Act of parliament took knowingly a lease thereof for his own benefitt." That he who could do no wrong had knowingly granted the lease could not be admitted.[25]

As in the case of the Montagu affair the king now stepped in. By asserting that the officers had indeed acted at his command he seemingly destroyed the case which the Commons were building.[26] This time the House was more sure of its ground. Selden again stated the issue: "Whether a Crime committed by a subject as it is his act, yet whether he procuring the Kings command shal stay us from procedinge."[27] It did not stay them, though it gave them pause. In the end it was necessary to hold the Speaker in the chair by force while they passed resolutions condemning not only the customs officers but any other subjects who propagated wrong opinions about religion or tonnage and poundage. All such persons, including merchants who paid the duties and customs officers who collected them, persons who advised paying the duties and also persons who tried to introduce popery or Arminianism, all were to be deemed capital enemies to the kingdom.[28] It was simply not to be admitted that they had the king's command for what they did or said. As the Speaker struggled in the chair, Sir John Eliot made the formal obeisance that dissociated the king from such capital enemies. "Wee have professed in all things," he said, "to obey him as the highest under God. . . . Nothing hath bene done amongst us, but that which is agreeable to his Majesties justice; and as he is just, so we doubt not but he doth justly intend to performe, what we shall desire of him."[29]

It will be perceived that the Commons, while chastising the presumption of other subjects, had themselves climbed up to the king's heart. They did not say to themselves, "The king is wise and good.

[24] Ibid., 227.
[25] Ibid., 158.
[26] Ibid., 94.
[27] Ibid., 238.
[28] Ibid., 101–2.
[29] Ibid., 253.

Therefore let us do what he wants." Instead, they said, "The king is
wise and good. Therefore he must want what we want." Their frame
of mind shows up well in the case of Roger Manwaring, another of
the king's chaplains, who had defended the forced loan in a published
sermon. John Pym, demanding his punishment, could devote most of
his argument to demonstrating that Manwaring had in fact defended
the loan. To prove to the House that this was cause for punishment,
it was enough simply to state that the king must despise anyone who
approved what the Commons disapproved. "Great is the love and piety
of his Majesty to his subjects," said Pym, "and therefore it may be
easily judged, his abhorring this man that would draw him from justice and piety."[30] The Commons thus presumed to know what the
king wanted better than his appointed officials did, better even than
the king himself did.

In effect, the Commons were exalting the king to the point where
he would be beyond the reach of any mortals save themselves, to the
point too where his body politic might lose touch with his body natural. A host of ambitious schemers, according to the Commons' view,
continually caught the king's natural ear and misinformed him in order
to procure benefits to themselves. But the king in his body politic
always wanted what was best for his subjects, all his subjects, and
surely no subject could know better what that was than the combined
representatives of all his subjects. "If anything fall out unhappily,"
said Sir Robert Phelips, "it is not King Charles that advised himself,
but King Charles misadvised by others and misled by misordered
counsel."[31] When presented with evidence that the king had acted
against established law, the Commons either refused to believe it (thus
Sir Thomas Wentworth: "I detest him that does believe it, that the
King should direct this. We know the King cannot have knowledge of
himself of these things.")[32] or else they placed all the blame on those
who carried out the act (thus John Glanville: "Our law says that the
King's command contrary to law is void, and the actor stands single.
If there were a command, it was upon misinformation.").[33]

Even those who suffered for refusing to pay the forced loan could
not permit themselves to admit that the king had any knowledge of

[30] *Commons Debates 1628*, IV, 103.
[31] Ibid., IV, 139.
[32] Ibid., IV, 393.
[33] Ibid.

such evil doings. Sir John Eliot, fresh from prison, rhapsodized on the monarch's perfection: "The goodness of the King," he cried, "is like the glory of the sun, not capable in itself of any obscurity or eclipse, but only by intervenient and dark clouds it may seem to be eclipsed and diminished to us. So by interposition of officers the goodness of the King may be darkened to us."[34] It was the business of Parliament to dispel the clouds, to disabuse the king of the false counsel fed him by evil subjects, so that his true wisdom and justice could prevail.[35] The members of Parliament, to be sure, were themselves subjects, but they had been entrusted with the responsibility of representing their fellow subjects and of informing the king of any abuses committed by those who pretended to act under his commands. It was all right for them, but only for them, to climb up to the king's heart and speak the truths placed there by God, even when the king had not discerned them himself.

At the same time and more significantly it was proper for Parliament as the highest tribunal in the land to punish those who misled the king, to deprive them of the special privileges they had extracted from him by their lies, to reduce them to the level of other subjects. Throughout the reigns of James I and Charles I the Commons were kept busy putting down evil men and correcting the king's apprehensions of what he really wanted. It was not merely scheming customs officers who misled him into letting them collect unauthorized taxes or wicked clergymen who tried to mislead him back to Rome. The most overmighty subjects were the king's own ministers and the favorites with whom he surrounded himself at court. It required a good deal of nerve to take on men whom the king so directly approved, and the Commons might not have dared to do it without encouragement from rivals in his court. There was always the danger that he would respond by dismissing Parliament altogether, perhaps to follow

[34] Ibid., III, 173. Benjamin Rudyard repeated this figure of speech in the Long Parliament. (Rushworth, *Historical Collections*, IV, 25.)

[35] The Commons had spelled out this function at the opening of the reign of James I, in the famous Apology of 1604 (which may not, however, have been formally adopted); but James himself encouraged them in his opening speech in 1609, in which he acknowledged that Parliament could inform him of the grievances of his people, that he might not otherwise learn of. (*McIlwain, Political Works of James I*, 313–15). Something of the continuity of parliamentary memory may be judged from the citing of this speech in 1628, as a reason for proceeding with a remonstrance after the Commons had won acceptance of the Petition of Right. *Commons Debates 1628*, IV, 198, 205, 207, 213, 312.

the footsteps of other European monarchs toward absolute monarchy.

The Commons at first approached the problem obliquely, by going after the favorites of favorites. In 1621 they tackled Sir Giles Mompesson, a hanger-on of the Marquis (later Duke) of Buckingham, James I's chief favorite. Through Buckingham's influence, Mompesson had acquired various monopolies, which of course the king could not be thought to approve. Against Mompesson the Commons, guided by Sir Edward Coke, revived an ancient procedure that amounted to impeachment. Lacking adequate powers of judicature themselves, they presented him before the House of Lords, which obliged with a sentence of life imprisonment, and Mompesson escaped only by fleeing to the continent.[36]

With this success behind them, the Commons went after bigger fish, and the court of James I was so riddled with corruption that bigger fish were plentiful. The name of the lord chancellor, Francis Bacon, had surfaced in the pursuit of Mompesson and other monopolists, as one who might have conspired in the misleading of the king. When the House began to investigate, they came upon witnesses who demonstrated that Bacon had taken bribes in his own Court of Chancery. The Commons again made complaint to the Lords, and when the Lords inescapably found the chancellor guilty, the king was obliged to disown him.[37] It was a heady experience for the Commons. If they were egged on by courtiers, it was nevertheless the Commons that brought the charges and gained the experience in humbling over-mighty subjects.

Five years later, after Charles I succeeded to the throne and entrusted the Duke of Buckingham with a long string of offices and powers that offended the Commons and in fact endangered the kingdom, the Commons were ready to take on this Lord High Everything himself. Having perfected the process of impeachment, they drew up articles against him in June 1626, but Charles saved him by dissolving Parliament.[38] When they met again in 1628, they first drew up the Petition of Right and then set their sights once more on Buckingham.

This time, impeachment having failed, they prepared a remon-

[36] On the Mompesson case see *Commons Debates 1621*, II, 268 and *passim;* Robert Zaller, *The Parliament of 1621: A Study in Constitutional Conflict* (Berkeley, Calif., 1971), 59ff; Colin G. C. Tite, *Impeachment and Parliamentary Judicature in Early Stuart England* (London, 1974), 88–110.

[37] Zaller, *Parliament of 1621*, 58–74; Tite, *Impeachment*, 110–14.

[38] Tite, *Impeachment*, 178–207; Rushworth, *Historical Collections*, I, 302–56.

strance, informing the king of all that was amiss in his kingdom, things "either unknown to you, or else by some of your Majesty's ministers offered under such specious pretences as may hide their own bad intentions." The list was a long one—innovations in religion, innovations in government, incompetence in the army and navy—and at the end it came to the point: the source of all these troubles was the Duke of Buckingham.[39] In the debates that preceded the document Coke had set the tone by charging that "the Duke of Buckingham is the cause of all our miseries, and till the King be informed thereof we shall never go out with honor, nor sit with honor here. That man is the grievance of grievances."[40] Other members took up the cry, charging that "He is too great for a subject," that he acted "as if he were the King's own son." "No power under the King," said Selden, "ought to be so great as the power that this man has."[41] The Commons accordingly resolved, even before the remonstrance was drafted, that "the excessive power of the Duke of Buckingham and the abuse of that power are the chief cause of these evils and dangers to the King and kingdom."[42] When the king received the remonstrance, hard after the Petition of Right, he made no attempt to conceal his irritation. A week later he prorogued Parliament; and before the Commons met again an assassin robbed them of their prey.

No one can say how the confrontation would have progressed had Buckingham lived. It seems clear, however, that the Commons were isolating the king in his majesty, reducing his mightiest subjects to a level where they could be controlled by Parliament, fencing in divine right by keeping all subjects in their proper place—in the place, that is, of subjects. In effect, insofar as the Commons succeeded they were denying to the king the right to delegate authority except when it was exercised to the satisfaction of Parliament. The king was divine and unaccountable, but those he commissioned to act for him shared neither his divinity nor the unaccountability that went with it. To the Commons his agents were all subjects; and if they acted in the king's name, they must do so at their peril. It has been pointed out that the Commons could not have succeeded in their attacks without the king's concurrence, but it may also be asked whether the king could have

[39] *Commons Debates 1628*, IV, 311–17, quotation at p. 311.

[40] Ibid., IV, 115.

[41] Ibid., IV, 120, 246, 310.

[42] Ibid., IV, 237.

withheld his concurrence in the face of a determined House. God's lieutenant might have found it impossible to persist indefinitely in support of those whom the Commons counted as ungodly.

Unfortunately for Charles, he thought that he could beat the game by calling it off. After 1629 he got along without summoning Parliament for eleven years, during which some of the members must have ruminated about the possible consequences of exalting the king, especially a king who seemed to be moving the English church ever closer to Rome. The more Puritanical may even have pondered the God-given responsibility that Calvinist political thinkers had placed on minor magistrates or even on the people to correct an erring ruler. But when Charles, in desperate need of funds, convened what became the Long Parliament in November 1640, the Commons fell at once to the old business of pulling down those who had stepped above the proper place of subjects. The culprits included nearly everyone close to the king: the Earl of Strafford, Archbishop Laud, Chief Justice Finch, the judges of the King's Bench, most of the bishops. And again the charges were the same. Strafford had "ascended the Throne," had "assumed to himself Regall power," had tried to "make himself equal to Sovereignty."[43] Laud was even worse: "he went about to sett himself above the King, and to make his throne his footstole."[44] The bishops who followed him had played the monarch, had "laid their hands upon the crowne."[45] The judges of the King's Bench were guilty of "great Ambition."[46] Because all these men had elevated themselves above the level of subjects, they were all guilty of high treason.

The king himself must remain blameless. And again the members rang the changes on his perfection. As each of the victims of the Commons' anger pleaded the king's approval, the Commons turned the plea into an aggravation of the offense. All the king's officers, they said, were "tied to give the King faithfull counsell. And if for want of that he command them to doe anie thing against law, their guilt and punishment is not lessened but aggravated by his command."[47] To obtain the king's approval for an illegal act was to seek to lay the blame for it on God's lieutenant, to hide the wickedness of an overmighty subject behind the shield of the king's divinity.

[43] Rushworth, *Historical Collections*, VIII, 8, 457, 579.

[44] Notestein, *Journal of Sir Simonds D'Ewes*, 413.

[45] Ibid., 427n; Rushworth, *Historical Collections*, IV, 295.

[46] Rushworth, *Historical Collections*, IV, 325.

[47] Notestein, *Journal of Sir Simonds D'Ewes*, 408.

But while the Commons seemed to be resuming Parliamentary politics where they had left off in 1629, the charade could no longer be sustained. The fictions of divine right and the subjection of subjects had been strained too far, not only by the king but by the Commons themselves. In their earlier efforts to cut other subjects down to size the Commons had already begun to elevate themselves to an unsubject-like height. In their very insistence that the king's authority was inalienable and not to be shared, they had been discovering a way to share it themselves. They were, in fact, already in 1628 on the path that led a century and a half later to ministerial responsibility to Parliament. Phelips had then told them that "The use of parliaments is as well to give our counsels as our monies. . . . Never were we more glorious than when the King weighs not so much the counsel of them about him as the counsel of the parliament."[48] And Selden had wanted to include in the Petition of Right a clause asking "that all his [the king's] ministers should serve him as they will answer the contrary to the high court of parliament."[49] Having climbed to the king's heart, the Commons were eyeing his throne.

In 1628 and 1629 they had done no more than eye it. They did not accept Selden's proposal, and they did not see themselves as challenging the king's authority. They could not, however, take their eyes off the throne while so many of the king's subjects seemed bent on sharing it, and in the course of pulling down others they had moved ever closer to sharing it themselves. The movement had accelerated after the Commons' enforced ten-year recess came to an end in 1640; it accelerated not only because they found so many offenders to chasten but because the king's majesty had been somehow tarnished, his divinity diluted, by the company he kept during the years he had avoided theirs. The "visible God" had crept too far from the true God. The king's body natural had betrayed his body politic. The men who assembled at Westminster in November 1640 went through the motions of subjection; but despite their continued expressions of reverence for the monarch, despite the concentration of their wrath upon wicked counsellors, they spoke to the king now with a sternness that belied the subordination they pretended. Even before closing in on Strafford, they passed the Triennial Act and extracted the king's approval of it. Henceforth, he should be unable to avoid their company: Parliaments were to sit every three years whether he called them

---

[48] *Commons Debates 1628*, II, 251.

[49] Ibid., III, 317.

or not. Lord Digby, who was later to vote against the attainder of
Strafford and to withdraw to the king's side, was one of the strongest
supporters of the Triennial Act; and he gave as his reason that it would
be no good "to punish and dispel *ill Ministers . . .* if there be not a way
setled to Preserve and *keep them good. . . ."*[50]

To prevent the king from ruling without Parliament was one way
to keep ministers good. But the apparatus of impeachment, by which
Parliament was doing it, was clumsy. The Scottish Estates showed a
better way when they were able, in September 1641, to gain the king's
agreement to choose his Scottish counsellors only with the "advice
and approbation" of the Estates there. A month later the English Parliament fell to discussing the same idea, the boldest maintaining that
"all wee had done this Parliament was nothing unless wee had a negative voice in the placing of the great Officers of the King and of his
Councellors, by whom his Majestie was ledd captive."[51] If the king
was to be a captive, he must be the captive of the Commons. And the
members achieved sufficient agreement to close their Grand Remonstrance of December 1 with a demand for parliamentary approval
of counsellors.[52]

Although the Grand Remonstrance did not produce at once the
ministerial responsibility it demanded, it did signal an end to the politics of divine right, as Sir Edward Dering observed in opposing it:
"When I first heard of a Remonstrance . . . I thought to represent
unto the King the wicked Counsels of pernicious Counsellors . . . I
did not dream that we shou'd remonstrate *downward*, tell stories to the
People, and talk of the King as of a third Person."[53] But that was where
the exaltation of the king had led. In barring others from climbing
into the seats of majesty, the Commons had elevated themselves to
the point where they were contending with the king less as subjects
than as rivals. And that kind of contest could not be conducted under
the old ground rules. Ultimately it required a transfer of divine sanction from the king to his people and their representatives.

The divine right of kings had never been more than a fiction, and
as used by the Commons it led toward the fiction that replaced it, the

[50] Rushworth, *Historical Collections*, IV, 147.

[51] Willson H. Coates, ed., *The Journal of Sir Simonds D'Ewes from the First Recess of the
Long Parliament to the Withdrawal of King Charles from London* (New Haven, Conn.,
1943), xxix–xxxii, 45.

[52] Rushworth, *Historical Collections*, IV, 451.

[53] Ibid., IV, 425.

sovereignty of the people. Although the two may seem to lie at opposite poles, they were more closely linked than at first it would seem.
By accepting the king's divine right, by insisting that his authority
was pure and indivisible, the Commons had come a good way toward
making that authority unworkable except on the terms they dictated.
By elevating the king they prepared his destruction; and by humbling
mighty subjects they made way for the rise of the humble, made way,
indeed, for the new fictions of a world where all men are created equal
and governments derive their powers from those they govern. That
was surely not the intention of the men who sat at Westminster and
sang the praises of a perfect king, but they were not the first persons
on whom history has played Whiggish tricks.

CHAPTER 2

The Enigma of Representation

T HE FICTION that replaced the divine right of kings is our fiction, and it accordingly seems less fictional to us. Only the cynical among us will scoff at Lincoln's dedication to "government of the people, by the people, and for the people." Sober thought may tell us that all governments are of the people, that all profess to be for the people, and that none can literally be by the people. But sober thought will also tell us that the sovereignty of the people, however fictional, has worked. In England and America at least, it has worked for three centuries, providing the few with justification for their government of the many and reconciling the many to that government. It has furnished the stability that die-hard adherents of divine right had declared impossible, yet it has also provided the leverage for political and social changes that have brought our institutions into closer proximity to its propositions.

Those propositions are not simple. In one way or another they all affirm the power, the authority, and the rights of the people over their government, even while sustaining the power, authority, and prerogatives of the government by virtue of their authorization of it. The people are the governed; they are also, at least fictionally, the governors, at once subjects and rulers. How such a contradiction could win acceptance among a governing elite as well as among the many whom they governed is logically puzzling but historically explicable. The explanation will take us from the Parliament that challenged the king in seventeenth-century England to the convention that drafted the United States Constitution in 1787, but it must begin with a closer look at the central enigma of popular sovereignty, the institution that embodies its contradictions most glaringly.

Representation in England began before representative government or the sovereignty of the people were thought of. It began in the thirteenth century as a mode of insuring or facilitating, and eventually of obtaining, consent to the king's government. The king summoned representatives from counties and boroughs to come to his Parliament armed with powers of attorney to bind their constituents to whatever taxes or laws they agreed to. The power of attorney had to be complete *(plena potestas)*, so that a representative could not plead that he must go back and consult his constituents. His consent, given in Parliament, must be as much theirs as if they had come in person.[1] "As if." Representation from the beginning was itself a fiction. If the representative consented, his constituents had to make believe that they had done so.

The way in which any group of subjects was first persuaded to pretend that one of them could substitute for all of them is not altogether clear. It is possible that originally a representative could consent only in the name of individuals who specifically empowered him and that those who did not, even though in the same community, were not bound by his actions. Although the records do not disclose such a situation in the first English Parliaments, we can observe it in the first representative assemblies gathered in England's colony of Maryland in the 1630s. While Charles was doing without his own representative assembly in England, he did not extend so free a hand in governing to those whom he authorized to found colonies in America. The charter he granted to his friend, Lord Baltimore, gave Baltimore power to make laws for Maryland but only with the consent of the free men *(liberi homines)* who settled there.[2]

Baltimore delegated his authority to a governor, and in the first

[1] Gaines Post, "Plena Potestas and Consent in Medieval Assemblies," *Traditio* (New York, 1943), 355–408; cf. H. G. Koenigsberger, "The Powers of Deputies in Sixteenth-Century Assemblies," *Album Helen Maud Cam*, II. Studies Presented to the International Commission for the History of Representative and Parliamentary Institutions (Louvain and Paris, 1961), XXIV, 211–43; J. G. Edwards, "The Plena Potestas of English Parliamentary Representatives," *Oxford Essays in Medieval History Presented to Herbert Edward Salter* (Oxford, 1934), 141–54; J. C. Holt, "The Prehistory of Parliament" in R. G. Davies and J. H. Denton, eds., *The English Parliament . the Middle Ages* (Manchester, England, 1981), 1–28.

[2] Francis N. Thorpe, *The Federal and State Constitutions . . .* , 7 vols. (Washington, D.C., 1902), III, 1671, 1679.

year after the arrival of the settlers the governor apparently summoned the free men to get their consent, as prescribed, to a number
of laws. We have no records for this assembly or of how many persons
attended it. But for the next assembly in 1638 the records show that
some free men attended in person while others delegated representatives, each of whom was entitled to his own vote and also to all the
votes of those who had selected him as their representative. He did
not represent anyone who had not specifically and individually
empowered him; and a man could even change his mind, revoke the
assignment of his vote, and attend in person. Thus we find in the
records on the second day of the meeting: "Came John Langford of
the Ile of Kent gentleman . . . who had given a voice in the choice of
Robert Philpott, gentlemen, to be one of the Burgesses for the freemen of that Iland; and desired to revoke his voice and to be personally
present in the Assembly; and was admitted." One could also transfer
one's proxy, as it was called, from one man to another after the session
began. Thus "Richard Lusthead desired to revoke his proxie [given to
Richard Gannett] and was admitted and made Robert Clark his proxie."
The records imply that elections of representatives were held in particular neighborhoods, but those who voted against the winner were
not bound to recognize him as their representative. Thus Cuthbert
Fenwick came to the assembly and "claimed a voice as not assenting
to the election of St. Mary's burgesses and was admitted."[3]

The result was a politically bizarre situation: within the assembly
some men had only their own vote, while others had the votes of all
their proxies in addition to their own. On one occasion an aspiring
politician named Giles Brent had enough proxies (seventy-three) to
constitute a majority of the assembly all by himself. In the 1640s the
assembly was gradually reduced to a strictly representative body, with
each community in the colony choosing, by majority rule, a representative who would stand for the whole community, including the
minority of free men who had voted against him. And he would cast
a single vote in the assembly, regardless of the size of the community
he represented.[4]

The original development of the fiction of representation in England

[3] *Archives of Maryland*, I. Proceedings and Acts of the General Assembly January 1637/8
–September, 1664. (Baltimore, 1883), 1–39.
[4] The development can be followed in Ibid. I, 74–75, 81–82, 115–18, 167–70, 214,
259, 272, 339–56.

may not have followed this pattern. At the time when representation began in England, local communities were already more developed than they could be in a newly founded colony, and the first writs that summoned knights of the shire in the thirteenth century specified that they be empowered to consent for themselves *and* for the whole community of the county (*pro se et tota communitate comitatus illa*) from which they came.[5] But the Maryland example exhibits graphically the original (and continuing) character of the representative as the agent of those he represented.

Whether in Maryland or England or anywhere else in the Anglo-American world, when representatives ceased to be, where they had ever been, mere proxies for individuals, the communities they represented were geographically defined. In England they represented counties or boroughs. In Maryland and Virginia they represented plantations or hundreds or counties, in New England they represented towns, in the Carolinas, parishes. It was possible to stretch the fiction of one man standing for another or for several others to the point where he stood for a whole local community, even for those within the community who had not specifically authorized him. But, in England and America at least, the community was geographically defined. It was the Isle of Kent or the borough of St. Mary's; it was Shropshire or Staffordshire, Norwich or Bristol; it was never the worshipful company of grocers or cordwainers, never the tobacco farmers' union or the association of shipowners. In the eighteenth and nineteenth centuries the fiction of representation was sometimes explained and defended as a means by which all the different economic or social "interests" in a country had a voice in its government, but representation in England and America has never in fact been based on anything but geographically defined communities.

The one interest, other than geographical, that the English House of Commons could be said to represent in the seventeenth century was, as we have seen, the interest of England's gentry, men whose birth and wealth were insufficient to give them a seat in the House of Lords but sufficient to make it seem desirable to them, to the king, and to some of their fellow subjects that they be present at the seat of government. They did not come, however, simply as gentlemen or as

[5] *Calendar of the Close Rolls Preserved in the Public Record Office . . . Edward I* (London, 1900–1908), 135–36 (June 14, 1290). I am indebted for this reference to Professor Eleanor Searle.

representatives of gentlemen. Whatever their powers might be, at home or abroad, they sat at Westminster as representatives, not of their class, but of localities.

It does not follow that particular communities were singled out for representation because the people within them had desired it. Representation began as an obligation imposed from above; and over the years, especially in the sixteenth century, the king or queen expanded the obligation by assigning representatives to new boroughs, not because the residents demanded it, but rather because powerfully connected country gentlemen persuaded the monarch to enfranchise boroughs where they could count on controlling the elections. As a result many small communities were given representation while larger ones were overlooked. By the opening of the seventeenth century most of the 462 members of the House of Commons (increased from 296 at the beginning of the sixteenth century), were country gentlemen not actually resident in the boroughs that elected them.[6]

The number of persons who participated in the choice of representatives within a county or borough similarly expanded without their asking for it. Voting for county members had been restricted by a statute of 1430 to adult males with a freehold in land that produced forty shillings a year in rent or produce. At the time forty shillings was a substantial sum, but by the seventeenth century inflation had rendered the amount nominal and expanded the suffrage in the counties to perhaps a fifth of adult males. Voting in the boroughs was determined by custom and varied greatly from place to place; in some it extended to virtually all free male inhabitants, in others it was confined to the members of the governing corporation of the borough. Borough voting expanded during the seventeenth century when the House of Commons began deciding election disputes. Such disputes generally arose when an ambitious candidate brought unqualified voters to the poll and swamped his opponent with them. If the erring candidate was favored by the majority of the House of Commons, the House would declare him elected, and the suffrage in that borough would henceforth be legally widened.[7]

The composition of the House of Commons was thus determined in large measure by the king, in assigning representation, or by the

[6] Neale, *Elizabethan House of Commons*, 140–61.

[7] Derek Hirst, *The Representative of the People? Voters and Voting in England under the Early Stuarts* (Cambridge, England, 1975).

Commons itself in deciding disputes. But neither king nor Commons sought to make the legal basis of representation anything but geographical. The members might in fact be chosen from a narrow social stratum but they remained representatives of counties and boroughs. No gentleman could present himself at the House of Commons without certification from a government officer that he had been chosen by a majority of voters as the representative of a specific county or borough. And that county or borough was thought to include everyone residing within its bounds, all the king's subjects, whether qualified to vote or not.

This local attachment of every representative in the House of Commons may have been an historical accident arising from the way in which the gentry had sought to obtain seats in Parliament. But by the seventeenth century the local geographical definition of representation had become an essential ingredient in it, just as representation had itself become an essential ingredient of the English government. Once again, the behavior of Englishmen who had moved to America may illustrate the point. The colony of Massachusetts was founded by a trading company, the Massachusetts Bay Company, in which the stockholders, designated as "freemen," were empowered to meet four times a year in a "General Court," to make laws for the Company and for its colony, and to elect the officials of the Company, that is, a governor and eighteen "assistants." The Company was given power, like Lord Baltimore in Maryland, to govern the colony as it saw fit but was not required to obtain the consent of the inhabitants for its laws. The majority of the Company determined in 1629 to transfer the meeting place of the Company to the colony, and once there the small number of freemen (stockholders) who had made the voyage opened their ranks to all orthodox male Puritan church members. They accompanied this move, however, with a transfer of legislative authority to the elected governor and assistants.[8]

Now the charter did not authorize such a delegation of the freemen's legislative power. On the other hand, neither did it offer to ordinary settlers who were not freemen (i.e., who were not Company members) any right to be consulted about the laws that the Company might make. But in 1632, when the assistants, acting in their newly assigned legislative capacity, levied a tax, the people in Watertown

[8] E. S. Morgan, *The Puritan Dilemma: The Story of John Winthrop* (Boston, 1958), 84–94.

refused to pay it on the ground that the government did not have authority "to make laws or raise taxations without the people." Governor John Winthrop explained to them that the assistants were like a Parliament, that they were elected by the freemen and therefore could do the things that Parliament did in England.[9]

This apparently satisfied the people of Watertown for the moment, but in truth the assistants were not like a Parliament, for they were elected at large and did not represent particular districts or towns. Apparently this fact was quickly recognized, for two months later Winthrop recorded that "Every town chose two men to be at the next court, to advise with the governour and assistants about the raising of a public stock, so as what they should agree upon should bind all."[10] Two years later the freemen of the towns revoked the legislative power of the assistants and insisted that all laws be made in the General Court, which was now to include representatives ("deputies") elected by the freemen of each town.[11] Non-freemen still did not share in the election, just as the majority of Englishmen were excluded from voting for members of Parliament, but this defect seems not to have affected the viability of the fiction. What was needed was not that every man, woman, and child share in the choice of a representative but that the choice be perceived as that of a geographical community. A representative had to represent the people of a particular place; he ceased to represent when he lost his local identification. A representative assembly had to be *assembled*. It had to be composed from the parts of the whole. The fiction of representation would collapse if it was stretched to have all legislators chosen at large by all voters, even in so small a society as Massachusetts Bay in the 1630s. This local character of representation was present at the beginning in England as well as in England's colonies, and it has remained to this day essential to the credibility of the fiction.[12]

Closely linked to the requirement that the representative be attached to a locality was the need already noticed that he be perceived as a subject of government. In order to represent other subjects he must be himself a subject. The Massachusetts assistants, though annually

---

[9] Ibid., 107–10. John Winthrop, *The History of New England from 1630 to 1649*, James Savage, ed. (Boston, 1853), I, 84.

[10] Winthrop, *History*, I, 91.

[11] Ibid., 152–54; Nathaniel B. Shurtleff, ed., *Records of the Governor and Company of the Massachusetts Bay*, (Boston, 1853), I, 117–19.

[12] See the discussion of instructions in Chapter 9, below.

elected, were on the other side of the fence from the governed. Though bound by the laws they enforced, they were perceived as rulers, not ruled, just as the king and his appointed council, though bounded by law, were rulers, not ruled. King and council, governor and assistants were there to exercise authority over the whole society; representatives were there to give or withhold the consent of their particular counties or towns or districts to what the rulers did. Although the distinction began to blur very early, it remained an essential ingredient in the fiction of representation and in the way people thought about government. In Massachusetts the Reverend John Cotton, who was by no means simple-minded, thought that a political system which confounded rulers and ruled—i.e., a democracy—was a contradiction in terms. "If the people be governors," he asked, "who shall be governed?"[13] And in his view and John Winthrop's the representatives of the people, the deputies whom the various towns sent to the Massachusetts General Court after 1634, were subjects, mere substitutes for the people who chose them.[14] They were like the first representatives whom the king summoned to Parliament in order to have them bind their local constituents to obey the laws and pay the taxes proposed to them by the king and his council of barons and other magnates. The consent given by the elected knights and burgesses was the consent of the particular localities that they represented, and the very act of consent identified them as subjects.

If representatives had in truth been, or had remained, mere subjects, if they had been merely the agents of their constituents, empowered only to consent for other subjects to measures propounded by the authority of a government of which they were not strictly speaking a part, then the fiction of representation would have been a much simpler and more plausible matter than it has ever in fact been. It is possible that in England the House of Commons continued for some time after its inauguration to be considered in the way that its members so often pretended to consider it, as a gathering of mere subjects, representing various communities of subjects throughout the land. As late as 1677 a member of the House of Commons could argue that

[13] Cotton to Lord Say and Seal, in Thomas Hutchinson, *The History of the Colony and Province of Massachusetts Bay*, Laurence S. Mayo, ed. (Cambridge, Mass., 1936), I, 415.

[14] Morgan, *Puritan Dilemma*, 156–60; Winthrop, "A Reply to the Answer . . ." and "Arbitrary Government . . . ," *Winthrop Papers* (Boston, 1929–), IV, 380–92, 468–88.

"We do not take ourselves to be part of the government, for then the government is no monarchy."[15] The meaning was still familiar enough so that no one felt called upon to deny the statement. But by this time it was a little archaic, for the members of Parliament had long since ceased to behave like mere subjects. They were not content to give or withhold consent to measures presented to them by the king and his council. Instead, from early on, they had concocted measures of their own, presenting them as petitions to the king, but nevertheless in effect making governmental policy, making laws.[16]

Similarly in the colonies representative assemblies took the initiative in government almost from the beginning. In Maryland the freemen and their proxies, even before representation was fully developed, did not wait for Lord Baltimore or his governor to present them with laws for passage: they made their own and presented them to him, laws regulating servitude and inheritance, laws about planting corn and selling liquor and trading with the Indians.[17] In Massachusetts, once the General Court resumed legislative authority in 1634, there was no doubt that the representatives would share in that authority. But they went further. The General Court was also the supreme judicial authority of the colony. Winthrop insisted that the deputies sent by the towns should not share in this authority, because they were mere subjects; but the deputies demanded the right to sit in judgment on judicial matters, and they got their way.[18] In Virginia the authority to make laws lay in the Virginia Company, resident in London, but the Company called a representative assembly in the colony in 1619, and that assembly presented the Company with a series of laws which, with the Company's approval, became the first laws enacted by a representative assembly in America.[19]

As soon as representatives began to make laws and policy for the larger society to which their communities belonged, they did not cease

[15] William Cobbett, *Cobbett's Parliamentary History of England* (London, 1806–20), IV, 839.

[16] See the discussion of petitions in Chapter 9, below. By 1530 laws were regularly enacted "by authority" of Parliament. Geoffrey R. Elton, ed., *The Tudor Constitution* (Cambridge, England, 1960), 228–34, *Studies in Tudor and Stuart Politics and Government* (Cambridge, England, 1974), II, 29.

[17] *Maryland Archives*, I, *passim*.

[18] Barbara A. Black, "The Judicial Power and the General Court in Early Massachusetts 1634–1686," (Ph.D. dissertation, Yale University, 1975).

[19] Susan M. Kingsbury, ed., *The Records of the Virginia Company of London* (Washington, D.C., 1906–35), III, 153–77, 482–84.

to be subjects but they ceased to be mere subjects. By the same token, though they did not cease to be the agents of local communities, they ceased to be merely that. The laws they made were to bind not only their own communities but the whole realm, the whole nation, the whole society. In making policy for the larger body they had to think in different terms from the needs and desires of their localities; sharing regal authority, they had to think regally, to think for the nation rather than the neighborhood. The well-being of the whole society might be different from that of any one part or even from that of the sum of all the parts. Insofar as they assumed authority and directed their attention to whatever they perceived as the welfare of the whole, representatives necessarily lost something of their character as subjects and as local agents and took on the trappings of a national ruling class.

Logically this meant a transformation in the meaning of representation, but chronologically, historically it was not so much a transformation as a paradox or conflict present in representation from the beginning or almost from the beginning. The very power that a local community was required to give its representative opened the way for him to elevate himself above the community. The king required the local community to give him full power *(plena potestas)* to act for them so that the inhabitants could not repudiate his actions if they did not like what he did. Moreover, the persons selected by a community to represent it in Parliament were from the outset those who could command the assent of that community by virtue of their own power and prestige. The character of the representative as a subject rather than a ruler was thus a little dubious at the outset. And his attachment to the locality he represented was also vitiated as early as the fourteenth century when nonresident country gentry began to buy and bully their way into possession of borough seats, elbowing out local but lesser dignitaries. A statute of 1413 required that a representative be a resident of the borough that chose him, but the lawyers in the House of Commons quickly interpreted this to mean that he need not be a resident of the borough that chose him.[20] Some connection was maintained through the practice of giving instructions to the representative

[20]J. S. Roskell, *The Commoners in the Parliament of 1422* (Manchester, England, 1953); May McKisack, *The Parliamentary Representation of the English Boroughs during the Middle Ages* (Oxford, 1932); Sir Simonds D'Ewes, *A Compleat Journal of the Votes, Speeches and Debates, both of the House of Lords and House of Commons throughout the whole Reign of Queen Elizabeth* (London, 1693), 168–71; Wallace Notestein, Frances H. Relf, and Hartley Simpson, eds., *Commons Debates 1621* (New Haven, Conn., 1935), II, 49–52.

to vote for or against this or that measure or to secure legislation conferring some local advantage. But the representative's full power meant that his votes would be valid even if in direct violation of such instructions.[21]

As representatives assumed the mantle of authority they stretched the fiction of representation to justify the attenuation of their ties to local constituencies. It may be counted as a step in this direction when they began as early as the fourteenth century to argue that they collectively represented the whole realm and could give the consent of every Englishman to what they did in Parliament. The English Parliament had never contained representatives from every town or village community. We have already seen that although every county sent representatives, only selected boroughs, and boroughs capriciously selected at that, were required or allowed to do so. But Sir Thomas Smith was able to state as a truism in 1583 that "everie Englishman is entended to bee there [in Parliament] present. . . . And the consent of the Parliament is taken to be everie mans consent."[22]

From this premise it was possible, though it might require an unusual logic, to argue that each representative could and must speak and act, not for the local community that chose him, but for all the people of the realm. Sir Edward Coke, who was good at this kind of logic, may have been the first to state the idea in so many words. "Though one be chosen for one particular county, or borough," he said, "yet when he is returned and sits in parliament, he serveth for the whole realm, for the end of his coming thither, as in the writ of his election appeareth, is generall."[23] From the fiction that one man may stand in the place of a whole community and bind that community by his actions, Coke has extrapolated the more extended fiction that one man may stand for the entire people of a country, most of whom have had no hand in designating him for that purpose.

The classic statement of this notion, of course, was to come in the

---

[21] See below, Chapter 9.

[22] Hannah Pitkin, *The Concept of Representation* (Berkeley, Calif., 1967), 85; Quentin Skinner, *The Foundations of Modern Political Thought* (Cambridge, England, 1978), II, 55; Sir Thomas Smith, *De Republica Anglorum*, L. Alston, ed. (Cambridge, England, 1906), 49.

[23] *The Fourth Part of the Institutes* (London, 1797), 14; *Journals of the House of Lords*, III, 307 (April 16, 1624). Cf. John Cook, *Redintegratio Amoris* (London, [1647]), 20–21: "though every several Shire and Burrough make their several Elections, yet they [representatives] are sent not only to vote for the good of their own County or Town, but for the general good of the Kingdom. . . . so every Member sits in the House for the good of the whole Kingdom, as if chosen by all the people."

next century, when Edmund Burke explained to the electors of Bristol why he owed them nothing but the courtesy of listening to their wishes before acting as he thought best for the whole country.[24] But already in Coke's formulation we are very close to the point where representation becomes representative government. At the time when Coke wrote, whatever authority representatives could claim over other subjects presumably came from the king. But it was only a short step from representing the whole people to deriving authority from them.

When Englishmen took that step in the 1640s, they did not affirm the sovereignty of each county or borough. It did not even occur to them to think that way. They were replacing the authority of the king, and the king had been king of all England. It was not a question of particular counties or boroughs declaring their independence from his rule any more than it was particular towns or counties in his American colonies that declared independence in 1776. There would have been no logical barrier to thinking of the people of every village as a sovereign body, but that is not what happened. The people whose sovereignty was proclaimed were the whole people of the country or colony, far too numerous a group to deliberate or act as a body. It was their representatives who claimed for them the authority that only a representative body could exercise. The sovereignty of the people was not said to reside in the particular constituencies that chose the representatives, it resided in the people at large and reached the representatives without the people at large doing anything to confer it.

Again, there would have been no logical barrier to having the people confer authority by a nation-wide election at large of any number of men to serve as rulers, but that is not what happened. What happened was that representatives elected by particular towns and counties assumed powers of government over a whole country and claimed that their powers came, not from the town or county that chose them, but from the sovereign people as a whole. And while it would have been logically possible for a national election to confer powers of government on any number of men, such a procedure would scarcely have suited the members of Parliament in their contest with the king. The people to whom they attributed supreme power were themselves fictional and could most usefully remain so, a mystical body, existing as a people only in the actions of the Parliament that claimed to act for them.

It would perhaps not be too much to say that representatives

---

[24] *Works*, (Boston, 1866), II, 95.

invented the sovereignty of the people in order to claim it for themselves—in order to justify their own resistance, not the resistance of
their constituents singly or collectively, to a formerly sovereign king.
The sovereignty of the people was an instrument by which representatives raised themselves to the maximum distance above the particular set of people who chose them. In the name of *the* people they
became all-powerful in government, shedding as much as possible the
local, subject character that made them representatives of a particular
set of people.

As much as possible. The English Revolution actually went awry
when the Long Parliament became too long, when the representatives
declined to return to their constituents for reelection or rejection. The
representative's national authoritarian character cannot be magnified
to the point of eliminating entirely his character as a local subject
without at the same time destroying the fiction of representation and
putting an end to representative government. The conflict cannot be
eliminated, it has to be muted and contained. One element may be
emphasized over the other at different times and places, and the history of representative government may be read as a dialectical process
in which one element rises or falls at the expense of the other. But if
either is wholly missing representative government either ceases to be
government or it ceases to be representative. When the local, subject
character of the representative is emphasized too much, it becomes
difficult to perceive him as a proper repository of the national authority with which the sovereign people have supposedly invested him.
When his national function as ruler of the whole people is emphasized, he may lose credibility as the spokesman of other subjects in his
local community. The fiction of representation has to sustain a continual strain from opposite directions.

The dimensions of the conflict have not always been apparent even
to those engaged in it, but we may perceive it in operation at a slightly
later stage in Algernon Sidney's explanation of the representative's
national authority. "T'is not," Sidney argued in the early 1680s,

for *Kent* or *Sussex*, *Lewis* or *Maidstone*, but for the whole Nation, that the
Members chosen in those places are sent to serve in Parliament: and tho it be
fit for them as Friends and Neighbours (so far as may be) to hearken to the
opinions of the Electors, for the information of their Judgments, . . . yet they
are not strictly and properly obliged to give account of their actions to any,
unless the whole body of the Nation for which they serve, and who are
equally concerned in their resolutions, could be assembled. This being
impracticable, the only punishment to which they are subject, if they betray

their Trust, is scorn, infamy, hatred, and an assurance of being rejected, when they shall again seek the same honour.[25]

Sidney here takes pains to distinguish the representative's obligations to the whole nation from his obligations to the electors who choose him as their agent. Yet he relies on the electors to remove him if he betrays his trust. What trust? The trust reposed in him by Kent or Sussex, by Lewis or Maidstone? No, the trust reposed in him by the whole body of the nation, which cannot be assembled for removing him—and by the same token was never assembled for entrusting him in the first place. If he betrays the trust so mysteriously placed in him, he is supposed to be subject to scorn, infamy, and hatred. But whose scorn, infamy, and hatred? Is it not likely that the man who wins scorn, infamy, and hatred from the rest of the nation may win praise, fame, and love in Kent or Sussex, in Lewis or Maidstone? And conversely the man who is faithful to his trust for the nation may win scorn, infamy, and hatred in Kent or Sussex, Lewis or Maidstone.

Sidney was not troubled by this contingency and would probably have responded to it, as he did to other objections, that while a representative assembly was not infallible, nevertheless "a house of commons composed of those who are best esteemed by their Neighbours in all the Towns and Counties of England" would at least be less "subject to error or corruption than such a man, woman or child as happens to be next in blood to the last King."[26] In the worst possible case, in other words, representative government will probably compare favorably with hereditary monarchy. A group of men popularly chosen, however strong their local attachments and whatever their weaknesses, are a safer repository of power than a hereditary king.

Because representative government rests on conflicting fictions or on a single fiction with glaring internal contradictions, it has often required such left-handed defenses. It is a *pis aller*, better than the alternatives. But Sidney's ignoring of the possible conflict between local and national interests is a reminder that representative government, in order to work, in order to mute the conflict within the fiction, requires that the different communities represented be able and willing most of the time and on most issues to perceive their own local interests as being involved in, if not identical with, the interests of the larger society.

That perception was more easily sustained while the authority of

[25] *Discourses on Government* (London, 1698), 451.

[26] Ibid., 424.

government was derived from the king than it was when the representative body professed to derive it from the people at large. When authority came from the king, government was palpably something other, a force against which representatives protected their constituents or to whose actions they bound themselves and their constituents to acceptance. Representatives, like those they represented, could be thought of as acted upon rather than as actors. By the same token, those communities that did not send representatives to Parliament did not seem so sharply distinguished from those that did. They were all subjects of the same national government, and the representatives who protected the subjects in Lewis or Maidstone could be more easily thought of as protecting those in, say, Sheffield or Birmingham, from the same external authority.

Moreover, that authority itself was less likely to be swayed by any combination of local interests. A king might become a tyrant, pursuing his own interests rather than those of his subjects. But he was not as likely as the majority in a representative assembly to place the interests of particular parts of his realm above the interests of others or of the whole.[27] Because the monarch was not likely to be geographically partial, there was less need than in popular governments for every community to have its own representatives to protect its special interests against those of other communities. Protection was needed rather against the more general danger of arbitrary government by the monarch, and this could be furnished by one set of representative subjects as effectively as by another.

Before representatives took over full command of government there was accordingly little agitation by excluded communities for inclusion in the representative body. The great expansion of representation in Parliament in the sixteenth century came, as we have seen, not because of demands by formerly excluded communities but because the rising and expanding gentry wanted seats in the House of Commons and because the king wanted them there. In the colonies, where the king's authority was diluted by distance and representatives were correspondingly more powerful (in fact if not in theory), there was some-

---

[27] Cf. James Madison, "Vices of the Political System of the United States," in *Papers*, William T. Hutchinson, Robert Rutland et al., eds. (Chicago and Charlottesville, 1962–), IX, 357: "In absolute Monarchies, the prince is sufficiently neutral towards his subjects, but frequently sacrifices their happiness to his ambition or his avarice. In small Republics, the sovereign will is sufficiently controuled from such a sacrifice of the entire Society, but is not sufficiently neutral towards the parts composing it."

what more concern about extending representation equitably. But even here, in Pennsylvania and in the southern colonies, where representation was most inequitable, there seems to have been little concern about the matter until shortly before the American Revolution.

When the king's authority was removed, as it was in England during the Commonwealth period and in America after 1776, the conflict of local interests with the sovereignty of the people at large became much more acute. In a Parliament where representatives chosen by a handful of voters had total authority over communities that could not vote at all, there were immediate demands for a more rational and equitable way of exercising the newfound sovereignty of the people. A rational plan of parliamentary representation in England was in fact adopted in the Commonwealth period, only to be abandoned for nearly another two centuries after the restoration of the monarch in 1660. And in the independent American states after 1776 the apportionment of representation became a major concern, because particular communities and regions feared that without adequate representation they would not be adequately protected from their sovereign compatriots.

In this transformation, government remained, as it must, something other, something external to the local community, but that something was no longer a king. It was now the representative body itself, or at least the representatives of other localities, acting rather than acted upon, exercising an authority derived from a people who could not exercise it themselves. When the authority of representatives was thus magnified, their function as the agents of a subject population was necessarily diminished. With the fictional people suddenly supreme, actual people, as embodied in local communities, found their traditional rights and liberties in jeopardy from a representative body that recognized only a fictional superior. The members of a Parliament as agents of local communities had viewed themselves, and had often acted, as protectors of popular rights against the arbitrary actions of a higher authority. When the Parliament, or more especially the House of Commons, itself became the government, who was left to protect actual people from its arbitrary actions?

The king had claimed his authority from God, and God was known to rule the universe by laws, laws which had been drawn out into positive enactments that defined right and wrong and which it was the king's duty to observe and enforce. The king could do no wrong. And if his government, misled by evil counsellors, did wrong, his High Court of Parliament could call it to account. But who could call

Parliament to account when Parliament did wrong and there was no king? Was Parliament bound by its own laws? If Parliament made the laws, could Parliament not unmake them? *Quis custodiet ipsos custodes?* Was there any way that the people themselves, the whole people, the fictional people, could materialize and act apart from their representatives in order to protect themselves?

These questions have troubled the advocates of popular sovereignty from its inception to the present day. New answers, new devices to bring the facts toward the fiction are invented from time to time. America's answers have been somewhat different from England's. But the paths taken in both England and America were first laid out in seventeenth-century England when Parliament challenged the king and replaced divine right with the sovereignty of the people. If we would understand how our own fictions came into existence and continue to operate, we must return to the stormy years when English men and women first tried them out.

CHAPTER *3*

Inventing the Sovereign People

WHEN PARLIAMENT began to "tell stories to the *People*" in the Grand Remonstrance of 1641, the members had no intention of deposing their king. They had been troubled by his attempt to rule without them, by his levying of taxes without their consent, and perhaps most of all by his filling positions in the church with men whom they suspected of covert Catholicism. But it took seven more years and successive purges of dissidents before those in the remaining "Rump" could bring themselves to consider doing away with a monarch and monarchy. Long before then, however, they were prepared to go beyond remonstrances and petitions. In February 1642, in the famous militia ordinance (so called because, though passed by both houses of Parliament, it did not receive the king's consent and so could not be called a law) they withdrew command of the country's militia from the king and took it upon themselves. Resistance began in April when the militia garrison at Hull interdicted the king's entrance to the city. Thereafter each side gathered troops. Before the summer was over king and Parliament faced each other in civil war.

Even then Parliament kept on pretending that the king as king was on their side, his regal and legal body remaining with them at Westminster while his misled person marched an army against theirs.[1] But

[1] Rushworth, *Historical Collections*, IV, 679, 691–703; V, 47, 140, 340, 383; *The Subjects Liberty Set Forth* (London, 1643), 5; *Symbolum Veritatis: Truths Notable Conspiracy* (London, 1643), 5–6: "So then the King is here at London after a more full and ample manner than he is at Oxford or elsewhere."

while Parliament and its adherents continued the old pretense, the fictions that centered in the divine right of kings were not adequate to support the challenge that Parliament was now mounting to the king's authority. A new ideology, a new rationale, a new set of fictions was necessary to justify a government in which the authority of kings stood below that of the people or their representatives. The sovereignty of the people was not a repudiation of the sovereignty of God. God remained the ultimate source of all governmental authority, but attention now centered on the immediate source, the people. Though God authorized government, He did it through the people, and in doing so He set them above their governors.

The idea was not wholly novel. It was at least as old as the Greeks, and in the preceding century it had served to justify appeals for rebellion by Protestants against Catholic kings and by Catholics against Protestant kings. These "monarchomachs" had fastened upon the people a duty to monitor their government's compliance with the will of God and to oust or slay any monarch who failed the test of orthodoxy, Catholic or Protestant as the case might be.[2] The new popular sovereignty as expounded by the adherents of Parliament in the 1640s owed much to the monarchomachs, as it also owed something to the doctrine of divine right that it replaced; but the change of emphasis was crucial: duty toward God gave way to the rights of men.

The shift can be seen in the transformation of one of the arguments justifying resistance to a heretical king. The monarchomachs had assigned a key role in such resistance to subordinate magistrates, those under the king, on the ground that, though appointed by the king, their authority came directly from God. When the king's commands ran counter to the will of God, it was their duty to obey Him from whom their authority came. In England the same argument came into play at first in the usual form to prescribe and justify resistance by royally appointed officials against the king's commands.[3] But as the conflict developed, the terms gradually shifted: by 1647 it was being argued that government officials, however appointed, gained their authority from the people and so were accountable only to the people for their actions in office. They must serve the will of the peo-

[2] See in general Quentin Skinner, *The Foundations of Modern Political Thought* (Cambridge, England, 1978).

[3] [Charles Herle?], *An Answer to Mis-led Doctor Ferne* (London, 1642), 4–6.

ple, not the contrary commands of whoever may have appointed them.[4] Even the biblical text most commonly used to discourage popular resistance to government (Romans XIII, "Let every soul be subject unto the higher powers") could be interpreted to justify it simply by affirming the people to be higher than their government: "Though it be not lawful for inferiours to resist superiours . . . . Yet is it very commendable for the superiour to resist the inferiour. Therefore it is undoubtedly lawful for the people, or their Representative, to resist the King . . . . The people's power is the higher, yea the supream power."[5]

Although such a direct reversal of common parlance was unusual, revolutions in thought frequently take the form of shifts in emphasis, with old ideas not repudiated, but put to new uses. The old ideology of divine right had not generally excluded the people from a nominal role in the creation of kings. Some vague sort of popular consent or choice in the distant past, renewed from time to time in the coronation ceremony, was at least implied. Even the most ardent Royalists had hesitated to base the king's authority (or his commission as God's lieutenant) on mere conquest. Although the descent of England's kings from William the Conqueror invited such an attribution, English publicists had often preferred to base William's title to the throne (and that of his successors) on some ground other than his subjugation of their countrymen. To that end they posited a contractual act in which he accepted English laws and Englishmen accepted him. The origin of English government could thus be placed in the actions of Englishmen themselves in a comfortably distant and nebulous past. It was not necessary, then, for the supporters of Parliament against Charles I to invent a popular basis for government, but simply to expand and make more explicit the supposed role of the people in originating and defining government.[6]

The definition, of course, would have to confer on Parliament

---

[4] "This is the *grand Error*, that subordinate officers are accountable only to the king, and the king to God, whereas all *Judges* and *Magistrates* are intrusted by the people." John Cook, *Redintegratio Amoris* (London, [1647]), 10. Cf. *A Brief Discourse Examining . . . the Nature, Rise and End of Civill Government* (London, 1648), 5.

[5] Peter English, *The Survey of Policy* (Leith, 1653), 178.

[6] J. G. A. Pocock, *The Ancient Constitution and the Feudal Law* (Cambridge, England, 1957). But cf. John Wallace, *Destiny his Choice: the Loyalism of Andrew Marvell* (Cambridge, England, 1968), 22–30.

powers of government independent of, and preferably superior to, any that the people might have granted to the king. The immediate objective of the change in fictions was to magnify the power not of the people themselves, but of the people's representatives. It did not originate in popular demonstrations against the king but in the contest between king and Parliament, a contest that had escalated to a point scarcely contemplated by the voters who chose the members of Parliament. Accordingly, the first formulations of popular sovereignty in England, from which it never quite escaped, elevated the people to supreme power by elevating their elected representatives.

The most articulate spokesman for the new ideology was Henry Parker, a barrister who became secretary to the Parliamentary army. Already in 1642 he and other Parliamentarians envisaged a nation that existed before it had a king or any other governing officer. According to this view, the people of the nation, exercising their God-given powers, chose to be governed by kings in hereditary succession (they might have chosen any other form of government). In making the choice they set limits to the king's powers in fundamental laws and provided for possible subsequent limitations by their representatives in Parliament. The powers they conferred on the king were conditional upon his observance of those limitations. If he violated the trust placed in him, the people through their representatives could rightly resist him and in the last resort depose him—though Parliamentary spokesmen long denied any intention of doing so.[7]

The new Parliamentary fictions strained credulity as much as the old. The divine right of kings had emphasized the divine character of the king's authority without giving much attention to the act in which God was supposed to have commissioned him. Similarly the sovereignty of the people, emphasizing the popular character of governmental authority, rested on supposed acts of the people, both past and present, that were almost as difficult to examine as acts of God. The very existence of such a thing as *the* people, capable of acting to empower, define, and limit a previously nonexistent government required a suspension of disbelief. History recorded no such action.

[7] Henry Parker, *Some Few Observations upon his Majesties late Answer* [London, 1642]; *Observations upon some of his Majesties late Answers and Expresses* [London, 1642]; *A petition or Declaration* (London, 1642); *The Contra-Replicant* [London, 1643]; Margaret Judson, *The Crisis of the Constitution* (New Brunswick, N.J., 1949), Chapter 10, and "Henry Parker and the Theory of Parliamentary Sovereignty," *Essays in History and Political Theory in Honor of Charles Howard McIlwain* (Cambridge, Mass., 1936), 138–67.

But the impossibility of empirical demonstration is a necessary characteristic of political fictions. In the absence of historical record Parker and his friends could reconstruct the original donation of the people in terms that gave to Parliament a determining power in its dispute with the king. That Parliament represented the whole kingdom in assenting to laws and taxes was, as we have seen, already an accepted part of the old ideology.[8] Parker and his friends built this lesser fiction into a foundation for popular sovereignty. It was true, they acknowledged, that the people as such could not have assembled in order to confer power on anyone. The "vastness of its owne bulke" made direct action by the people impossible.[9] Whole nations in general were "not congregable, nor consultable, nor redeemable from confusion." It therefore followed that "both Kings and laws were first formed and created by such bodyes of men, as our Parliament now are." And Parker easily slipped from imaginary bodies "such as our Parliament now are" to England's Parliament as it now was and allegedly had been from time immemorial. "We may truly say of it," he argued, "that by its Consent Royalty it selfe was first founded, and for its ends royalty it selfe was so qualified and tempered, as it is."[10]

Since by this reasoning Parliament had in effect created the king and set limits on him, it was obvious that Parliament was the best judge of those limits: "from its supreme reason, the nature of that qualification and temperature ought only to be still learned, and the determination thereof sought. For who can better expound what Kings and lawes are, and for what end they were both created, then that unquestionable power, which for its own advantage merely gave creation to them both?"[11]

This formulation involved a circularity that neither Parker nor other Parliamentary spokesmen ever acknowledged: it made Parliament its own creator. But it had the great advantage of endowing Parliament not simply with a part of the powers of government, but with the people's inherent power to begin, change, and end governments. And however circular the reasoning, the attribution attained a degree of plausibility from the election of the House of Commons by what passed for a popular vote. Although it was a small minority of the population

[8] See above, pp. 48–49.
[9] Parker, *Observations upon some*, 15.
[10] Parker, *Contra-Replicant*, 16.
[11] Ibid.

who voted, only a stretch of the imagination was required to envisage parliamentary elections as the act in which *the* people endowed Parliament with their sovereign power.

That the direct action of the suppositious people should remain fictional apart from the element of reality in parliamentary elections was quite in accord with the needs and wishes of Parliament in the contest with the king. Parliament needed popular support, needed men to fight the armies that the king raised, and needed money to pay them, but it did not want any body of people outside Parliament to take matters into their own hands. Although the new ideology might safely encourage a greater degree of popular participation in government than the old, its purpose remained the same, to persuade the many to submit to the government of the few. It would not do to encourage the unruly to shelter under an illusion that they were the people. Mere people, however many in number, were not *the* people, and the sovereignty of the people must not be confused with the unauthorized actions of individuals or of crowds or even of organized groups outside Parliament.

That the new ideology invited such confusion was apparent from the beginning. It was impossible to appeal to the people to resist their king without seeming to appeal to individual, actual people or groups of people. Indeed the sovereignty of the people would have lost much of its usefulness for Parliament if it had been necessary to disavow any connection between *the* people and actual people outside Parliament. The outcome of the contest with the king would depend on the number of warm bodies that each side could muster, and Parliament counted on its own claims to represent the people as a means of enlisting popular support.

The king and his adherents were not unaware of the advantages that the new fiction, if accepted, must give their opponents. Royal government, like any other government, rested on opinion, and the contest between king and Parliament was necessarily a contest of opinions. The fact that Royalists discounted the role of the people as a source of authority did not reduce their need for popular support, and ultimately their own appeals to people became appeals to *the* people. While cavalier fought roundhead in battle, their spokesmen fought the war of fictions in print. Official proclamations and pronouncements, remonstrances and declarations, accusations and rebuttals, all designed for public consumption, all aimed at winning popular support, accompanied every move by either side. And along with these lengthy official appeals came an equally unprecedented outpouring of unofficial pamphlets and newsletters addressed to a popular audience.[12]

Because the new fictions did strain credulity, Royalists did their best to make the strain unbearable. And if sheer logic had determined the outcome, the sovereignty of the people might well have fallen back into obscurity under the Royalists' onslaught. Where, they asked, did the people come from who were supposed to have exercised sovereignty in starting the government, either in England or anywhere else? They must have been without mothers or fathers, "like grasshoppers and locusts bred of the wind, or like *Cadmus* his men sprung out of the earth."[13] All mortal men that anyone had ever seen were born in subjection to authority. If they were born subjects, they could scarcely confer on others a power or authority they did not themselves possess. The whole concept of the will of the people was ridiculous anyhow, "for the people, to speak truly and properly, is a thing or body in continuall alteration and change, it never continues one minute the same, being composed of a multitude of parts, whereof divers continually decay and perish, and others renew and succeed in their places." It followed that "they which are the people this minute, are not the people the next minute."[14] Moreover, the Parliament that claimed to represent this protean entity in fact represented only a small fraction of it. Women, children, and even the majority of adult males had no hand in the selection of representatives. And while some of the nation's smallest boroughs and towns were assigned representatives, some of the largest were not.[15]

But even as they ridiculed the idea of a sovereign people embodied in a Parliament, royalists could not resist the temptation, by taking

[12] George Thomason (d. 1666) collected and dated these publications as they appeared. His collection, now in the British Library and available on microfilm, is the basis of most of this chapter and the next, as it is of most historical studies of the period.

[13] Dudley Digges, *A Review of the Observations upon some of his Majesties late Answers and Expresses* (Oxford, 1643), 4. Cf. Robert Filmer, *Observations upon Aristotle's Politiques* (London, 1652), 14.

[14] Ibid., 40.

[15] Dudley Digges, *An Answer to a Printed Book* (Oxford, 1642), 15; *A Plain Fault in Plain English* (London, 1643), 6; William Prynne, *A Plea for the Lords* (London 1648), 9; *The Anarchy of a Limited or Mixed Monarchy* ([London ?], 1648), 14. The deficiencies of popular representation continued to serve as a Royalist argument against popular sovereignty in the 1680s. See George Hickes, *A Discourse of the Soveraign Power* (London, 1682), 22–24; Paul Lathom, *The Power of Kings from God* (London, 1683), 20; John Wilson, *A Discourse of Monarchy* (London, 1684), *passim*.

the idea at face value, to turn it against their opponents. Suppose that Englishmen were sprung from the earth and able unanimously to agree to delegate whatever powers they possessed, or some part of those powers, what part had they delegated to Parliament and what part to the king? And to whom, if anyone, had they delegated power to alter whatever distribution they had originally made?

A reference to the writs that summoned voters to the polls suggested a realistic answer to these questions. The small minority of the population who voted did so on command of the king, and his writ specified the purpose for which he required them to choose representatives, namely to advise him and give consent to acts of his government, "to be our Counsellors, not Commanders." There was nothing in the writs to suggest that representatives were empowered to do anything else, certainly not, as the king reminded them, "to alter the Government of Church and State."[16] If the people indeed possessed the power to make and break governments and could also impart that power to others, what evidence was there that they had ever imparted it to Parliament? "Clearly," said Sir John Spelman, one of the abler Royalists, "there is no such trust imparted to the [House of] Commons. Their trust is limited by the writ to advise with the *King*, not to make Acts and Ordinances in any case against him."[17]

Even supposing that the House of Commons represented the whole people for whatever purposes, by the very reasoning that assigned sovereignty to the people, those who chose representatives must also have power to dismiss them. The spokesmen for Parliament argued that the people could revoke the powers that they had supposedly bestowed on the king. If that was the case, said the Royalists, they could also revoke the powers they bestowed on their representatives.[18]

To make this last point, Royalists assumed the voice of voters and announced their intention to recall Parliament for "having broken the trust we reposed in you."[19] "We advise all our Knights and Bur-

[16] Rushworth, *Historical Collections*, IV, 591.

[17] *A View of a Printed Book* (Oxford, 1642), 33. See also *Animadversions upon those Notes* [London, 1642], 7; William Ball, *Tractatus de Jure Regnandi et Regni* ([London], 1645), 15; Robert Filmer, *The Free-Holders Grand Inquest* [London, 1648], *passim*.

[18] *A Complaint to the House of Commons* (Oxford, 1642), 23 (Parliamentarians printed in London a tract with precisely the same title, denouncing this one); *Animadversions upon those Notes*, 12; John Maxwell, *Sacro-sancta Majestas* (Oxford, 1644), 101.

[19] *A Complaint to the House of Commons*, 23; *The Declaration of the County of Dorset* ([London], 1648), 4; *A Brief Discourse of the Present Miseries* ([London], 1648), 24–25; *The Commons Dis-Deceiver* ([London], 1648), 7; *A Publike Declaration and Solemne Protestation* ([London], 1648), 5.

gesses," they said, "to vote no more against our gracious Soveraigne
. . . . And as we doe protest against such Ordinances as are made
against the King, or without His Consent, so shall we withdraw our
trust and power of representation from such as shall goe on to abuse
it."[20] One group of "gentlemen and Freeholders" from a dozen counties, eight cities, and fifty-two boroughs addressed their representatives by name, repudiated their actions, and declared that they did
"revoke and resume all that trust, power and authority we formerly
delegated and committed to them."[21] Royalist authors even suggested
that the people might withdraw all power from the House of Commons and locate it in the king alone.[22] If the people were sovereign,
they could confer power wherever they chose. And this was no idle
threat. As the struggle wore on, though the Parliamentary armies got
the better of it, their spokesmen in the press were ready to concede
that "the greater party are for the King."[23]

Insofar as Royalists rejected popular sovereignty altogether, they
were arguing a lost cause. But in challenging Parliament's claim to be
the sole repository of that sovereignty, they expanded the dimensions
of the fiction and contributed to its future success as the basis of modern government. Political fictions, we have already observed, may
impose restraints on the few who govern as well as on the many who
are governed; and the sovereignty of the people could be used to restrain
the governing few in Parliament, as divine right had been used to
restrain the king. The Royalists were the first to try to use it this way,
and they were followed by others with larger ends in view.

The objective for both, insofar as they accepted the new fiction,
was to bring the facts of political life somewhat closer to it, not only
to make Parliament more responsive to those who chose it, but to
make more plausible the very existence of the imaginary body that
could create both kings and parliaments and set limits on their actions.
If that body itself could not be seen or heard at any given time or
place, it might nevertheless give proof of its existence, like the existence of God, if those in power could be made to recognize as ema-
nating from it a set of principles, commandments, limits, a set of
"fundamental constitutions," superior to the government itself. Such

[20] *Sober Sadnes* ([Oxford ?], 1643), 46.

[21] *A Remonstrance and Declaration of Several Counties, Cities, and Burroughs* (London,
1648), 8.

[22] Maxwell, *Sacro-sancta Majestas*, 101.

[23] *Salus Populi Solus Rex* ([London], 1648), 18; *A Warning, or a Word of Advice* (London,
1648), 3.

a recognition might require an act of faith, as had the recognition of the king as God's lieutenant, but it might have given to Parliament a more credible claim to the powers it exercised in the name of the people than it was able in fact to achieve in the 1640s and 1650s. The development of popular sovereignty after king and Parliament went to war lay more in the efforts of Royalists and radicals against Parliament than in the blind equating of popular with parliamentary power as uttered from Westminster.

The limitations of the Parliamentary view became apparent in the first responses to the Royalist challenge, which did not go beyond hurt surprise and dogmatic denials. Implicitly acknowledging Royalist popularity, Parliamentary spokesmen complained of desertion. Those who forsook Parliament for the king, they said, "forsake themselves, their Religion, Lawes, and Properties, and all that can properly be called theirs."[24] Parliament was not simply the representative of the people, it *was* the people: "the *Parliament men* are no other than *our selves*, and therefore we cannot *desert them*, except we *desert our selves*."[25] Or, as another Parliamentary apologist put it, "their judgement is our judgment, and they that oppose the judgment of the Parliament oppose their own judgment."[26] Desertion of Parliament was not only self-destructive, it was wicked. "There can be nothing under Heaven," Parker declared, "next to renouncing God, which can be more perfidious and more pernitious in the people than this."[27] Others suggested that those guilty of "ungrateful and unworthy disrespect unto the Parliament . . . may onely learne better, when better taught by the *Parliaments* lash."[28] From such premises it is no surprise to find lawyers on the Parliamentary side arguing that Parliament "can do no wrong," that "no dishonourable thing ought to be imagined of them," and that "Kings seduced may injure the commonwealth, but that Parliaments cannot."[29]

That so infallible a body should be subject to recall or rebuke by those who chose it was unthinkable. Though Parliament might prop-

---

[24] *Considerations for the Commons* [London, 1642].

[25] *The Vindication of the Parliament and their Proceedings* (London, 1642), 7.

[26] *Plain Dealing with England* (London, 1643), 2.

[27] *Observations upon some*, 16.

[28] *Some more new Observations* (London, 1642).

[29] John Marsh, *An Argument, or Debate in Law* (London, 1642), 15; *The Vindication of the Parliament and Their Proceedings*, 8, 16; *Reasons why this Kingdom ought to adhere to the Parliament* [London, 1642], 7; *Animadversions Animadverted*, [London, 1642], 5.

erly withstand the king whom it, acting for the people, had created, the people had no similar right in relation to Parliament because the people and Parliament were identical. The people's act in conferring power on their representatives was one which "once pass'd they cannot revoke." Moreover the power they conferred was total: "The people," according to one of the most ardent Parliamentary spokesman, "have reserved no power in themselves from themselves in Parliament."[30]

In endowing the people with supreme authority, then, Parliament intended only to endow itself. That intention directed its response to popular pressure even in the traditional form of petitions. When "the most substantiall Inhabitants of the Citie of London" petitioned for less intransigence in Parliamentary negotiations with the king, Parliament replied that its status as trustee for the whole kingdom did not permit it to accommodate a part of the kingdom (that is, the petitioners), and in a burst of candor admitted that "we love not to be sollicited at all by the people in any case whatsoever, except when we do manifestly faile of our Dutie."[31] It did not say who was to judge when such failure was manifest. By 1647 when Parliament was petitioned for a wide spectrum of reforms, including greater religious freedom, it ordered the petition to be burned by the common hangman.[32]

The Parliament that assumed this haughty position is properly known as the Long Parliament. Elected in 1640, it remained the governing body of the kingdom until 1653. During that time the majority of its members departed to join the king or died or were driven out, and most were not replaced in new elections. The army it created forced the resignation of eleven members in the summer of 1647, and in December 1648, in Pride's Purge, forcibly barred 110 more from their seats, leaving only a couple hundred members in the House of Commons. It was this ever-dwindling minority, most of them elected in 1640, who took upon themselves to speak until 1653 the will of the people.[33]

Thanks to its armies, Parliament survived the Royalist challenge

---

[30] Charles Herle, *A Fuller Answer to a Treatise Written by Doctor Ferne* (London, 1642), 25; William Bridge, *The Wounded Conscience Cured* (London, 1642), 36–37; *The Vindication of the Professors and Profession of the Law* (London, 1646), 88–89.

[31] *The Petition of the most substantiall Inhabitants of the Citie of London* (London, 1642).

[32] Don M. Wolfe, ed., *Leveller Manifestoes of the Puritan Revolution* (New York, 1944, 1967), 131–41.

[33] See in general David Underdown, *Pride's Purge* (London, 1971, 1985) and Blair Worden, *The Rump Parliament* (Cambridge, England 1974).

in the field. But the very tenuousness of its claim to represent the people, combined with its long duration and increasing remoteness from its constituents, invited challenges that went beyond the Royalist one, challenges in which the relationship of popular sovereignty to actual people was explored as searchingly as it ever has been. While the issue of the war remained in doubt, the most ardent advocates of the new fiction were content to join ranks behind Parliament.[34] By the summer of 1645, as the king's forces tottered toward surrender, voices from within the ranks began to expose the deficiencies of the Parliamentary claim and to call for reforms that would narrow the gap separating the fiction from fact.

The voices came from many directions. The impending overthrow of the king, his execution in 1649, and the establishment of a republican government set men to reexamining all their old assumptions about themselves and the world they lived in.[35] One group, believing that the Fifth Monarchy predicted in the Book of Revelation was at hand, called for immediate establishment of a theocratic government by saints. Another group, who came to be known as Diggers, decided to abandon virtually all the relationships and institutions that had hitherto bound them to other men. Armed only with spades and mystical visions, they began to dig the earth of common lands and called for an end to private property and social distinctions. These gentle people were too few in number and too imaginative in their goals to affect seriously the shape that popular sovereignty would ultimately assume. But another group, tagged by their opponents as Levellers, though they failed to achieve most of their goals, came a good deal closer.[36] For the goals they set were not beyond reach, and many have in fact been reached in the development of popular sovereignty that still continues.

---

[34] But as early as January 1643, the author of *Plaine English* (London, 1642 [3]), considering the possibility of a betrayal by Parliament, called for a popular association to support the army as "a good second string in case the Parliament should unhappily miscarry." (p. 28.)

[35] The best account is Christopher Hill, *The World Turned Upside Down* (London, 1972).

[36] The Levellers have, deservedly, attracted more attention from scholars than any other group of the period, and their writings were voluminous. See in general Theodore H. Pease, *The Leveller Movement* (Washington, D.C., 1916); Joseph Frank, *The Levellers* (Cambridge, Mass., 1955); A. S. P. Woodhouse, ed., *Puritanism and Liberty* (London, 1938); Wolfe, *Leveller Manifestoes*; William Haller and Godfrey Davies, eds., *The Leveller Tracts* (New York, 1944).

That the Levellers came as close as they did to success in their own time was owing to their influence in yet another group that was dissatisfied with Parliament, namely, the army that fought its battles. Both the army and the Levellers in and outside it were committed to the supremacy of Parliament over the king. But like the Royalists, with whom at some points they nearly joined forces, they became increasingly discontented with the existing Parliament. And their discontent prompted them, as it had the Royalists, to think more seriously about the meaning of popular sovereignty than the members of Parliament were willing to do.

What initially prompted the dissatisfaction of the Levellers and the Army and indeed of other dissatisfied groups was not so much what Parliament was or was not as what it did or failed to do. Parliament's quarrel with the king had been heavily influenced by his religious policies. The members feared that he wished to lead the Church of England back to Rome and that he might even call in Catholic troops from France or Ireland to effect that goal, a fear heightened if not confirmed by his efforts to obtain foreign aid after the war began. Parliament in its hostility to Catholicism probably enjoyed wide popular support. But it did not follow that Englishmen were agreed in their religious views. With the removal of restraints after 1641, religious and ecclesiastical beliefs proliferated. Some favored a continuation of episcopacy, some a presbyterian form of national church, and others, representing a wide variety of theological doctrine, favored freedom for any group to organize its own independent church with no nation-wide organization prescribed.

The members of Parliament, as it happened, came increasingly to favor a national Presbyterian church, and they were encouraged in this direction by the need for military assistance from Scotland, where Presbyterians were in control. By 1645 it was apparent that Parliament, given its way, would force Presbyterianism on all. The men who made up the army, as it happened, had come more and more to favor Independency, that is religious freedom and the independence of individual congregations. Oliver Cromwell in particular, who led the cavalry in spectacular victories over the king's forces, was an advocate of religious freedom, as was John Lilburne, a lieutenant colonel as intrepid with pen and ink as Cromwell was with the sword. Lilburne, along with Richard Overton, a printer, and William Walwyn, a London merchant, produced a torrent of tracts that earned for them and their adherents the name of Levellers. They were all Independents in their views of the church, and it was in opposition to Parliament's Presbyterian policies that they first formulated their proposals for reform.

The proposals themselves, though they directed changes in parliamentary policies, went far beyond specific measures. They proposed to change what Parliament did by changing what it was and at the same time to set limits, in the name of the people, on what it could do. They wanted not only to give more people a hand in electing Parliament but also to give *the* people a way of exercising their sovereignty outside Parliament and with a necessary superiority to Parliament. That the Levellers and most other reformers of the period failed was owing to the fact that they took the new fictions too literally, endowing *the* people with capacities for action that so ideal a body— ideal in the philosophical sense—can never possess. But by the same token they exposed the failure of Parliament to take its own fictions seriously enough and alerted those who accepted the new fictions to the need for limiting the actions of any governing power, whatever its alleged source of authority.

The Leveller proposals belied the name fastened on them by their opponents. The term "Leveller" implied a desire to level social and economic differences and would have accurately described the Diggers (to whom at their first appearance it was applied, probably as part of the continuing effort to discredit the Levellers). It might also have been applied to a few isolated pamphleteers of the time, who denounced the voters for electing to Parliament "the noblest and richest in the County," arguing that "it is they that oppresse you, insomuch that your slavery is their liberty, your poverty is their prosperity."[37] The Levellers themselves complained very little about the social composition of the House of Commons. They expressly disclaimed, and wanted the House to disclaim, any intention of levelling men's estates.[38] Their proposals for reforming the House were accordingly directed not so much against its domination by a social elite as against its bizarre geographical distribution of seats and its long duration. They wanted annual elections and an assignment of seats among the counties of England proportioned to their population. They would have enlarged the suffrage, excluding only women, chil-

---

[37] *A General Charge. Or Impeachment of High Treason* (London, 1647), 11. See also *Tyranipocrit Discovered* (Rotterdam, 1649), which calls for limiting incomes to £100 a year.

[38] Wolfe, *Leveller Manifestoes*, 288, 390.

dren, criminals, servants, and paupers from voting,[39] and they would have denied the House of Commons the right to expel a member without the consent of his constituents. To such a reformed House of Commons they would have given all the powers of the central government, eliminating the House of Lords entirely from government along with the king.[40]

The expansion of suffrage and of representation might well have resulted in some broadening of the membership of the House of Commons to include men of less exalted rank; but if that was the aim of the Levellers they did not say so. The elimination of the House of Lords, to be sure, would bar the highest ranks of the aristocracy from any automatic share in political authority. But in proposing the abolition of the House of Lords the Levellers did not propose the abolition of lordship. Indeed they invited any lord who still cherished political power to stand for election to the House of Commons,[41] and it is not unlikely, given the economic leverage of most lords and the popular deference generally shown them, that many would have won seats in a Leveller-type House. That this outcome would have bothered the Levellers is not apparent. The sovereignty of the people, as they saw it, did not require, indeed forbade, any radical change in the social structure.

It did require, however, more than reform in the election and distribution of representatives in a more powerful House of Commons. Although the Levellers' proposed reform of the House aimed at enabling it to speak more truly what they took to be the will of the people, they never claimed, as Henry Parker had, that Parliament could *be* the people. And as they became more and more disillusioned with the existing Parliament, they thought more and more in terms not merely of reforming it but of finding additional, alternative, more direct ways

[39] The precise extent to which the Levellers would have expanded the franchise has been a matter of some dispute among historians. See C. B. MacPherson, *The Political Theory of Possessive Individualism* (Oxford, 1962); Keith Thomas, "The Levellers and the Franchise," in G. E. Aylmer, ed., *The Interregnum* (London, 1972); R. Howell and D. E. Brewster, "Reconsidering the Levellers," *Past and Present*, no. 46 (1970), 68–86; and G. E. Aylmer, "Gentlemen Levellers?," ibid., no. 49 (1970), 120–25.

[40] Wolfe, *Leveller Manifestoes*, 226–28, 269, 295–99. These reforms were proposed again and again, not only in manifestoes but in the publications of Lilburne, Overton, and Walwyn.

[41] Richard Overton, *A Defiance against all Arbitrary Usurpations or Encroachments* (London, 1646), 21; *A Remonstrance of Many Thousand Citizens, and other Free-born People of England* ([London], 1646), 7.

of expressing the will of the people, thereby to curb any future Parliament that escaped popular control as this one had.

The Levellers indeed had identified the central problem of popular sovereignty, the problem of setting limits to a government that derived its authority from a people for whom it claimed the sole right to speak. How could the people, assuming there was such a thing, speak for themselves and give orders to the government they had supposedly created? In particular, how could they address a Parliament that claimed in their name an authority that knew no bounds?

The first line of approach to popular limitation of Parliament proceeded from a direction marked out by the Royalists. Royalists had repeatedly argued that the people could endow their representatives only with whatever powers the people themselves possessed. The Royalist view of what powers the people possessed was, of course, itself limited: the people had a power to consent to legislation and not much else. When it became apparent that Parliament was bent on establishing Presbyterianism as the state religion, those who took a larger view of popular powers but who favored religious freedom picked up and expanded the Royalist argument. Early in 1645 Walwyn reformulated and transformed it to bar parliamentary regulation of religion: "The people of a Nation" he said, "in chusing of a Parliament cannot confer more then that power which was justly in themselves: the plain rule being this: That which a man may not voluntarily binde himselfe to doe, or to forbear to doe without sinne: That he cannot entrust or refer unto the ordering of any other."[42] Richard Overton reiterated the point the following year, telling the members of Parliament: "neither you, nor none else can have any Power at all to conclude the People in matters that concerne the Worship of God. . . . for wee could not conferre a Power that was not in our selves, there being none of us, that can without wilfull sinne binde our selves to worship God after any other way, then what (to a tittle,) in our owne particular understandings, wee approve to be just."[43] The argument was made most dramatically in 1648 when the Levellers in the army discussed the question with their officers. In answer to the officers' suggestion that the civil magistrate might have some limited power to suppress blasphemy and regulate religion, Thomas Collier, a chaplain with Baptist leanings, asked how the magistrate could get such a power.

[42] A Helpe to the right understanding of a Discourse concerning Independency (London, 1644 [5]), 4.

[43] A Remonstrance of Many Thousand Citizens, 12.

God himself, he acknowledged, could give it to him: "if he have his commission from God we have nothing to do to limit him." But divine right would have to be proved: "If he have his commission from God let him show it."[44] It went without saying that no one could show a commission signed and sealed by the Almighty. Divinity was departing from government.

Once it was admitted that there were powers which the people could not confer on their government, it was natural both to extend the limitation on what the people *could* confer and also to limit the extent of powers that they *did* confer, or had conferred. Overton provided a theoretical basis for the first kind of limitation by positing an equal power in all men over their own bodies. From this individual property in the self must be derived all the powers entrusted to government. The whole purpose of the entrustment was for the "severall weales, safeties and freedomes" of those who granted it. Therefore, he argued, only those powers could be entrusted which served that purpose, "for as by nature, no man may abuse, torment, or afflict himselfe; so by nature, no man may give that power to another, seeing he may not doe it himselfe."[15] John Cook, a barrister and a Leveller sympathizer, put it more positively: "free men can give away their freedom no further then as it conduceth to justice universal and particular."[46] In other words, in the language of a later age, some human rights and powers were inalienable.

While Overton and Cook were formulating these precocious theories, Overton and Lilburn and others were also groping for some embodiment of specific popular rights in fundamental laws that would override any contrary ones enacted by Parliament. In this quest they were handicapped by the historical fictions they had created in arguing for the abolition of the king and House of Lords. While Royalists had usually avoided basing the title of English kings on William's conquest, the Levellers embraced the attribution as a means of discrediting not only the king and the Lords but also most of English law, including the common law (which had traditionally been regarded as the bulwark of liberty). All were products of the "Norman yoke," which freeborn Englishmen must now shake off. And Levellers con-

[44] Woodhouse, *Puritanism and Liberty*, 164.

[45] *An Arrow Against All Tyrants* (London, 1646), 4.

[46] *Redintegratio Amoris*, 32. Independent sects continued to argue for religious liberty on this basis, while Presbyterians maintained that the people could convey to government the power to judge *in sacris*, as well as in other matters.

tinued to decry the common law and the lawyers whose learning was
required to decipher its Latin and French language intricacies.[47] Consequently, as Lilburn and his friends searched for a legal expression
of the will of the people outside Parliament they had to press backward of 1066 for "fundamental constitutions and customs"[48] or else
content themselves with the concessions that had been wrung from
subsequent monarchs. These last, including Magna Carta and the
Petition of Right, they regarded as "but a part of the peoples rights
and liberties . . . wrestled out of the pawes of those Kings, who by
force had conquered the Nation, changed the laws and by strong hand
held them in bondage."[49]

The Levellers had reached this position even before the king was
subdued. After his armies were defeated and the king was himself a
prisoner, it was no longer necessary to search the past for fundamental
constitutions or to rest the liberties of the people on the concessions
of tyrants. It was time for a full statement of popular rights and for
spelling out the limits of the powers that the people could and would
confer on their representatives in a reformed and supreme House of
Commons. What the Levellers proposed was an "Agreement of the
People" to be signed by every Englishman who agreed to transfer to
his representatives the powers specified therein. (What would happen
to those who did not agree is not altogether clear.)[50]

The specific prohibitions and injunctions to be laid on the kingless, lordless Parliament in this Agreement reflected the experience of
the preceding years. Among other things, besides the limitations contained in Magna Carta and the Petition of Right, Parliament was
excluded from power over religion, power to impress men for the
army or navy, power to grant legal privileges or exemptions to any
individual or group, power to imprison for debt or to impose severe
penalties for trivial offenses, or to require accused persons to answer
incriminating questions, or to "levell mens Estates, destroy Propriety,

---

[47] *Englands Lamentable Slaverie* [London, 1645], 3–4; John Lilburne, *The Just Mans
Justification* (London, 1646), 11–13; Lilburne, *Regall Tyrannie Discovered* (London,
1647), 25; *An Alarum to the Headquarters* [London, 1647], 4–5; *Englands Proper and
Onely Way* [London, 1648]; R. B. Seaborg, "The Norman Conquest and the Common Law," *The Historical Journal* 24 (1981), 791–806.

[48] The phrase is used in *The Copy of a Letter from Colonell John Lilburne* [London, 1645],
14.

[49] *Englands Lamentable Slaverie* [London, 1645], 3–4.

[50] Wolfe, *Leveller Manifestoes*, 223–34, 291–303, 311–21, 397–410.

or make all things Common."[51] Many of the provisions were less than precise in their wording, the product of compromise and discussion not only among the Levellers themselves but also between the Levellers in and outside the army on the one hand and officers of the army on the other.

As a result of such discussions the Agreement went through a number of metamorphoses, and several different versions of it were published at different times. For our purposes, however, the specific provisions are less important than the concept it embodied of the people acting apart from their representatives in Parliament. In the first published version, November 3, 1647, the reasoning was made plain: "No Act of Parliament is or can be unalterable, and so cannot be sufficient security to save you or us harmlesse, from what another Parliament may determine, if it should be corrupted; and besides Parliaments are to receive the extent of their power, and trust from those that betrust them; and therefore the people are to declare what their power and trust is, which is the intent of this Agreement."[52] Accordingly the final version expressly forbade any representative "to render up, or give, or take away any part of this Agreement."[53] The response of the sitting Parliament to the proposal was as might have been expected: the Agreement of the People, the House of Commons proclaimed, was seditious, "destructive to the Being of Parliaments, and Fundamental Government of the kingdom."[54] A Parliament claiming omnipotent authority from the people could not afford to admit the possibility of the people being embodied anywhere outside the walls of Westminster.

If there was ever a possibility that the Agreement of the People could have been implemented, it would have been through the army, which by 1647 had begun to think of itself as representing the people more directly than Parliament. Parliament had recruited the "New Model army," as it was called, in the spring of 1645, and it had achieved almost instant success. Parliament had less success in raising the money to pay it. In the spring and summer of 1647, as Parliament moved

[51] Ibid., 301.

[52] Ibid., 230. See also Haller and Davies, *Leveller Tracts*, 426: "That which is done by one Parliament, as a Parliament, may be undone by the next Parliament: but an Agreement of the People begun and ended amongst the People can never come justly within the Parliaments cognizance to destroy."

[53] Wolfe, *Leveller Manifestoes*, 409.

[54] Rushworth, *Historical Collections*, VII, 867, 887.

nevertheless to disband it, the enlisted men formed their own organization to protect themselves, electing two "agitators" from each regi-
ment. In June the soldiers took a "Solemn Engagement" not to disband
until their demands were met, and their demands included not only
their own back pay but some of the political changes that the Levellers
had called for. On the same day that they took the Engagement, one
of them, the famous Cornet Joyce, abducted the king from his Parliamentary keepers, thus giving the soldiers a trump card in politics; for
the king, though no longer a military force, was still a force to be
reckoned with politically. The soldiers now created a Council of the
Army, consisting of their agitators and of two officers from each reg-
iment, along with a number of staff officers. It was in this body and
its committees that the terms of the Agreement of the People were
hammered out, and it was this body that might have found a way to
implement it by some sort of submission to popular vote.[55]

Although the Levellers themselves continued to press for adoption
of the Agreement of the People as a fundamental constitution, the
Council of the Army, increasingly dominated by Oliver Cromwell
and his son-in-law Henry Ireton, sidetracked their efforts and made
of the army itself the instrument for supposed popular control of Parliament. The soldiers in their June 1647 Engagement had made the
point that they "were not a meer mercinary Army, hired to serve any
Arbitrary Power of a State, but called forth and conjured by the several Declarations of Parliament, to the Defence of our own and the
People's just Rights and Liberties."[56] With the king in their possession at Hampton Court they had marched on Westminster in August
1647 and forced the resignation or withdrawal from Parliament of
Presbyterian leaders. When the king escaped to the Isle of Wight and
Royalists rallied to him in a second Civil War, the army again acted
not only to put down the Royalists but to put an end to Parliamentary
negotiations with him. On December 6, 1648, Colonel Pride at the
doors of the House of Commons barred the entry of all members who
favored such negotiations. Within two months the remaining Rump

<hr>

[55] Woodhouse, *Puritanism and Liberty*, 1–178. Mark Kishlansky, "The Army and the
Levellers," *The Historical Journal* 22 (1979), 795–824, and *The Rise of the New Model
Army* (Cambridge, England, 1979), argues that the influence of the Levellers in the
army was never as large as has been supposed. Cf. Norma Carlin, "Leveller Orga-
nization in London," *The Historical Journal* 27 (1984), 955–60; and Barbara Taft,
"The Council of Officers' Agreement of the People," ibid., vol. 28 (1985), 169–85.

[56] Rushworth, *Historical Collections*, VI, 565.

had tried, convicted, and beheaded the king, and in March 1649, abolished both monarchy and the House of Lords.

In taking charge of government the army continued to act through
Parliament. It was a Parliament that owed its existence more to the
army's dictates than to direct election, but the army justified its dictates in the name of the people. Even while it continued to discuss a
possible Agreement of the People, spokesmen for the army explained
that though it was itself recruited by Parliament it was actually the
proper agent of the people: "It is true, the Army received their Commission from the Parliament, and so did the Parliament theirs from
the people; so that the Army are as equally intrusted by the people,
as they are by the Parliament, or the Parliament by the people." Just
as Parliament had earlier claimed to be supporting the king's true self
in resisting him, now the army's dominance of Parliament was "not
disobedience and opposition to the Parliament but the defence of the
Parliament." Parliament rightly considered must want what the army
wanted, because the army wanted what the people wanted.[57]

In the wake of Pride's Purge, a stronger identification with the
people was offered up, perhaps without the army's having to seek it.
William Sedgwick, an army chaplain, after arguing that power had
reverted from Parliament to the people, proclaimed that "This Army
are truly the *people of England*, and have the nature and power of the
whole in them." They were, he said, "the very breast and strength of
England." They had in them "the soule and life of the nation." They
were "unquestionably to be entitled *the people of England*." In the light
of such a perfect identification with "the *whole kingdom* in their true
and right sense" it was ridiculous for the army to concern itself further
with an Agreement of the People.[58]

The reasoning by which Sedgwick arrived at this conclusion revealed
a tendency that would shape many future apologies for whatever powers claimed to act for the people. He spoke of the people only "in their
true and right sense," which was not the more literal sense that the
Levellers had in mind. The army, according to Sedgwick, were "truly
the people, not in a *grosse heape*, or in a *heavy*, *dull body*, but in a *selected*,
choice way: They are the people in *virtue*, *spirit* and *power*, gathered up
into *heart* and *union*, and so most able and fit for the worke they have

---

[57] *A Just Vindication of the Armie* (London, 1647), 5, 11. See also *Englands Remedy*
([London], 1647), 16–17; and *A Cleare and full Vindication of the late Proceedings of the
Armie* (London, 1647).

[58] *A Second View of the Army Remonstrance* (London, 1648), 11–12, 26.

in hand: The people, in grosse, being a monster, an unweildy, rude
bulke of no use."[59]

As the authorization of government moved farther and farther from
any actual designation by popular choice, characterizations of the people as such became less and less flattering. They were the "giddy multitude," "beasts in men's shapes," who would destroy themselves if
given a chance. It was "not *vox*, but *salus populi*" that must determine;
"major reason" must prevail over "major voice."[60] These were not the
sentiments of Royalists but of advocates for both Parliament and the
army. Thus the Reverend John Goodwin, a frequent spokesman for
the powers that be, justified Pride's Purge on the grounds that it was
proper "to save the life of a lunatique or distracted person even against
his will" and went on to argue that "if a people be depraved and corrupt, so as to conferre places of power and trust upon wicked and
undeserving men, they forfeit their power in this behalf unto those
that are good, though but a few. So that nothing pretended from a
non-concurrence of the people with the Army, will hold water."[61]
That the people in mass were not to be trusted with their own welfare
was apparent from "the *childish Love* the Common people beare the
gaudy person of a King."[62] They must be saved from themselves, for
they were "so much deluded with the greatnesse of the King" that
they thought it had been improper to resist him.[63]

The Levellers did not share this view of the people and continued
to press for an Agreement of the People, to be implemented by the
express consent of individuals throughout England and to be treated
also as a contract between representatives and their constituents. After
the king's execution, which went beyond the deposition that the Levellers favored, they protested vehemently against "England's New
Chains" imposed by the army and by the Rump in governing without
the authorization of the people and without regard to the limits that
would have been set by an Agreement of the People.[64] The army
responded in March 1649, by arresting Lilburne, Overton, Walwyn,
and Thomas Prince (a merchant who had recently emerged as a leader

[59] Ibid., 13.
[60] *Salus Populi Solus Rex*, 19.
[61] *Right and Might Well Met* (London, 1648), 15.
[62] *A Perswasive to a Mutual Compliance* (Oxford, 1652), 22.
[63] English, *The Survey of Policy*, 17–18, 85.
[64] *Englands New Chains Discovered* [London, 1648]; *The Second Part of Englands New-Chaines Discovered* [London, 1649].

of the movement). From the Tower of London these four continued to denounce the new regime, but the shrillness of their protests betrayed the forlornness of their cause. Although they retained a following among the common soldiers, it was not enough to matter. A mutiny led by their supporters in May 1649, was quickly put down; and with it perished all hope for an Agreement of the People. In September the indefatigable Lilburne issued an appeal for popular action to elect a new representative assembly to bypass and overthrow the existing Parliament and establish the principles of the Agreement. But by this time the feebleness of the response made clear that the Leveller cause was dead.[65]

[65] *Englands Standard Advanced* [London, 1649]; *The Levellers (Falsly so called) Vindicated* [London, 1649]; *An Outcry of the Youngmen and Apprentices* [London, 1649]; *The Remonstrance of Many Thousands of the Free-People of England* (London, 1649).

CHAPTER 4

The People's Two Bodies

T HE DEMISE of the Levellers and their Agreement of the People
left unanswered the question of how actual people might
exercise the acknowledged sovereignty of *the* people over a
government whose claim to represent them was becoming
increasingly difficult to credit. The credibility of the kingless government was only made the more dubious by an effort to shore it up
through an "Engagement" (not to be confused with the soldiers' Solemn Engagement of June 1647) to which all citizens were supposed to
subscribe. The new engagement stated simply that the subscriber would
"be true and faithfull to the Commonwealth of England, as it is now
established without King and House of Lords."[1] In place of an Agreement of the People that would limit the government, this offered the
Rump Parliament and its military masters a blank check to govern as
they pleased, unhampered even by the traditional restrictions that had
hedged in the older royal government.

In support of so bald a bid for power, spokesmen of the army and
the Rump offered arguments that handed the sovereignty of the people to the strongest battalions in a new kind of divine right. All government, the apologists now discovered, rested on force, and that was
the way God wanted it. It was the solemn duty of all men to obey
whoever had the force, because "it is not possible that any can attain

---

[1] S. R. Gardiner, ed., *The Constitutional Documents of the Puritan Revolution* (Oxford,
1889), 298.

to the height of power without Gods disposall of it into his hands."[2] It was no use to question the authority of the existing government because there was no rival government and "nothing can binde to that which is not in being." It followed "that they that possess the places and performe the duty *de facto* must *de jure* and *ex debito*, receive the dignity annext to the publike authority."[3]

While thus glorifying brute force ("the power of the Sword is, and ever hath been, the Foundation of all Titles to Government") Marchamont Nedham, who was to gain an undeserved reputation as a political thinker, proclaimed the superiority of the existing government both to monarchy and to the kind of government envisaged in the Agreement of the People. The Agreement, he charged, with its inclusion of the Leveller provision for annual elections and extension of the suffrage, would have resulted in "unlearned, ignorant Persons, neither of Learning nor Fortune, being put in Authority." The "self-opinionated Multitude" would have elected "the *lowest of the People*" who like some of their Roman predecessors would have occupied themselves with "Milking and Gelding the Purses of the Rich," an outcome that would have proved "the ready Road to all licentiousnesses, mischief, mere Anarchy and Confusion."[4]

Though the Agreement of the People had become a lost cause, such hysterical denunciations of it indicated the thinness of the existing regime's popular support. Nedham wrote to persuade people to take the engagement, but the engagement itself prompted others to challenge the legitimacy of the regime. In the earlier Solemn League

[2] J. D., *Considerations concerning the present Engagement* (London, 1649), 15. See also *The Bounds and Bonds of Publique Obedience* (London, 1649), *Plenary Possession Makes a Lawfull Power* (London, 1651). There is a curious resemblance between the arguments for the engagement and some of those for religious toleration, on the grounds that it is not possible for mortals to determine which religion (or which government) is the right one. The casuistry used to defend the engagement is placed in a larger perspective by John Wallace, *Destiny his Choice*, and by Quentin Skinner, "Thomas Hobbes and the Engagement Controversy," in Aylmer, *The Interregnum*, 79–98. Hobbes's *Leviathan* (1651), growing out of the engagement controversy, furnished a philosophical justification for absolute government that left little room for divine right on the one hand or popular sovereignty, as usually conceived, on the other. Although his arguments were powerful, their influence on the growth of the fictions we have been tracing lay less in attempts to refute them than in a simple revulsion from them.

[3] *A Disingag'd Survey of the Engagement* (London, 1650), 21.

[4] *The Case of the Common-Wealth of England Stated* (London, [1650]), 74–79.

and Covenant of 1643, Parliament had exacted a promise "to preserve and defend the King's Majesty's Person and Authority, in the Preservation and Defence of the true Religion and Liberties of the Kingdoms [of England, Scotland, and Ireland], that the World may bear Witness with our Consciences of our Loyalty, and that we have no Thoughts or Intentions to diminish his Majesty's just power and Greatness."[5] Now the remains of the House of Commons had not only killed the king but transformed the government to exclude king and kingship and the House of Lords too. In the engagement, they were asking the people to sanction after the fact actions that by their own admission had not had and did not have the sanction of the people.

The response from those who had the courage to make it was to deny that the members of the House of Commons could confer supreme power on themselves: "if such a grant could create a right, few men that could get strength would lack preferment."[6] If the government by king, Lords, and Commons, sworn to in the Solemn League and Covenant, was to be altered, it must be done by the people themselves, not by representatives chosen by the army out of representatives chosen by the people to be a part of that government which the army and the Rump had destroyed ("It being beyond the power of the constituted, and onely in the Constitutors to make such an alteration in the fundamental Constitution").[7] The engagement itself was sufficient evidence that the people had not authorized the change: "if they had, to what end were this *Engagement* tendered to them? they had in effect subscribed it before, and would no doubt bee faithfull to that which they had given being to." Although those who spoke up against the engagement did not offer any plan of how the people might go about setting up a new government if they in fact wished to, they were clear that they could not have done it in elections to the House of Commons: "A Power to constitute a new fundamentall and Supreme Government was never committed, granted or entrusted, either anciently or lately to that House, that ever wee heard or can believe. All that (to our understandings) they can claime from the People, is a power to bee of the Government and Constitution, as one *integrall*;

---

[5] Gardiner, *Constitutional Documents*, 187–90; Rushworth, *Historical Collections*, V, 478–79.

[6] *An Exercitation concerning Usurped Powers* ([London?], 1650), 73.

[7] Ibid., 8.

not to bee the Constitutors of it, as efficients, or the sole and pleni-
potentiarie transformers of it, or the founders of another."[8]

The opponents of the engagement, like the Levellers before them,
had fastened on a distinction that was to become central to the later
development of the fictions that made up the sovereignty of the people: the distinction between the power to legislate embodied in an
elected representative assembly, on the one hand; and on the other
hand what today would be called the constituent power—that is, the
power to begin, end, or alter the government of which that assembly
was a part. The constituent power had to be superior to the legislative
power. It had to be considered the work of the people as opposed to
their mere attorneys or representatives. The army was in effect claiming such a power, claiming to *be* the people when it purged the House
of Commons of members who had allegedly betrayed their trust. Such
a claim, however hard to believe, respected the distinction, as the
claim of the House of Commons itself to alter the government could
not.

The army asserted its claim again when Cromwell successively
dissolved the Rump and then the "Barebones Parliament" whose
members he had appointed to take its place. But by this time the claim
was even harder to believe, as Cromwell took it entirely to himself. In
December 1553, he decreed a new constitution, the "Instrument of
Government," in which he gave himself most of the powers formerly
held by the king, assisted by a Council of State and an elected Parliament. In a "Humble Petition and Advice" of 1657 the elected Parliament created a new House of lifetime lords and invited Cromwell to
call himself king.[9] Cromwell, satisfied with the substance, refused the
title. His death in 1658 was followed by another series of changes,
including the recall of the surviving members of the Long Parliament
and finally the restoration of the monarchy in 1660.

Most of these changes were made in the name of the sovereign
people. Although many of the Royalists who welcomed the return of
the king were ready to reaffirm his divine right, others perceived that
divine right was no longer necessary to monarchy. In the years since
1642 it had become apparent that popular sovereignty did not necessarily dictate one form of government rather than another. While the
engagement of 1650 had called for a republic, the Solemn League and

---

[8] *A Plea for Non-Scribers* ([London?], 1650), 26–27.
[9] Gardiner, *Constitutional Documents*, 334–45.

Covenant of 1643 and the Humble Petition and Advice of 1657 had called for monarchy. The sovereignty of the people offered no obstacle to the restoration of the king.

What popular sovereignty did require, in the eyes at least of those who thought seriously about it, was a means by which some body or bodies capable of doing so could speak decisively and authentically for the people, so as to contain government, whether monarchical or otherwise, within the framework and the limits which that speaking body prescribed for it. It was widely acknowledged that the people could not speak for themselves—there were too many of them. And the question of who could speak for them was complicated by the perceived alienation of the majority of the population from those who were most eager to speak, most eager to affirm the sovereignty of the people.[10] To many this seemed at first a temporary, circumstantial difficulty. As time passed, they reasoned, the adherents of monarchy would come to recognize the benefits of popular power. But the problem of reconciling the wishes and needs and rights of actual people with the overriding will of a fictional sovereign people was not temporary. It was, indeed, inherent in the new fictions. Until and unless it could be worked out, the sovereignty of the people would pose graver threats not only to the wishes but also to the rights and liberties of actual people, than the divine right of kings had ever done. The way to work it out lay in taking a lesson from the older problem of reconciling divine right with human weakness.

Over the centuries the keepers of the old fiction had divided the king's person into two bodies, one symbolic, eternal and divine, the other concrete, time-bound and human. The division had provided a means by which one part of the government (Parliament) could hold the nominally supreme part (the king) to a given standard of conduct. The real power could be asked, if not required of right, to conform to the ideal, the human to the divine. The old fictions had also been clear in distinguishing God's lieutenant from his subjects and in giving his subjects rights and privileges which he could not violate without endangering his claim to divinity and thus to authority. To begin with at least, the new fiction lacked these distinctions. When Parliament or the army claimed to be the people, it left no room for any higher expression of their will. And when the people became sovereign they seemingly ceased to be subjects and so could no longer claim the rights

[10] See Chapter 3, note 23.

of subjects against themselves, as John Lilburne and the Levellers had discovered in prison. By the 1650s it was apparent that the new fiction, in the absence of a clear distinction between sovereign and subject, and in the absence of any higher expression of popular will, could endow an existing government with absolute and arbitrary powers beyond anything that England's kings had ever exercised. Under the guise of popular sovereignty a Parliament that held no elections, or an army that defied its creators, or a Protector who made and broke governments at will could claim to be acting as sole agents of the very people they oppressed. The new fictions, by placing authority and subjection, superiority and inferiority in the same hands, could deprive people, who were actually subjects, of effective control over a government that pretended to speak for them—a form of tyranny that popular sovereignty continues to bring to peoples all over the world.

What was needed was what the Levellers had been groping for, a division resembling that between the king's two bodies, a division that would protect the people as subjects from the people as rulers, a division between the power to govern and the power to determine the form and limits of government. In the years after 1649, as Cromwell and his handpicked Parliaments gave England a taste of arbitrary government, a number of individuals, following the lead of the Levellers, were casting about for a way to give the people two or more bodies, so that one could control the other and protect actual subjects from acting rulers.

Most of those who grappled with the problem recognized the need to establish or restore a set of fundamental laws or "fundamental constitutions" that would embody the will of the people in some enduring way, superior to the changing needs and ambitions of the persons who might be designated to conduct the day-to-day operations of government.[11] Some contented themselves with setting down specific prohibitions and injunctions, without attempting to say how an elected Parliament could be prevented from violating them. But a few, addressing themselves to the structure of government, tried to work out schemes that would give a separate and superior institutional voice to the people, to protect them as subjects from themselves as governors.

[11] *The Onely Right Rule for Regulating the Lawes and Liberties* (London, 1652), 4–5; *No Return to Monarchy* (London, 1659), 6–7; *Speculum Libertatis Angliae* (London, 1659), 6; *A Mite of Affection* (London, 1659), 10; Henry Stubbe, *A Letter to an Officer of the Army* (London, 1659), 61.

One of the most perceptive was Isaac Penington, Jr., whose father had represented London in the Long Parliament. Penington, himself a mystical revolutionary, started from the premise that "They who are to govern by *Laws* should have little or no hand in making the *Laws* they are to govern by."[12] He recognized that the people as such could act only through representatives, and he accepted Parliament as the body through which they had generally acted. But in 1651, when he wrote, Parliament consisted of the Rump, which had assumed all the powers of government. As he looked at the result Penington concluded that this Parliament not only was unrepresentative but that it was performing functions from which it ought to have been excluded even if it had been perfectly representative. Parliament, like the people themselves, was "of a *great bulk* . . . and therefore not fitted for many motions, but only for such as are slow and sure."[13] Ideally Parliament should exercise the people's sovereign power only "in such ways as were proper for the people to exercise it in were they capable of joynt and orderly acting."[14] As the people were bound to be subjects of government as well as its theoretical masters, the members of Parliament ought themselves to keep the character of subjects. They should not attempt to administer the government; they should be what the name of the House of Commons implied, ordinary people; and they should return as rapidly as possible to being mere subjects, so as to feel the effects of the measures they passed as representatives.

In prescribing what those measures should be Penington did not attempt to exclude Parliament from making constitutional changes in the structure of government. He described its powers as constitutive, corrective, and alterative, as extraordinary powers, "above the ordinary standing Power," by which he seems to have meant the executive or "administrative" power.[15] He refrained from specifying how those who were to exercise this power should be selected. They were apparently to be chosen at least indirectly by popular vote, but they were clearly to be distinct from Parliament. What had gone awry in England was that Parliament had assumed this ordinary standing power that formerly centered in the king. As a result there was no body to guard the interests of subjects and serve as a buffer between government and people. "The proper use of Parliaments," he said, "is to be a curb to

[12] *The Fundamental Right, Safety and Liberty of the People* (London, 1651), 3.
[13] P. 27.
[14] P. 5.
[15] Pp. 5, 13–15.

the extravagancy of Power, of the *highest standing Power:* But if they themselves become *the standing Power*, how can they be a fit curb for it? . . . So that if Parliaments succeed in the place of the *supream administring-power*, there will be as much need of somewhat else to stand between the people and them, as there was of them to stand between the people and *Kingly Power:* for they coming into that place and Authority, the people are in as much danger of them, as they were of the Power of Kings." [16] Penington's solution was not to create a new representative body but to restore Parliament to its old character, with a recognition of its supremacy over those, however chosen, who would exercise the ordinary powers of government.

Penington's analysis was not highly original. Others also saw the need to distinguish executive from legislative powers. [17] The virtue of his scheme lay in its recognition that the people were actual subjects as well as fictional sovereigns, and needed protection as subjects from those who exercised their powers as sovereigns. Penington offered a way to conform the structure of government to the people's two characters without creating any new and unfamiliar institutional apparatus.

The same could not be said of another, more acute analysis and prescription that also sought to locate the people's rights as subjects within the structure of a government that recognized their sovereignty. James Harrington, whose writings were much more widely circulated and better known than Penington's, offered in his *Commonwealth of Oceana* a model of government so bewildering in its detail that it could scarcely have had a wide reading. But its analysis of England's society and politics was carried to the public in simpler form in a variety of briefer tracts, including many by Harrington himself. [18]

---

[16] P. 13.

[17] *Mercurius Politicus*, July 1–8, 1652; R. V., *Certain Proposals Humbly Presented to the Parliament* (London, 1653), 8; Marchamont Nedham, *The Excellencie of a Free State* (London, 1656), 212; *Lilburns Ghost* (London, 1659), 5.

[18] Harrington's own writings are in J. G. A. Pocock, ed., The *Political Works of James Harrington* (Cambridge, England, 1977). His principal thesis is anticipated in *A Copy of a Letter from an Officer of the Army in Ireland* [London, 1656]. Subsequent formulations of it include *XXV Queries Modestly and Humbly . . . propounded* (London, 1659); *The Leveller: or, The Principles and Maxims concerning Government and Religion* (London, 1659); *The Armies Dutie* (London, 1659); *A Commonwealth and Commonwealthsmen* (London, 1659); *The Humble Petition of Divers Well-affected Persons* (London, 1659); *A Model of a Democraticall Government* (London, 1659); *A Modest Plea for an Equal Common-wealth* (London, 1659).

Harrington was convinced that the distribution of political power in any stable government must depend on the distribution of land. In England both land and power had once been in the hands of the king and nobility, but during the preceding century land had become much more widely distributed among the gentry and yeomanry. The Civil Wars, he argued, were the product of the resulting imbalance, as government adjusted to the change. Stable government in England must now be, as it had become, republican, with political power widely distributed. Harrington wished in effect to freeze the situation by forbidding the accumulation of more than a certain amount of land by a single person and by keeping the government continuously attuned to the resulting structure of society. There would still be a numerous and not very aristocratic aristocracy, and there would still be a much more numerous body of ordinary people, a substantial portion of which, if not the majority, would be landowners. The government in turn would contain a large house of representatives, larger and more representative than the existing house of commons, and also a small house of lords or senate, the one directly, the other indirectly, elected by popular vote.

Harrington despaired of establishing his republic by the action of the people or their representatives. Instead he looked to a conquering hero, a Cromwell, to put the scheme in practice. Once in place it would provide its own stability through a variety of devices such as rotation in office and secret ballots. The essential device, however, in which the differing characters of the people as sovereign and as subjects would be embodied, was in the limitation of the popularly elected representatives to approving or rejecting without amendment whatever laws might be formulated by the senate. Representatives were to be limited to their local character as subjects. They were to be as near as possible a replica of the people at large, and like their constituents they would be not only too numerous but too incompetent intellectually to devise laws and develop policy. They would nevertheless be fully competent to understand how a proposed law, devised by the republican senate, would affect them as subjects, and therefore to reject or accept it.

Harrington, as we shall see, was to have a long-continuing influence on the subsequent history of popular sovereignty, especially in the American colonies, but his deliberating senate and yes-or-no house of representatives was perhaps the least successful of his proposals. Although the separation of powers within the structure of government became a standard ingredient of Anglo-American government, and although the separation included a division of legislative powers between two houses, it was not the separation that Harrington had envisaged for protecting the people as subjects from the people as rulers. The future, especially in America, lay closer to the route that the Levellers had begun to explore, in giving the putative people a commanding voice outside the government they created and embodying their rights as subjects in the commands they thereby gave to their government.

The Levellers' scheme of an Agreement of the People to achieve this end had foundered on its too literal application. In order to take effect the Agreement of the People would properly have required the signature of every man, woman, and child to be governed and protected under it. But the idea behind it, of the people acting apart from their government, to create and limit government, lay at the heart of popular sovereignty. After the demise of the Agreement, a number of persons continued to think about it, about giving the people a controlling voice outside the structure of government.

One who thought seriously about the theoretical implications of such extralegal or para-legal popular action was George Lawson, a moderate clergyman who had supported the Parliamentary cause.[19] Lawson borrowed the jargon of earlier political theorists in order to distinguish the powers of the people in their supposed natural condition, before they formed a society, from the powers of the government that the society created. The people in their "original state of liberty" (what would later be called a state of nature), had first to come together and form a "community." That community would then enjoy "real" majesty or sovereignty, which was the power to create a "commonwealth" with a government of whatever form the community might designate. The government thus created had the lesser power of "personal" majesty or sovereignty, to which the people became subject. As subjects they could not resist or alter the government which, acting as a community, they had created, provided those thus endowed with personal majesty acted according to the conditions imposed by the community at the outset. In England, according to Lawson, the community had placed personal majesty in the collective hands of the king and Parliament. When the king deserted Parliament, he destroyed

---

[19] Lawson's ideas are examined at length in Julian H. Franklin, *John Locke and the Theory of Sovereignty* (Cambridge, England, 1978), 53–86. They are expounded in *An Examination of the Political Part of Mr. Hobbs his Leviathan* (London, 1657) and *Politica Sacra et Civilis* (London, 1660).

the government and all the personal majesty it possessed. In doing so
he left Parliament with no residual powers. Once the king deserted it,
Parliament as Parliament ceased to exist, as did the commonwealth of
which it was a part.

What remained was the community, which was not destroyed by
the destruction of the commonwealth. Having gone through this exercise in definition, Lawson came to the crucial question of how the
community, deprived of both king and Parliament, could act at all.
Although he was too preoccupied with his definitions to face the question clearly, he did face it and suggested, in different publications,
two possible answers.

Lawson's first suggestion, made in passing without elaboration,
was one that had already surfaced among those who were disen-
chanted with the succession of governments claiming power over them.
It was simply an affirmation of the continuing endurance and superiority of local institutions when the central government failed. As early
as 1645 William Ball had argued that "Counties, cities, and Townes
corporate" could take arms against a Parliament that betrayed them,
because counties, cities, and towns were "essential."[20] Later the Levellers' proposals had included a reduction in the power of the central
government and a magnification of local administrative powers, a suggestion that was echoed by later reformers.[21] Lawson in envisaging
the destruction of the commonwealth and survival of the community
suggested that the community was embodied in the counties. The
community, he said, could not act through Parliament to alter the
government because Parliament was part of the commonwealth. Instead,
"the People must return unto the original State of Liberty, and to a
Community, which in *England* is not a Parliament, but the fourty
Counties."[22] The idea was appealing because it is much more plausible to conceive of the people acting without and apart from government in small local neighborhoods than in a whole kingdom or nation,
but it left unanswered the question of how forty counties could constitute a single community in the absence of king or Parliament.

Lawson's other suggestion, also unelaborated, was simply a repe-

[20] William Ball, *Tractatus de Jure Regnandi et Regni* ([London], 1645), 13.
[21] Wolfe, *Leveller Manifestoes*, 190, 303; J. W. *A Mite to the Treasury*, 10–11; *The Fundamental Lawes and Libertyes of England* [London, 1653], 4; *Sagrir. Or Doomes-day drawing nigh* (London, 1654).
[22] *Examination of the Political Part*, 15.

tition of the sleight of hand that Henry Parker had engaged in when he spoke about the people acting through a body "such as our Parliament now are." Without identifying the body that still called itself a Parliament, Lawson suggested that "If the Government be dissolved, and the Communitie yet remains united, the People may make use of such an Assembly as a Parliament, to alter the former Government and constitute a new; but this they cannot do as a Parliament, but considered under another Notion, as an immediate Representative of a Communitie, not of a common-wealth."[23] In other words, if Parliament called itself a convention or by any name other than its old one, it might safely proceed to erect whatever government it chose, a procedure to which Englishmen would resort in 1660 and again in 1689.

A much more detailed and more daring suggestion came from Sir Henry Vane, who had cut his teeth on political controversy twenty years earlier in a dispute with Governor John Winthrop in Massachusetts Bay. In 1656 in *A Healing Question*, he proposed to the army and to Cromwell a way of giving substance to the army's claim to be the people. Vane was impatient with the array of governments that had assumed larger and larger powers in the name of the people while distancing themselves farther and farther from actual people. The army, he decided, was the closest thing to an embodiment of the people. In a sense they could be thought of as the people acting in a military capacity. And in that capacity they had become "irresistible, absolute, and comprehensive in their power, having that wherein the substance of all Government is contained."[24] It was time for them to use that power to achieve the goals for which they had fought the king and unseated an irresponsible Parliament; they must exercise the sovereignty of the people to establish fundamental constitutions of government.

Vane did not go into detail about the specific content of these constitutions, though he made clear that they should include an injunction against the establishment of a particular religious denomination and that they might also bar the legislature from participating in the execution of the laws it made. The way to bring about the establishment of fundamental constitutions was through a "General Council, or Convention of faithful, honest, and discerning men, chosen for that

[23] *Politica Sacra*, 35–36.
[24] *A Healing Question* [London, 1656], 10.

purpose by the free consent of the whole Body of adherents to this Cause."[25] It was up to the commanding general of the army to arrange for the elections and to set the time and place of meeting. Perhaps the most significant of Vane's prescriptions was that this "Convention is not properly to exercise the Legislative Power, but onely to debate freely, and agree upon the particulars that, by way of fundamental Constitutions, shall be laid and inviolably observed, as the conditions upon which the whole Body so represented, doth consent to cast it selfe into a Civil and Politique Incorporation, and under the visible form of Government therein declared." When the document was completed, it was "to be by each individual member of the Body subscribed in testimony of his or their particular consent given thereunto."[26]

It will be obvious that what Vane proposed differed little from the old Agreement of the People, which had been drafted by agitators elected from army regiments and by the army's General Council. Not surprisingly it pleased Cromwell as Protector no better than the Agreement of the People had pleased Parliament. Neither wished to be exposed to so direct and commanding an expression of popular will. Cromwell and his Council of State pronounced the proposal seditious and imprisoned the author.

The charge of sedition against both Vane and the Levellers may remind us that popular sovereignty remained, like the fictions that preceded it, a way of reconciling the many to the government of a few. It originated, not so much in discontent among the governed many, as in disagreement among the governing few. Those who invoked it were wary of having it invoked against them, as jealous of their own exclusive claim to speak for the people as the king had been of his claim to speak for God. To set up a convention with a higher claim to popular authority than Parliament or Protector was a little like setting up the pope with a higher claim to divine authority than the king.

But popular sovereignty, like divine right, had a life and logic of its own that made demands on those who used it. As a fiction it required the *willing* suspension of disbelief, which meant that perceived reality must not depart so far from the fiction as to break the suspension. As the king must not behave in a way that would betray his claim to be God's lieutenant, a Parliament (or new-style king) must not become so isolated from the people as to render absurd the claim to speak for

[25] P. 20.
[26] P. 20.

them. On the other hand, a fiction taken too literally could destroy the government it was intended to support. A government that surrendered to direct popular action would cease to govern. The fiction must approach the fact but never reach it.

The governments that succeeded one another from 1642 to 1660 were unable to strike the proper balance. Each successive change brought a greater isolation from the people and a greater distrust of any motions made by others in their behalf. The proposals by Vane and the Levellers may have been too literal in calling for subscription by individuals to give direct popular endorsement of fundamental laws. But the idea of an elected convention that would express enduring popular will in fundamental constitutions superior to government was a viable way of making popular creation and limitation of government believable. It was fictional, for it ascribed to one set of elected representatives meeting in convention a more popular character, and consequently a greater authority, than every subsequent set of representatives meeting as a legislature. But it was not too fictional to be believed and not so literal as to endanger the effectiveness of government. It never came into use in England, but it was reinvented in the American Revolution. There is no evidence that the men who met at Philadelphia in 1787 knew that they were acting out Henry Vane's *Healing Question* or George Lawson's distinction between community and commonwealth. But the inner dynamic of popular sovereignty recreated Vane's proposal and Lawson's distinctions (without his bewildering nomenclature) in America of the 1780s as it had created them in England of the 1650s.

The unwillingness of Parliament or Protector to consider such proposals in the 1640s and 1650s is symptomatic of their failure to achieve a willing suspension of disbelief in their claim to speak for the people. Perhaps no government without a king could have made good its claim, for it was widely agreed at the time that the people, if able to speak for themselves, would have repudiated any other government. Nineteen out of twenty, it was said, would have preferred the government they got when Charles II returned.[27] That estimate may exaggerate the proportions, but even the apologists of the various governments of the interregnum acknowledged that they lacked a popular

[27] *A Copy of a Letter Concerning the Election of a Lord Protector* (London, 1654), 36. By 1681 Bishop Burnet was ready to declare that the protectorate had not enjoyed the approval of 99 out of 100. *A Sermon Preached before the Aldermen . . . Jan. 30, 1680–1* (London, 1681), 16.

majority. What was more important, by the end of the 1650s they
probably lacked a majority of those who mattered, those whose positions in society assured them of deference from the rest. Harrington
may have been right in thinking that the redistribution of land in the
preceding century had greatly increased the numbers who mattered.
But they were still a small percentage of the whole: the bulk of the
population was without property, without the religious zeal that ani-
mated the contest with the king and the contests that followed among
the victors, without even the ability to read the tracts in which they
debated with one another. Most of the population belonged to what
Richard Baxter called "the rabble that cannot read," and they were all
too ready to follow what he called the "sensual gang" among their
betters, rather than the saints.[28]

As long as the literate, propertied saints commanded a majority of
their own kind, they could carry the rest of the country with them.
For a time they could suppress stage plays and maypoles and the Book
of Common Prayer. For a time they could levy heavier taxes than the
people had ever borne before. But there were limits to the lengths
they could go in measures for which there was so little popular enthusiasm.[29] Without strong support among those who mattered, the limits would shrink. And as the succession of interregnum governments
wore on, more and more of those who mattered worried about the
absence of the restraints that had protected all subjects under the king.
None of the proposals by such as Vane and Harrington and Penington
met with serious consideration, and it was questionable whether any
of them, even if adopted, would have offered a security comparable
to what Englishmen had claimed under the "ancient constitution,"
under Magna Carta and the Petition of Right, and the common law.
If the mass of the people preferred a government by king, Lords, and
Commons to a Protector who acknowledged no effective superior,
perhaps that was what popular sovereignty demanded in seventeenth-
century England as the most effective way of maintaining the will of
the people in fundamental law. It was not only the "sensual gang" and
their following among the "rabble" who seemingly deserted the good
old cause for the ancient constitution but men who took popular sovereignty seriously. Seen in this light, the Restoration was not a repu-

[28] Richard Baxter, *A Holy Commonwealth* (London, 1659), 236; Keith Thomas, *Religion
and the Decline of Magic* (New York, 1971), 162; Keith Wrightson, *English Society
1580–1680*, 206–21.

[29] David Underdown, *Revel, Riot, and Rebellion* (New York, 1986).

diation, but a triumph, of popular sovereignty, the new fiction settling into a viable relation with fact. Unfortunately neither Charles II nor those who engineered his return were able to see the usefulness of popular sovereignty in this light, and the lessons of the 1640s and 1650s had to be learned anew in the 1670s and 1680s, and again in the 1770s and 1780s.

CHAPTER 5

The Cautious Revolution

THE DECADE of England's radical experiments in government drew toward a close in 1659 when the Rump Parliament, dissolved in 1653, reassembled at Westminster. The army had created the Rump in 1648 when Colonel Pride purged the House of Commons of all members who favored continued recognition of the already disabled monarch. Recall of the Rump was itself a sign of the general disenchantment with the intervening regimes, and the clock was put back farther in February 1660 when General George Monk undid Pride's Purge by reinstating the excluded members. In less than a month the reconstituted body finally dissolved itself to make way for a new Parliament on the old plan. Although it was called a Convention because not summoned by a king, the members quickly demonstrated their conviction that a restored Parliament required a restored king. Two weeks after convening they had Charles II proclaimed in London.

The Convention Parliament, as it was now called, continued to sit for the rest of the year and showed something of the old Parliamentary independence. In their first address to the king, presented by Denzil Holles, a veteran of the Long Parliament of 1641, they assured him that they were "the true representative of the whole nation." As such they proceeded to pass bills to abolish feudal tenures of land and to confirm both Magna Carta and the Petition of Right. They even passed bills reminiscent of an earlier day to punish breaches of the sabbath, drinking of healths, and profane cursing and swearing.[1] But at the

[1] William Cobbett, *Cobbett's Parliamentary History of England* (London, 1806–20), IV, 53–54, 146–51, 162, 164.

beginning of the next year, 1661, new elections produced a Parliament whose members, sitting for the next eighteen years, showed at the outset a deference to the king that seemed to spell the total demise of popular sovereignty. As one of its first measures the new Parliament ordered the Solemn League and Covenant of 1643 burned by the common hangman. By a specific act the members disclaimed any legislative authority apart from the king, and with his approval restricted popular petitions, emasculated the Triennial Act, and restored the Church of England to preeminence by laying severe penalties on any kind of dissent from it, Catholic or Protestant, lay or clerical.[2]

The clergy of the restored church responded gratefully with reaffirmations of the divine right of the king. For the next thirty years, with assistance from secular writers of the same persuasion, they did their best to dismantle the whole apparatus of opinion that located the origin and justification of government in the people. Government, they found, did not originate in a compact between king and people or among the people themselves. Who had ever seen this celebrated document, they asked, where was it kept? Nowhere, because such contracts "never had any existence but in their nodles that invented them."[3]

The people, it now appeared, had nothing to do with starting governments. They could not confer powers of government on anyone, because they had no such powers themselves. Governments began in the natural authority of fathers over their children. Men were not born free (it went without saying that women were not) and never had been since Adam's time. Nor could the people place limits on government in the fundamental constitutions that had been so much talked of. Even if the unthinkable were admitted, that the people could designate the person to be their king, they could not reserve any powers to themselves, since they never had any powers to reserve. It followed that the laws drafted by the people's representatives in Parliament derived their only authority from the monarch who endorsed them. The king alone possessed sovereignty, "which the House of *Commons* share as little in as they which sent them; which is *not at all*."[4] The king could do no wrong, and if he did, the people must bear it. God

[2] Ibid., IV, 207, 217, 242–44, 290–94.

[3] *Protestant Loyalty Fairly Drawn* (London, 1681), 6. The number of sermons and pamphlets affirming these views is too numerous to cite. Cf. B. Behrens, "The Whig Theory of the Constitution in the Reign of Charles II," *Cambridge Historical Journal*, VII (1941), 42–71, and John Miller, "Charles II and his Parliaments," Royal Historical Society, *Transactions*, fifth series, vol. 32 (1982), 1–23.

[4] L. Womock, *A Short Way to a Lasting Settlement* (London, 1683), 23.

forbade resistance to him, whatever he did.

The arguments were all familiar from the Royalist tracts of the 1640s, but then they were defensive. Now they were dominant. Their prevalence in sermons and the public press may have been due in part to government censorship or to fear of it. But twenty years of war and uncertainty were widely blamed on popular sovereignty and the delusions that it allegedly fostered: "Were we not inchanted into a Freestate," asked one minister in 1661,

till there were nothing but chains to be seen? and into Keepers of liberties till there was not one priviledge of the Subjects remaining? and into a Committee of Safety till no man was safe, but every man stood in fear of his life? and into the purity of the Gospel, till our Orthodox faith was even taken away?[5]

In this atmosphere it was tempting for the king and his ministers to believe that they could take England toward the kind of government that continental monarchs, freed of parliaments, had been creating. This was the time when Charles II's cousin, Louis XIV, was establishing the most absolute regime in French history. With help from Louis, Charles and his brother and successor James moved, at first cautiously and then recklessly, in the same direction. Had they succeeded, England might well have become a satellite of France, with a despotic monarch whose divine right was conveyed from Rome by way of Paris. Although they did not succeed and probably could not have succeeded, even if they had gone about it with more political intelligence than either of them could summon, it took their subjects nearly thirty years to become convinced that survival of the ancient constitution required once again the removal of the reigning monarch. When that was done, in 1689, the divine right of kings died a lingering death. So strong, however, was the continuing revulsion from the good old cause of the 1640s and 1650s that the men who ousted James II were extremely cautious about affirming the sovereignty of the people.[6] Although they could scarcely have done without it in 1689, the

[5] Thomas Reeve, *The Man of Valour* (London, 1661), 111 (pagination continuous with the same author's *A Dead Man Speaking* (London, 1661). Cf. *The Primitive Cavalierism Revived* (London, 1684), 5–6.

[6] J. P. Kenyon, *Revolution Principles: The Politics of Party 1689–1720* (Cambridge, England, 1977). Cf. H. T. Dickinson, "The Eighteenth-Century Debate on the Sovereignty of Parliament," Royal Historical Society, *Transactions*, fifth series, vol. 26 (1976), 189–210; Howard Nenner, *By Colour of Law: Legal Culture and Constitutional Politics in England, 1660–1689* (Chicago, 1977), 155–96.

way they used it and the way it found expression in English institutions during the next two centuries bore the marks of its stunted growth during these years of royal ambition—years when divine right sponsored one foray after another toward absolute monarchy.

A variety of circumstances saved England from going the way of France and insured the survival and eventual revival of popular sovereignty, however attenuated, as the nation's guiding political fiction. One was the mendacity of Charles II—as much a liar as his father—whose habitual dissimulation, even with his own chosen ministers, eventually provoked distrust in everyone, including the members of his Parliaments, who had to deal with him. Another was the foolhardiness of his brother James, when he ascended the throne in 1685, in ignoring or underestimating the hostility not only of the general public, but of the ruling elite, to Roman Catholicism. But probably the crucial difference that distinguished English politics from French was the fact that the Restoration had restored Parliament and it was Parliament that restored the king and continued to sustain him. In spite of, or perhaps partly because of, the long periods from 1629 to 1640 and again from 1642 to 1660, when the traditional interplay of Parliament and king had been interrupted, and in spite of the equally long period from 1661 to 1679, when the members had not been obliged to face an election, they exhibited a strong sense of institutional continuity and of their obligations to their constituents. Repeatedly in their debates they cited proceedings in the Parliaments of James I and Charles I, and even Elizabeth, though few of the members could have been personally present in the sessions held before 1640.[7]

It would be too much to say that the House of Commons after 1660 deliberately adopted a policy of withholding a permanent revenue from the king in order to insure his dependence on their meetings. But neither the Convention Parliament of 1660 nor its successors under Charles II voted the king enough supplies to meet his needs. To be sure, if Charles had been willing to curtail his needs, he might have been able to get along for a considerable period on what they gave him. But Charles cheerfully accumulated debts; and when the Com-

[7] See, for example, Anchitell Grey, ed., *Debates of the House of Commons, from the year 1667 to the year 1694* (London, 1763), I, 213; VII, 49; VIII, 34, 167, 213. Political pamphleteers also showed a surprising familiarity with former parliamentary debates. See for example *A Letter from Major General Ludlow to Sir E. S. Comparing the Tyranny of the First Four Years of King Charles the Martyr, with the Tyranny of the Four Years Reign of the Late Abdicated King* (Amsterdam, 1691), in which Ludlow accurately quotes speeches in Charles I's Parliaments at a time when Ludlow himself was a child.

mons discovered that he lied to them regularly about what he needed money for, they became increasingly wary of granting the sums he asked for without some kind of assurance that he would spend it as he promised and as they specified in granting it. As a result of the king's expanded needs and the Commons' parsimony, Parliament was in session during most years of his reign and after the first ten years in pretty continual agitation about his and his ministers' conduct of government and about the dangers that he and his brother posed to their religion.[8]

Religious zeal or, to give it a less attractive name, bigotry had been a moving force in the rise of popular sovereignty. The monarchomachs of the sixteenth century had called up the power of the people for the express purpose of dethroning or killing rulers with whose religious views they disagreed. It was not religious liberty they sought, but the elimination of wrong religions. Although James I, in defending the divine right of kings, had exhibited his commitment to the right religion by identifying the pope with Antichrist, his Parliaments had all found him insufficiently zealous in the persecution of Catholics at home and in support of the Protestant cause abroad. Charles I's Parliaments found him equally lax and took alarm at the favor he showed to churchmen who seemed to be moving the English church toward Rome. One historian has even suggested that the English Civil Wars should be considered not as the first modern revolution but as the last of the religious wars (though it is evident in the twentieth century that we have not yet seen the last of those).[9]

Although the Long Parliament of 1641, once it freed itself of royal control, had expended little of its energies on stepping up the persecution of Catholics, the penal laws against them, being of long standing, remained on the books when Charles II returned to take the throne. Thereafter under the guidance of a new archbishop Parliament enacted additional laws to punish any kind of dissent from the restored Church of England. But Charles II himself was no bigot, and his political ambitions included the gaining of freedom of movement from the Church as well as from Parliament. His first trial of the waters was a Declaration of Indulgence in 1662, by which he would have sus-

---

[8] For the general history of the whole period from 1660 to 1689, covered in this chapter, I have found particularly useful J. R. Jones, *Country and Court: England, 1658–1714* (Cambridge, Mass., 1979).

[9] John Morrill, "The Religious Context of the English Civil War," Royal Historical Society, *Transactions*, fifth series, vol. 34, 155–78.

pended the operation of laws against both Catholic and Protestant dissent from the Church of England, thus associating religious liberty with the exercise of the royal prerogative in defiance of parliamentary statutes. The storm of protest with which he met convinced him that the time was not yet ripe. When he tried again ten years later, his Parliament had already become suspicious of his good faith (with good reason—unknown to Parliament, Charles had already made a secret treaty with France in which he had agreed to declare his conversion to Catholicism). The House of Commons responded with a resolution "that penal statutes, in matters ecclesiastical, cannot be suspended by by act of parliament." They then proceeded to pass a bill imposing on all officeholders a total renunciation of Catholicism and its doctrines, and they obliged the king to withdraw the Declaration and sign the bill into law (the Test Act of 1673) before they would grant the supplies which, as usual, he badly needed.[10]

No affirmations of popular sovereignty accompanied this display of parliamentary power, but two years later another unsuccessful foray toward absolutism resulted in a widely read denunciation of divine right. The Earl of Danby, at this point the king's chief minister, managed to drive through the House of Lords a bill to match the Test Act of 1673. It would have required of all officeholders an oath renouncing any right "upon any pretence whatsoever" to take arms against the king or those commissioned by him and forswearing any attempt to alter the established government. The bill never reached the Commons because Danby and the king thought it better to prorogue the Parliament for a lengthy cooling-off period. But the opposition to the bill, led by the Earl of Shaftesbury, publicized its terms in a pamphlet that revealed how they had condemned it in parliamentary debate as a revival of the absolutist theories of Archbishop Laud, and how they had argued the need for resistance to a king who violated the laws established by his Parliaments. Such laws, they said, might well be alterations of the government, "For what is the business of Parliaments but the alteration, either by adding, or taking away some part of the Government . . . ?" It was possible, they said, to be too much in favor of the king by trying to give him more power "than the Law and Constitution of the Government had given." But while condemning divine right and excusing resistance, the opposition lords had not gone so far as to restate the principles of popular sovereignty, however

---

[10] *Parliamentary History*, IV, 517–71.

much their views seemed to imply such principles. They had taken their stand against divine right reluctantly, for according to the pamphlet "they several of them begg'd, at the first entrance into the Debate, that they might not be engaged in such disputes, as would unavoidably produce divers things to be said, which they were willing to let alone."[11]

Indeed no one was eager to resort to the doctrines that had led to 1649, and the Commons did try at first to keep their efforts to control the king within the limits they had honored in the 1620s, blaming everything on evil counsellors' "encroaching upon Royal Power," preventing the king from the good things he would otherwise do, "intercepting" his grace and favor to his people.[12] When die-hard Royalists reminded the other members that the Civil Wars had begun with the same sort of "cry against evil Counsellors," they were answered that "some about the king" were making him think it was 1641 and "would bring us to that."[13] If by "that" was meant civil war, it did not come, but it did come close enough to set men, in and out of Parliament, to looking once again for a way to insure themselves of a king who not only could do no wrong but would do no wrong. And the worst wrong a king might do would be to inflict Catholicism on his people.

Charles II's thrusts toward absolutism had been worrisome enough, but he never fulfilled his secret promise to Louis XIV by avowing himself a Catholic. His brother James, however, more earnest than Charles, was correctly assumed to be a Catholic. As it gradually became evident that Charles would have no legitimate children, James, then Duke of York, became heir apparent. A Catholic king was an alarming prospect, and the alarm was raised to the point of panic by a charlatan with a tale of conspiracy that won the instant acceptance of nearly everyone except the king and the alleged conspirators.

In the fall of 1678 one Titus Oates, a renegade clergyman who had lived among Jesuits, testified before the Privy Council that the Jesuits were planning to murder the king (thus bringing his Catholic brother to the throne). They were also planning to set fire to London again (they had already been blamed for the great fire of 1666)[14] as well as organizing English Catholics to welcome a foreign invasion. It did not

[11] *A Letter from a Person of Quality to his Friend in the Country* ([London?], 1675), 25, 29, 33; Jones, *Country and Court*, 190.

[12] Grey, *Debates*, IV, 374, V, 329–330; VI, 351.

[13] Ibid., V, 243, 335.

[14] *Parliamentary History*, IV, 334–35.

matter that their alleged enterprises seemed to conflict with each other or that the king himself caught Oates out in several lies. To cast doubt on the existence of the plot was to invite suspicion of complicity in it, and the Duke of York, as the principal beneficiary, became increasingly suspect.[15]

The king himself, though rightly unimpressed by Oates and all his crew, was obliged to send his brother out of the country for a time and to contend with a succession of Parliaments that impeached his ministers and tried to exclude James from succession to the throne. In this contest, in which Charles dissolved four Parliaments in a little over two years' time, he repeatedly offered to accept measures that would protect the Church and keep the regular administration of government in Protestant hands in the event of a popish succession. But he was unbending in his insistence that he would not consent to any alteration of the succession.[16] Over this question Parliament and the nation first divided into Whigs, who supported exclusion, and Tories, whose fear of altering the Constitution by meddling with the succession outweighed their fear of a popish king.[17] The clergy, though it was their church that was threatened, were mainly Tory, and along with other Tories they filled the presses with a deluge of sermons and pamphlets extolling divine right in general and hereditary succession in particular. In this campaign they enlisted the posthumous support of Sir Robert Filmer, a Royalist of the 1640s whose writings had hitherto appeared only in fragments. These were now reprinted along with his hitherto unpublished magnum opus, *Patriarcha*, which, as its title implies, derived all authority from paternity and furnished a more respectable rationale for hereditary succession than the Tories might have been able to construct on their own.[18]

It was the Whigs, in their efforts to alter the succession, who revived the sovereignty of the people. The form in which they cast the arguments for it reflected both the cause in which they invoked it and the caution with which Englishmen now wished to limit the application of ideas that had formerly justified not merely the exclusion but the

[15] Grey, *Debates*, VI, *passim;* J. P. Kenyon, *The Popish Plot* (London, 1972).

[16] Grey, *Debates*, VII, 158–59, 433; VIII, 234–35, 291–92.

[17] J. R. Jones, *The First Whigs: The Politics of the Exclusion Crisis 1678–1683* (London, 1961).

[18] John Locke, *Two Treatises of Government*, Peter Laslett, ed., (Cambridge, England, 1964), 57; Robert Filmer, *The Freeholders Grand Inquest* (London, 1679); *Patriarcha* (London, 1680).

killing of a king. Limitations on the monarch—Magna Carta, the Petition of Right—had been a distinguishing mark of the ancient constitution to which England had presumably returned in 1660. But in the
hysteria induced by the popish plot, the Whigs feared that James or
any other Catholic sovereign, once on the throne and backed by
unscrupulous and sinister forces at home and abroad, would sweep
away any constitutional barriers to Catholicism and to the arbitrary
government that went with it. When the king's friends in Parliament
pressed for the limitations he had suggested as an alternative to alteration of the succession, the Whigs treated the opportunity as a ruse:
"I should be glad to be shown," said Sir Nicholas Carew, "any bonds
and fetters that a Prince, when he comes to the crown, shall not easily
break."[19] The only safeguard worth having was the exclusion of the
duke or any other Catholic from the throne.

   In pursuit of their objective the Whigs had to overcome the prevailing notions of divine right, in which hereditary succession was so
firmly ensconced. To challenge that succession, it was convenient, if
not essential, to remove its sanctity by placing the origin both of government and of kingship in popular choice or compact. But the Whigs
drew back from pursuing this thought, at least publicly, to the point
of making Parliament (as Henry Parker had in 1642) the successor to
the primeval assembly that began and defined the government. The
"original compact" was best left undisturbed in the distant, indeed the
fictional, past, lest its resurrection in the present produce another rash
of Levellers, Diggers, and Ranters on the one hand, or a Protector
backed by a New Model army on the other. A change in the succession, though necessary for keeping out Catholicism, must not invite
any change in the structure of government, not even to an elective
monarchy.

   The Whigs' brand of popular sovereignty accordingly stressed
adherence to the ancient constitution of king, Lords, and Commons.
They strenuously denied the Tory contention that legislative authority derived solely from the king and reaffirmed the claim of the early
1640s that the power of Parliament, conferred directly by the people,
was coordinate with that conferred at the same time on the king. But
this did not mean that Parliament was superior to the king. Although
they affirmed the right of the people to resist a popish monarch, their

[19] Ibid., VII, 238.

actual efforts to exclude James all assumed the unaltered continuance of the existing government and would thus have required the consent of the king and the House of Lords as well as the Commons. The history of England, they could easily show, recorded more than one instance in which Lords and Commons with the consent of the monarch, had determined the succession to the throne, the latest conveniently located in the reign of the revered Elizabeth.[20] Both their strategy and the application of popular sovereignty on which it rested required the cooperation of a reigning monarch who had not, yet at least, forfeited his throne. The king could thus defeat their efforts by dissolving Parliament: they were unwilling to go as far as Parliament did in 1641 by resorting to an ordinance (that did not carry his assent) in place of a law.

The Whigs were unwilling to go that far because it would probably have meant civil war with the attendant miseries and uncertainties that were still fresh in memory. The Whigs were led, moreover, by a peer, the Earl of Shaftesbury, whose conception of popular sovereignty assigned a primary role in government to the nobility.[21] There were, he maintained, only two ways for a monarch to sustain his authority. One was a standing army, which was Cromwell's way, to be abhorred by all good Englishmen. The other was through his nobility: "If you will not have one," he told his fellow peers in the House of Lords, "you must have the other, or else the Monarch cannot long support itself from tumbling down into a Democratical Republick." It went without saying that no one wanted England to tumble down there.[22] Shaftesbury would gladly have seen the popular character of the House of Commons enlarged by a more equitable distribution of representation, but he would have confined both voting and officeholding to "the optimacy," that is, to substantial propertyholders. The existing electorate contained too many persons "of a mean and abject Fortune in the World." Such men were too easily

---

[20] *The Great and Weighty Considerations* (London, 1680); *A Word Without Doors Concerning the Bill for Succession* [London?, 1679]; *A Letter From a Gentleman in the City to One in the Country* (London, 1680); *A Dialogue at Oxford Between a Tutor and a Gentlemen* (London, 1681).

[21] Cf. J. G. A. Pocock, "Machiavelli, Harrington, and Political Ideologies in the Eighteenth Century," *William and Mary Quarterly* 22 (1965), 549–83.

[22] *Notes Taken in Short-hand of a Speech in the house of Lords . . . Octob. 20, 1675* [London, 1679], 3.

"Corrupted and Seduced by the inveiglements of a little Money for a Pot of Ale: whilst those whose Circumstances are more enlarged, have their thoughts so likewise, being thereby raised beyond such low alurements."[23]

Even the most daring affirmation of popular sovereignty published at this time, *Plato Redivivus*[24] by Henry Neville, was extremely cautious in allowing the people a role in government except under the guidance of their betters. Anarchy, Neville felt, was the inevitable result of letting the people, under the influence of some popular leader, alter the established government. And "that which Originally causes this Disorder, is the admitting (in the beginning of a Government, or afterwards) the meaner sort of People, who have no share in the Territory, into an equal part of Ordering the Commonwealth."[25] Neville followed Harrington in linking power to the possession of property. Given the wide distribution of property in England and the relatively small share of it in the king's possession, the stability that all Englishmen longed for was not to be had by enlarging the king's prerogative, as the proponents of divine right contended, because the king had "a greater Power already than the condition of Property at this present can admit, without Confusion and Disorder."[26] Neville would have revamped the government to give more power to Parliament, but he did not propose like Harrington to have his changes introduced by some conquering hero. Neville was writing in 1681, and he rejected the very thought of a conquering hero. The sovereignty of the people in 1681 demanded that any changes be made, as the Whigs were trying to change the succession, legally, by the unanimous consent of king, Lords, and Commons.[27]

Neville was well advised to speak so cautiously. The Exclusion Crisis prompted at least two other Whigs, John Locke and Algernon Sidney, to write more sweeping defenses of popular sovereignty, but neither saw fit to publish what he wrote at the time. Sidney was hanged in 1683 for treason simply on the basis of a few pages of notes, seized in his quarters, in which he assigned the origin and limitation of government to the people, with a right to depose rulers who betrayed

[23] *Some Observations Concerning the Regulating of Elections for Parliament* (London, 1689), 11.

[24] (London, 1681).

[25] P. 68.

[26] P. 214.

[27] P. 257.

their trust.[28] Sidney's view of the way in which the people could act scarcely invited spontaneous popular uprising. The decay of the ancient constitution he attributed, like Harrington, to the decay of the nobility, and the loss of the military services of their tenants. With no command of men, they could neither protect the weak, nor curb the insolent. "By this means all things have bin brought into the hands of the King and the Commoners." Which meant that "That which might have been easily performed when the people was armed, and had a great, strong, virtuous and powerful Nobility to lead them, is made difficult, now they are disarmed, and that Nobility abolished."[29]

Sidney cast his whole treatise in the form of a line-by-line refutation of Filmer, whom he and other philosphically minded Whigs identified as the most formidable intellectual opponent of any form of popular sovereignty. Most of John Locke's *Two Treatises of Government* would have taken the same form, if he had not lost or suppressed the better part of the first treatise. Except for a few paragraphs added later, he evidently wrote both treatises between 1679 and 1681, and they were doubtless originally intended to justify exclusion. Locke was a protégé of the Earl of Shaftesbury, escaped with him to Holland in 1682, and sought refuge there again in 1683 when Sidney was executed for writing a much more restrained affirmation of popular sovereignty than Locke's.[30]

Locke is a special case, partly because his *Second Treatise* has become the classical exposition of popular sovereignty, and partly because it did not achieve that position until long after it was written. Until the present century, Locke's *Treatises,* first published in 1690, were thought to have been occasioned by the Revolution of 1688. Their exposition of the popular origin of government and of the right of the people to depose a king or any other ruler who betrays his trust was much more sweeping than can be found in any published tract of the Exclusion Crisis. Not surprisingly they seemed better designed to justify the revolution that immediately preceded their publication than the attempted exclusion of ten years earlier. Indeed, it now appears that Locke went farther than the other Whigs of 1688 were ready to go, and his work began to furnish the standard justification of the Glorious Revolution only after the government that rested on that revo-

[28] *The Arraignment, Tryal and Condemnation of Algernon Sydney for High-Treason* (London, 1684).

[29] Algernon Sidney, *Discourses Concerning Government* (London, 1698), 418–20.

[30] Laslett, ed., *Two Treatises,* 25–66.

lution had demonstrated its stability and the Revolution itself was comfortably far behind.[31] Insofar as Locke's writings gave shape to the fictions of popular sovereignty they did so after the application of the fictions to the government of England had been determined in the transactions that placed William of Orange and his wife Mary (James II's daughter) on its throne. Since those transactions took place without Locke's participation we may reserve further consideration of his version of popular sovereignty until we have examined them.

After the dissolution of his last Parliament in 1681, Charles took steps to insure that any future parliament he might have to call would be more compliant than those that had tried to exclude his brother. Since the majority of members sat for boroughs, he began a large-scale process to narrow and control the governing bodies and electorate of the boroughs by "regulating" their charters of incorporation. With the assistance of the courts, which were simultaneously discovering treason in all Whig activities, Charles was so successful that when he died in 1685, James succeeded to the throne with a minimum of organized opposition. A rebellion under Charles's bastard (and Protestant) son, the Duke of Monmouth, was quickly put down, and the new Parliament that assembled in May 1685, contained a great majority of Tories, returned by the newly sanitized borough electorate.

From the events that followed it is hard to escape the conclusion that James, despite years of experience in his brother's administration, was a political imbecile. He lectured his tame Tory Parliament like a testy schoolmaster, and when it proved less than wholly servile, he dissolved it and embarked on a campaign to pack the next one with candidates who would promise to vote for repeal of the laws against Catholics. Abandoning the Tories altogether, he made a bid for the support of dissenters by two declarations of indulgence, comparable to those on which Charles had burned his fingers in 1662 and 1672. Some dissenters took the bait, but the net result was to unite Whigs and Tories in common cause against a king who seemed bent on fulfilling every prediction made by those who had sought his exclusion.

Unfortunately for James, the Earl of Danby, in an earlier bid for popular approval, had arranged the marriage of James's daughter Mary to William of Orange, the champion of the Protestant cause against Catholic France. Mary shared none of her father's enthusiasm for Rome,

---

[31] See note 6 above.

and in the absence of any brother she stood next in line for the English throne. On June 10, 1688, she lost that position, when James, on top of his other sins, became father to another child, a son. Good Protestants did not want to believe it had happened, and with William's concurrence they spread the story that it had not in fact happened, that the child was smuggled into the queen's bed in a warming pan. The story was designed not only to preserve Mary's claim to the throne but to invite the intervention of William, ostensibly in her behalf. On October 10 William, with the assistance of a number of leading English politicians, issued a declaration detailing the king's many violations of English law and constitutional rights and the widespread suspicion that his alleged new heir was not borne by the queen. William called for a *free* Parliament, with the ancient qualifications for voting restored. To that body he would refer the question of the rightful succession to the throne as well as the redress of the grievances under which the country suffered.[32]

This was, in effect, an ultimatum, issued in advance of William's landing with an army to carry it into effect. The army did not have to strike a blow. By the end of the year James had fled to France, and a meeting of former members of Parliament had asked William to assume the administration of government temporarily and to summon a convention to make a permanent settlement of it.

The use of the word "Convention" rather than Parliament was deliberate. It was a recognition that James was still officially king, and that only a king could legally summon a Parliament. Before leaving, James had not only withdrawn the writs for electing a new Parliament but had thrown the Great Seal of England into the Thames. The Convention, though chosen in the same way as the old Parliament (before the corporations were regulated), with the same constituencies electing the same number of members, could not therefore, strictly speaking, be called a Parliament. But this legal technicality was not the only way in which it would differ from a Parliament in the eyes of those who now wished to reestablish the sovereignty of the people. A convention newly elected by the people, with no king to veto its acts, might be England's opportunity to establish its constitution through the kind of original contract that spokesmen for popular sovereignty had been talking about since the 1640s. With the collapse of royal authority the press was open as it had not been since Charles II returned; and a stream of broadsides and pamphlets, addressed to the

[32] *Parliamentary History*, V, 1–13.

Convention, explained to the members what large powers they bore by virtue of not being a Parliament.[33]

The spokesmen for popular sovereignty at this point, most of them anonymous, recognized that the members of the Convention might be reluctant to act the part that the fiction assigned them. Most of the members had formerly been members of Parliament, and they might consider themselves to possess a lesser authority than they would have had as a regular Parliament, summoned by royal writ. Actually, they were told, the opposite was the case. "Never," wrote the Reverend Edmund Hickeringill of Colchester, "had any *Englishmen a greater* Trust put upon *them, nor a greater* Power put into their hands . . . You *have* virtually in you, *the power of* all the Laws, *and all the* Kings *and* Parliaments *that* ever were *or ever* shall be *again* in England, *to the* Worlds End."[34] This was a little extravagant, but other writers also stressed that the Convention enjoyed "an opportunity we are like never to have again in the World."[35] It was the opportunity to recast the government in whatever form seemed best suited to serve the welfare of the people. The writers generally agreed that the best form was the ancient constitution, distinguished by the sharing of authority among a hereditary monarchy, a hereditary nobility, and a popularly elected body of representatives. But the important thing was for the Convention to recognize that it had the authorization of the whole people, already bound together in a community, to contract with whatever rulers they chose and to lay down the conditions on which those rulers might exercise authority. The Convention had "the *Golden Opportunity* to bring a *Crown* in one hand, with their *Terms* or *Conditions* in the other."[36]

[33] The fullest discussion of the Convention is Lois Schwoerer, *The Declaration of Rights, 1689* (Baltimore, 1981).

[34] *A Speech Without Doors: or Some Modest Inquiries Humbly Proposed to the Right Honourable the Convention of Estates Assembled at Westminster* (London, 1689), epistle dedicatory. The same point was made in "a Paper which was delivered to the house of Commons on Monday 28th January 1688 [i.e., 1689]. . . . said to be written by the Marquis of Halifax" (Rawlinson Ms. D1079, p. 8. Bodleian Library); "Remember that the Government being dissolved, we are in such a state at present as a people are where no government is yet set up. In such a state, the people are to meet in their Representatives, and agree upon their constitution, before they choose their governour for the Administration. . . . Redeem us from slavery, what you omit now is lost for ever."

[35] "Proposals to this present Convention," in *The Eighth Collection of Papers Relating to the Present Juncture of Affairs* (London, 1689), 33.

[36] "Good Advice Before it be Too Late," ibid., 25, also in Walter Scott, ed., *A Collection of Scarce and Valuable Tracts [Somers Tracts]*, 2d ed. (London, 1809–15), X, 201.

To make this point clear the authors read the Convention little lectures on the popular origin and dissolution of governments. Drawing on the distinctions developed in the 1640s and 1650s, especially by George Lawson, they explained that the Convention represented the Community which had come into existence prior to government by a "popular contract" among all the people. It was the community, acting through such representatives, that first established a commonwealth or government through a "rectoral contract," to which the community was one party and the king the other. While the rectoral contract was in effect, the people were subjects, and as individuals they had no right to judge or resist the government they had established. Nor could a regular Parliament sit in judgment on the king who summoned them, because the Parliament was itself a part of the government and not a party to the rectoral contract. The Convention, however, could do what a mere Parliament could not: "They may resolve whether the Constitution of the Kingdom and the Rectoral Contract, whence it arose, be violated on the King's part." They could do it because "they are the Parties Contracters with their Kings, and their Race: as to which they were, and must be considered as unsubordinate; for they were not Subjects in that Contract, nor their Kings Soveraigns, but by and after that Contract."[37]

Not only could the Convention judge the past performance of King James and cancel his contract, they could also commit the community to a new contract on the same, or on different, terms with a new king or queen. Although it might be appropriate to make Mary queen, there was no need to keep the crown in the family that had tried Englishmen's patience in four reigns. And it might be well, given the recent preaching up of divine right and hereditary succession, to make clear the community's freedom of action by placing the crown in someone whose heredity did not entitle him to it—who else but William, waiting in the wings with an army at his back?[38]

It would be important also to exercise the community's authority by setting out the explicit terms, ancient or novel, of the contract

[37] *A Discourse Concerning the Nature, Power, and Proper Effects of the Present Conventions in both Kingdoms* (London, 1689), 7, 8, and *passim; A Political Conference* (London, 1689), 21–31.

[38] *Reasons Humbly Offer'd for Placing his Highness The Prince of Orange Singly on the Throne, during Life* ([London], 1689); *Several Queries Relating to the Present Proceedings* (London, 1689), 9; *A Word to the Wise* (London, 1689); *Some Short Considerations Relating to the Settling of the Government* ([London], 1689), 7; *Reasons for Crowning the Prince and Princess of Orange King and Queen joyntly* ([London], 1689).

under which the government of the new commonwealth would operate. These would be the commonwealth's fundamental laws, its constitution. A Parliament, if authorized under that constitution, could
make laws, but not fundamental laws, for a law made by one Parliament could be repealed or altered by another and thus could not be
fundamental. Most of the fundamentals of England's ancient constitution were well known, but there were some that the Convention
should spell out more specifically, particularly the exclusion of any
future papist heir to the throne.[39]

Probably by design, those who argued for the Convention's
extraordinary powers made no mention of the State of Nature, a term
already rendered alarming by the scene it conjured up of uncontrolled
popular activity or of the war of man against man that Thomas Hobbes
had described. The point of the distinction between a community
without government and a settled commonwealth with a government,
was that the dissolution of government did not destroy the bonds of
community and reduce people to the state of nature that existed before
they joined together through the popular contract. It was equally
important to insist that the government *was* dissolved and needed
reconstituting (though the Convention might look like a Parliament to
those uninitiated in popular sovereignty, it was not) and at the same
time to insist that the community was *not* dissolved and could act
through its convention.

When the Convention, duly elected in the old manner of Parliaments, met on January 22 and got down to business, the members
showed none of the certainty of the pamphleteers about who they
were and what their business was. The majority of members were or
had been Whigs, but a substantial minority were Tories.[40] They were
agreed on one thing, that James, whether or not he retained the title
of King, must not be allowed to return to England, at least in the
immediate future. On the first day of their meeting, without extensive
debate, they voted an address of thanks to William for their preservation from popery and asked him to continue the administration of
government "till further application shall be made by us."[41] On Jan-

---

[39] *A Discourse Concerning the Nature*, 16; *A Brief Collection of Some Memorandums* [London, 1689], 7–8, 13.

[40] Schwoerer, *Declaration of Rights*, 152.

[41] *Parliamentary History*, V, 34.

uary 28, having waited six days, presumably for more members to show up, the lower house (organized like the parliamentary House of Commons) began debate on the state of the nation. By the end of the day they had adopted a resolution that embodied their agreement about James and their commitment to the basic tenets of popular sovereignty, while leaving uncertain the precise application of those tenets to their situation. The resolution read:

That King James the Second, having endeavoured to subvert the Constitution of the Kingdom, by breaking the original Contract between king and people, and, by the advice of Jesuits, and other wicked persons, having violated the fundamental Laws, and having withdrawn himself out of this Kingdom, has abdicated the Government, and that the Throne is thereby become vacant.[42]

The wording, which was more cautious than may at first appear, could not have satisfied the most radical of the Whigs or the most conservative of the Tories present. Tory views had been most effectively presented by Sir Robert Sawyer in a speech that revealed the kind of adaptation Tories could make to popular sovereignty and their skilfull use of its principles for their own purposes. Sawyer was clear that James had "stretched and strained" royal prerogative "to do the People mischief," that he had violated fundamental law, and by so doing abdicated the government and "that all our Obligations to him are Void." But it did not follow for Sawyer "that the People have the Power of disposing of the Crown." And even if they did, he denied that the Convention represented the people or was empowered by them to act for this purpose. If the government were devolved upon the people collectively, which he denied, then it would be the right of *all* the people to participate in the choice of a convention to establish a new government. The lower house of the Convention had been elected like a house of commons, by an electorate that, according to Sawyer, did not represent "so many as the 4th part of the Nation, for there are freeholders under 40 shillings a year and all Copyholders, and Women and Children and Servants." The Convention was thus merely the third estate in the existing government and not entitled to act for the whole community. What, then, was the state of the nation? Simply that the throne was empty, momentarily, as though the king had died, and the next heir in line should fill it. Sawyer did not say whether he

[42] Ibid., 50.

thought the heir was Mary or the king's newborn son (in which case a regency would be required.)[43]

Sawyer's views were the usual Royalist *reductio ad absurdum* of popular sovereignty and did not prevail. But the Whig response to them fell short of affirming the powers of the Convention in terms that the pamphleteers had urged. To Sawyer's charge that the Convention did not represent all the people, they answered only that it represented "the valuable part, and those that deserve a share in the Government."[44] But this was begging the question. They did not even try to deal with the distinction underlying his charge, between the people acting as a community before the creation of government and the freeholders acting as the third estate in a government already in existence. Sir Robert Howard came closest to it in saying that the government "is devolved into the People, who are here in civil society and constitution to save them."[45] This would seem to imply the continuation of the community, acting through the Convention, after the government, with its rectoral contract, had dissolved. But Howard did not pursue or clarify the distinction, and neither he nor any other Whig responded with it, as they might well have done, to the argument of the Tory Heneage Finch that an empty throne implied a state of nature, in which all private title to property would be lost.[46] The Whigs insisted that James's actions, whether his violation of the Constitution or his desertion of the kingdom, left the throne vacant, but they preferred to make the vacancy a direct consequence of the king's actions, not of their own as representatives of the continuing community. He had "demised," or "deserted," or "abdicated," but they shied away from the word "depose." It was not necessary, they said, to determine whether the Convention had power to depose him. "The Question," said Serjeant Maynard, "is not, whether we can depose the King; but,

---

[43] Grey, *Debates*, IX, 21–23; Lois Schwoerer, ed., "A Jornall of the Convention at Westminster begun the 22 of January, 1688 / 9," Institute of Historical Research, *Bulletin* 49 (1976), 242–63, at 252–54; "Notes of what passed in the Convention," in Philip Yorke, Earl of Hardwicke, ed., *Miscellaneous State Papers from 1501 to 1726* (London, 1778), II, 399–425, at 403. Sawyer seems to have been echoing an unpublished tract entitled "The Present State of the English Government Considered" (Rawlinson Ms. D836, ff. 65–74, Bodleian Library). Alan Simpson, "The Convention Parliament 1688–1689" (D.Phil. dissertation, Oxford, 1939), pp. 69–72, identifies the author as Roger North.

[44] Grey, *Debates*, IX, 13.

[45] Ibid., IX, 20.

[46] Ibid., IX, 18.

whether the King has not deposed himself."[47] Or, as Sir George Treby put it, "we have found the Crown vacant, and are to supply that defect. We found it so, we have not made it so."[48]

But the idea of a vacancy in the throne, however it came about, had unacceptable implications to many, if not all, Tories. It had been a premise of English law that the king never dies. Upon the demise of one king the throne was instantly filled by his lawful successor even if an infant. In declaring the throne vacant the Convention implied not only that the king had legally died, but that the people, acting through the Convention, had authority to name a successor other than his automatic legal heir. When the Commons' resolution came to the Lords, this proved a sticking point. The Lords were surprisingly ready to accept the idea of an "original contract" and thus the popular origin of government in a nebulously distant past.[49] But, given the Tory assumption that all authority of the existing government derived from the king (even if he did not get it directly from God), they did not wish to imply the dissolution of government as they thought the word "abdicate" and the vacancy of the throne seemed to do. In a committee conference with the Commons they objected that a vacant throne meant an elective kingship or even a commonwealth. The Commons denied that they had any leaning toward either, but they did aver that "the settlement of the constitution is the main thing we are to look after."[50] The Lords after a week of debate gave in, accepted the resolution as it stood, and immediately voted to offer the throne to William and Mary.[51] The Commons meanwhile were considering the main thing they were to look after, settling the Constitution.

It almost went without saying that the Constitution they would settle was the ancient constitution of the king, Lords, and Commons. But the terms of the relationship among the three had been so much in dispute throughout most of the century that settling the Constitution required the affirmation of specific principles, principles that would avert a repetition of the conflicts that had brought on the execution of one king and the abdication of another. After all the talk of an original contract that had now been broken, it was perhaps time for a new,

[47] Ibid., IX, 11–12.

[48] Ibid., IX, 13.

[49] Great Britain Historical Manuscripts Commission, *Twelfth Report, Appendix, Part VI: The Manuscripts of the House of Lords 1689–1690* (London, 1889), 15–17.

[50] *Parliamentary History* V, 66–108. Quotation is at p. 97.

[51] Grey, *Debates*, IX, 71.

more visible, more specific contract. When the Commons addressed this question on January 29, the day after declaring the throne vacant, the discussion disclosed how halting, not to say tentative, was their new commitment to popular sovereignty and how little eager were its Whig proponents to apply it to the Convention. It was the Tories who took the lead in urging a declaration of rights that would limit future kings. They may have been moved by a desire to place more limits on a monarchy originating in popular consent than on the one to which they had attributed divine right; or they may even have wished to thwart any change in the succession by imposing conditions that William would be unlikely to accept. But in any case Whig members proved more hesitant than Tories in claiming for the Convention, as representatives of the people, a power to bind a new king to new fundamental laws.[52]

It was not that the Whigs were averse to a clear statement of the principles that had been violated not only by James II but by Charles II and that must be protected in the future. William Sacheverell thought the Convention must "look a great way backward" not only to the actions of the king but also to the laws that compliant and corrupt Parliaments had passed. He could not, he said, "find three Laws, from twenty years upwards, that deserve to be continued." But Sacheverell's sweeping denunciation reveals at the same time the limitation or confusion of Whig thinking about the role of the Convention. His proposed remedy for the situation was to "secure this House, that Parliaments be duly chosen, and not kicked out at pleasure."[53] Sacheverell evidently identified the Convention with Parliament and "this House" with the regular House of Commons, His lawyer colleague, Henry Pollexfen, also a Whig, was less confused, but in differentiating the Convention from Parliament, he denied it any of the extraordinary powers that the pamphleteers would have conferred on it. He wanted action to fill the throne and reestablish the government, but he thought that "making laws to bind your Prince" was beyond the power of the Convention precisely because it was not a Parliament. "A Law you cannot make till you have a King," he told the members, "The thing you go upon is not practicable." The proper order of things, then, would be to fill the throne and then have Parliament, consisting of king, Lords, and Commons enact whatever laws were necessary to

[52] Schwoerer, *Declaration of Rights*, 184–98.
[53] Grey, *Debates*, IX, 33.

correct the evils of the preceding reigns. He obviously believed that ordinary legislation would have a greater binding power than any contract made by the Convention in the name of the community.[54]

This view did not immediately prevail. The House resolved that before filling the throne they would "proceed to secure our Religion, Laws, and Liberties;" and they appointed a large committee to draw up a list of grievances that needed correcting.[55] (The very idea of grievances of course implied a less than total interruption of royal authority.) That committee reported a list of twenty-three grievances (to which the House added five more), many of them identical with those William had listed in his declaration, but with some reaching back into the reign of Charles II.[56] To correct them all would have required new limitations on the royal prerogative. It was again the Whigs who held back from such a step by suggesting that the reaffirmation of ancient limitations on the king be separated from the assertion of new ones. And again they revealed their uneasiness about the validity of anything they might do as a convention with the throne still empty. In making the motion for a separation of old and new, Major John Wildman (himself an old Leveller turned new Whig) argued that "Things of Right and of Grace will have no effect, without distinction," as though the establishment of new limitations on the king could only be effected by grace. Wildman cited the Petition of Right of 1628 as the proper model. And Sir Richard Temple, in supporting him, observed that "The Throne must be filled before you deliver that Petition."[57]

The committee was sent back to revise its report and returned with what, after a few amendments, was agreed on by both Lords and Commons as a Declaration of Rights. It began with a preamble reciting the many ways in which James II "did endeavour to subvert and extirpate the Protestant Religion, and the Laws and Liberties of this kingdom." Without mention of any original contract, it stated that James had abdicated and left the throne vacant, specified a series of past royal actions (some of them applying to Charles as well as James) as illegal and another series as things that ought not to be done. It closed by offering the throne to William during his lifetime, with the

---

[54] Ibid., IX, 34.
[55] Ibid., IX, 32–37; Rawlinson Ms. D1079, p. 6. Bodleian Library.
[56] Schwoerer, *Declaration of Rights*, 200–203.
[57] Grey, *Debates*, IX, 51–52.

succession to lie in Mary and Mary's heirs, then to Mary's sister Anne, and then to William's heirs. The Declaration also contained two oaths, to be substituted for the old oaths of Allegiance and Supremacy, in which the testator swore his abhorrence of Rome and Roman power and promised "That I will bee faithful and beare true Allegiance to their Majesties King William and Queen Mary." The wording was designed to ease the consciences of hairsplitting Tories by omitting any affirmation that William and Mary were "rightful and lawful" sovereigns. It would thus be possible for die-hard Tories to accept them as de facto rulers without forswearing a continuing recognition of James.[58]

Such a compromise was in keeping with the ambiguities and the uncertain status of the Declaration of Rights. The things it declared illegal, which were presumably considered violations of existing laws or constitutional principles, included some that had not generally been so considered previously, such as suspending the execution of laws in particular cases or the maintenance of an army in peacetime. Some of the things asserted more tentatively as what ought not to be done had at least as ancient a basis as those declared unlawful, such as impediments to the freedom of speech and debate in Parliament.[59] But old or new, the statements of principles were not presented as a new original contract, and William was not asked to accept them as a condition of his accession to the throne. He had, of course, in his own Declaration before landing, indicted James's violation of most of them. And he had agreed to have the Declaration of Rights read at the outset of the ceremony that proclaimed him king on February 14. It could thus be interpreted as having his consent, prior to his accession to the throne. But the doubts that had surfaced in the Convention debates about the status both of the document and of the Convention's powers to establish it did not subside.

As soon as William was on the throne, he asked the Convention for money. The members therefore had to decide whether they were empowered to levy the taxes which, in their own Declaration, they had said that only a Parliament could levy. Their solution, after much soul-searching, was to declare themselves a Parliament without recourse to new elections. They felt much more comfortable sitting as a Parlia-

---

[58] The Committee report, known as the Heads of Grievances, and the Declaration of Rights are printed in Schwoerer, *Declaration of Rights*, 295–300.

[59] Schwoerer, *Declaration of Rights*, 281–91.

ment with the minor infraction of law involved in the original manner of their summons than they had felt in presuming to act as a convention of the continuing community after a presumed dissolution of the government. The Declaration itself, in its final wording, had avoided the implication that the king's abdication had dissolved the government: James had only *endeavored* to subvert it. They had presumed as a convention to fill the throne that James himself had made empty, but once the throne was filled it was possible for a Parliament to exist. Tories wanted a new election to make it fully legal (they also expected to gain more seats in such an election) but the Whigs (who expected to lose seats) were content to undertake the transformation (Tories derided it as a transubstantiation) which they effected by vote on February 20.[60]

The status of the Declaration of Rights still remained uncertain. But before the self-created Parliament was dissolved by royal proclamation a year later, it transformed the Declaration with a few amendments into a Bill of Rights. When King William signed the bill, on December 16, 1689, it became a regular statute (though it has curiously retained its unsigned title as the Bill of Rights).[61]

The seeming timidity of the Convention in assuming the powers that the pamphleteers urged on them in the name of popular sovereignty can be explained in many ways. The members all felt an urgent need to secure themselves against a return of James with a French army behind him. William alone stood between them and that possibility, and William privately made known to the members that he was not likely to stay, unless offered the throne without stipulations that would give him less authority than his predecessors. Although the Tories took the lead in proposing such stipulations, they were much less committed to popular sovereignty than the Whigs, and they did not follow through in support of placing conditions on the offer of the throne. The Whigs, on the other hand, while more committed than the Tories to popular sovereignty, were also more eager to exclude James. They wanted to take no chances on creating delays that might give him and Louis XIV an opportunity to mount an invasion. Moreover, both Tories and Whigs were eager for office under the new regime

[60] Grey, *Debates*, IX, 84–106; Cf. *Humanum Est Errare, or False Steps on Both Sides* [London, 1689], 7–10. Thomas Browne, *Some Reflections on a Late Pamphlet, Entitled A Vindication of Their Majesties Authority to fill the Sees of the deprived Bishops* (London, 1691), 10.
[61] Schwoerer, *Declaration of Rights*, 267–80.

and wary of offending William by seeming to impose conditions on him.[62]

These pragmatic considerations fell in with a mode of applying popular sovereignty that had predominated in England from its first inception. When the Long Parliament of 1640 assumed supreme powers of government, it claimed to represent the people so completely as actually to be the people. Leveller attempts at a higher expression of popular sovereignty in an Agreement of the People were turned away as seditious. The army, too, had claimed a higher expression of popular sovereignty and had made it good for a time by brute force. But that was what had rendered the doctrine *un*popular for so long. And when the Whigs revived it in the Exclusion Crisis, they had fastened their whole attention on an act of Parliament to exclude James and dismissed Charles's offer to accept limitations as worthless—which at that point it might have been.

The same attitude toward limitation made some Whigs in 1689 less than enthusiastic about wasting time on them while the throne lay empty and while James might be preparing a counterattack. Sir Henry Capel, a Whig leader who had been through the Exclusion Crisis, expressed this skepticism on the first day of debate. "I'm sure," he said, "it was the Sence of 2 Parliaments before the Crown fell to this unhappy King that it was fit to exclude him: but then wee were amusd with specious pretences of limitations. How will you limit him now?"[63] The answer that might have been given by the Levellers or Henry Vane or George Lawson or by the many pamphleteers who pressed it on the Convention was that the Convention should do it as a higher expression of popular sovereignty than Parliament could claim. Abstractly considered, apart from the problem of getting William to agree, it would have been a viable answer, as the United States demonstrated in 1787. But it was not to be the English answer, and to the members of the Convention, it did not seem viable.

The sovereignty of the people was a convenient, perhaps a necessary, fiction for a convention bent on disinheriting and displacing a monarch whose beliefs and conduct offended what was (probably rightly) assumed to be the vast majority of his subjects. But the sovereignty of the people, like other fictions, would lose its usefulness if taken literally. The Tories of the 1680s, like the Royalists of the 1640s,

[62] Ibid., 232–47.
[63] Schwoerer, ed., "A Jornall of the Convention."

recognized its vulnerability in this respect. They would have disarmed their opponents by demanding a literal application. It would
obviously have been impossible to gather the whole people together
to agree on "fundamental constitutions." The advocates of popular
sovereignty had admitted that from the beginning. What was only a
little less obvious was that a representative convention elected by all
the people was equally impossible. When Sir Robert Sawyer suggested that the Convention could not exercise the sovereignty of the
people because women, children, and servants had not participated in
its election, he was demanding a degree of literalness that he knew the
Whigs would not and could not agree to. To attempt such a thing was
to invite anarchy and a dissolution of the existing social structure.

The idea that anarchy and the absence of any social structure preceded the formation of government in the "state of nature" was part
of the fiction of popular sovereignty. But this was supposed to have
occurred in the distant past. No one, at least among those who enjoyed
the principal benefits of government, especially its protection of private property, wished to see a return to the state of nature. That was
the point of the distinction made by the pamphleteers between the
popular contract, creating a society or community, and the rectoral
contract in which the community created a government. The dissolution of government left the society intact, so there need be no return
to a state of nature. But even the most distinguished exponent of popular sovereignty displayed some confusion about the condition in which
a dissolution of government would leave the people.

John Locke was an unlikely person to invite anarchy. In describing
the state of nature as a state of perfect equality between man and man,
he was certainly not proposing that England would be returned to this
condition by the exclusion of James from the throne; and in writing
or revising his final and crucial chapter on the dissolution of government he began by insisting that "He that will with any clearness speak
of the *Dissolution of Government*, ought, in the first place to distinguish
between the *Dissolution of the Society*, and the *Dissolution of the Government*."[64] He went on to argue that the agreement which brought men
"out of the loose State of Nature, into *one Politick Society*," could usually be dissolved only by foreign invasion and conquest.[65] But while
dissolution of the society by foreign conquest would necessarily dis-

---

[64] Laslett, ed., *Two Treatises*, 424.
[65] Ibid.

solve the government along with the society, dissolution of the government by other means would not necessarily dissolve the society. Dissolution of the government could occur whenever those in charge of it grossly misused the powers entrusted to them and the society, remaining intact, reassigned the government "by the change of Persons, or Form, or both as they shall find it most for their safety and good."[66] Clear enough. But Locke, in a paragraph perhaps added to his text after James's abdication, described the dissolution of government through the executive's failure to execute the laws (James's suspension of the Test Act) as destroying "the Bonds of the Society," whereby "the People become a confused Multitude, without Order or Connexion."[67] Moreover, in the preceding chapter on tyranny, Locke had argued that when a prince puts himself into a state of war with his people, thus dissolving the government, his actions "leave them to that defence, which belongs to every one in the State of Nature."[68] If Locke himself could suggest that the dissolution of government might throw people into a state of nature, the members of the Convention may be excused for wanting to avoid the implication of a dissolution of government that would be involved in their considering themselves as representatives of the continuing society. It seemed much safer to think of themselves as part of the old government, temporarily, partially disabled by a vacancy in the executive branch.

The Convention's restraint meant that England did not achieve—and never would—a formulation and establishment of its constitution by a popular sanction or authority separate from its government. Popular sovereignty in England was to be exercised, as from its inception, by Parliament, or more particularly by the House of Commons. When enough time had passed and the government had acquired a stability unknown in the seventeenth century—Walpole's England was in no danger of returning to a state of nature—it was possible to look back on 1689 as a dissolution of government and persistence of the community. But even then the Declaration of Rights had to be interpreted not as an innovation but as a restoration of the ancient constitution, first established when wise ancestors emerged from a state of nature and created the government in which the House of Commons continued to speak for the people.

[66] Ibid., 429.
[67] Ibid.
[68] Ibid., 420.

Thus cautiously and casuistically the English reinstated popular sovereignty as the reigning fiction of government, with the unreformed Parliament as its beneficiary. The character of that body, as it developed in the eighteenth century, seemed to belie the fears generated by its earlier execution of one king and ouster of another. The day of the Levellers and Diggers and Fifth Monarchists was over. And if further proof was needed of the utility of popular sovereignty, rightly understood, it could be found in England's American colonies. There popular sovereignty sustained orderly government without ever generating the kind of ideas that had once threatened to turn the English world upside down.

CHAPTER 6

Colonial Peoples

WHILE ENGLISHMEN AT HOME were working out the implications and applications of popular sovereignty, those who settled England's American colonies were building societies where the authority of England's king was ostensibly undiluted by his unruly English Parliament. The first English colonies were founded while the divine right of kings remained the reigning fiction of English government. It was, moreover, the king and the king alone who authorized his subjects to settle the colonies and to govern them in his name. This was the case even after the 1630s. None of the colonies that later participated in the American Revolution was authorized by act of Parliament, and none was ever invited to send representatives to Parliament. Whether the king conferred powers on a corporation or a family or on several families together, or on the inhabitants themselves, the legal authority of England's colonial governments ultimately rested on the king of England and on him alone.

But authority that issued from a king three thousand miles away could never be as awesome as when his entourage of courtiers and emissaries exhibited his majesty close at hand. While English authority remained a key ingredient in colonial government before 1776, the facts of life in North America dictated to the English (if not to the Spanish or French) a degree of popular participation in government that would make the sovereignty of the people—the people of the colonies—a more plausible fiction, a fiction closer to fact, than in England itself. Although the settlers of most colonies departed from the mother country with the intention of establishing government resting on the king's grant (and thus entitling them to his protection in withstanding any enemies), unforeseen contingencies and geographical imperatives sometimes combined to render his grant inadequate. The Pilgrims who stepped ashore at Plymouth in 1620 had intended to settle within the boundaries of Virginia under the government of the Virginia Company of London. At Plymouth they were outside the jurisdiction of that government as prescribed in the king's charter to it. People moving from the Boston area to Hartford in 1636 similarly found themselves outside the boundaries of the government authorized in the royal charter to the Massachusetts Bay Company. Those who settled New Haven a couple of years later deliberately moved outside those boundaries, while Roger Williams and other founders of Rhode Island were banished from them.

In each case the settlers preferred government to anarchy. They agreed among themselves to submit to a government of their own devising, in what would later be called a social contract, and they sometimes set limits to it in what could be called a "fundamental constitution." The "Mayflower Compact," agreed to aboard ship before the settlers disembarked, was later hailed by John Quincy Adams as "perhaps the only instance, in human history, of that positive, original social compact, which speculative philosophers have imagined as the only legitimate source of government."[1] And the state of Connecticut now dubs itself the Constitution State because of the so-called "Fundamental Orders" that the settlers agreed to in 1639. These improvised devices were later confirmed or replaced by royal grants, but they furnished a factual foundation on which the sovereignty of the people could build.

The necessities of the colonial situation that produced compacts and fundamental orders also dictated the creation of popular representative assemblies, quite apart from any belief in popular sovereignty. We have already seen the beginnings of such assemblies in Massachusetts and Maryland as convenient substitutes for the meetings of all freemen as required in the royal charters of those colonies. Paradoxically, royal requirements not only created some colonial assemblies and gave legal standing to all of them, but also, as we shall see, could be a source of strength to them in contests with other appointed agents

[1]John Quincy Adams, *An Oration Delivered at Plymouth, December 22, 1802* (Boston, 1801), 17.

of royal authority within their governments. And even in the absence of royal directives or in contradiction to them, those entrusted with government in the colonies found it difficult in practice to do without representative assemblies. The Virginia Company of London, after a decade of trial and error, recognized that orders generated in England might produce confusion and disaster in a colony whose needs and changing circumstances could never be fully understood in London. In 1618 the Company accordingly instructed its governors on the scene to call a representative assembly to make laws for the colony, subject to veto by the Company, and gave assurances that its own orders would ultimately be subjected to veto by the assembly. When the Company nevertheless foundered six years later and forfeited the colony to the king, he pointedly declined to continue the assembly. But the men he sent to govern in his name found that they could not do the job effectively without the advice and consent of the people on the spot. Without royal advice or consent, successive Virginia governors regularly called meetings of elected representatives until 1639, when the king, on the point of calling his own neglected assembly in England, officially recognized the need for one in Virginia, a need provided for in the royal instructions to every subsequent Virginia governor.[2]

A similarly reluctant royal recognition of the pragmatic need for an assembly occurred in New York, which the English acquired from the Dutch in 1664. The Dutch had governed their sprawling colony (present-day New York, New Jersey, and Delaware) without benefit of an assembly. When the king assigned the new possession to his brother James, Duke of York, the duke saw no reason to trouble his government with a body that, in his view, would be more apt to contest his authority than facilitate its exercise. But the duke never visited his colony, and the men he appointed to govern it soon discovered, as the earlier Virginia governors had, that without a representative assembly to inform them of popular needs and conditions and to give prior consent, their decrees were difficult to formulate intelligently or enforce effectively. Knowing of the duke's feelings about assemblies and sensitive perhaps to the way in which an English assembly had handled his father, the New York governors nevertheless kept hinting to him that their task would be considerably lightened by a representative assembly. James's response was grudging:

[2]Charles M. Andrews, *The Colonial Period of American History* (New Haven, Conn., 1934), I, 183–88, 198–204; W. F. Craven, *The Southern Colonies in the Seventeenth Century* (Baton Rouge, La., 1949), 134–36, 159–64.

I have formerly written to you touching assemblyes in those countreys and have since observed what severall of your latest letters hint about that matter. But unless you had offered what qualifications are usual and proper to such Assemblyes, I cannot but suspect they would be of dangerous consequence, nothing being more knowne than the aptness of such bodyes to assume to themselves many priviledges which prove destructive to, or very oft disturbe, the peace of the government wherein they are allowed. Neither do I see any use of them which is not as well provided for, whilst you and your Councell govern according to the laws established . . . But howsoever if you continue of the same opinion, I shall be ready to consider of any proposall you shall send to that purpose.[3]

The eventual result was New York's first representative assembly, which met in 1683 and promptly fulfilled the duke's predictions by passing a formidable array of laws dictating the mode of government and affirming the rights of subjects. After the duke ascended the throne of England, his Privy Council disallowed this "charter of Libertyes and Priviledges" and dissolved the assembly.[4] But when James's short reign ended in revolution, William restored the assembly, which sometimes thereafter made life difficult for New York's governors, but without which they could scarcely have governed at all.

While colonial governments from the beginning depended more visibly on popular consent than the government of England, there was less occasion in the colonies than in England for the development or articulation of ideas about popular sovereignty. The colonists enjoyed a large degree of autonomy in their representative assemblies, but it would have been imprudent to invite royal interference by affirmations of a popular basis for government to justify that autonomy. To have done so might have raised a question that no one as yet wanted to confront: if the authority of colonial governments was thought to derive from an original grant by the people, what people could be supposed to have made the grant? The people of England? Or the peoples of particular colonies? Both together?

Only in New England or in areas settled by New Englanders did seventeenth-century settlers feel the need to go back to first principles either in criticizing or in justifying the actions of government. Puritans had been discussing the origin, functions, and limits of government for nearly a century before the founding of New England. While

[3] Andrews, *Colonial Period*, III, 113; M. G. Hall, L. H. Leder, M. G. Kammen, eds., *The Glorious Revolution in America* (Chapel Hill, N.C., 1964), 194.
[4] Andrews, *Colonial Period*, III, 115–19.

Mary Tudor reigned (1553–58), they had propounded radical ideas not only about the popular contractual origin of government, but about the obligations of the people who conveyed governmental powers, to see that those powers were properly used. Taking a cue from French monarchomachs, Puritans had determined that Mary's improper use of her authority (in restoring Roman Catholicism in England) obliged her subjects to depose her, an undertaking they were unable to effect before she died. Her successors, Elizabeth I and James I, while not living up to the standards that Puritans demanded, came close enough so that during their reigns there was much less discussion of popular initiatives in creating and monitoring government. James's assault on papal power with the divine right of kings as his weapon tended to stifle Puritan affirmations of popular sovereignty anyhow, since in that context any derogation of the king's direct commission from God seemed to make room for papal power, an outcome that no Puritan wished to bring about. But Charles I's Romish proclivities and his hostility to Parliament sent the Puritans back to first principles again and sent fifteen thousand of them to New England, with the charter they had somehow obtained for governing Massachusetts Bay.

In New England it was safer to talk openly about first principles than in Charles I's England, and in setting up government Puritans were not content to rest authority simply on the king's grant. John Winthrop, who brought the Massachusetts charter with him, was particularly concerned to derive his powers from popular as well as royal grant. He saw the office of governor, to which he was regularly elected, as endowed with a divine right of its own. But like the Puritans in Parliament later, he held that God operated through popular agencies, not only in designating persons to govern but in establishing government itself. Drawing on the same political traditions that Parliament revived in the 1640s, Winthrop held that the origin of any body politic lay in "The consent of a certaine companie of people, to cohabite together, under one government for their mutual safety and welfare."[5] Although the government of Massachusetts followed as nearly as possible the form prescribed by the king's charter, the people who submitted to it did so willingly by the very fact of moving to Massachusetts. Their migration, Winthrop explained, was an act of consent, indeed

---

[5] John Winthrop, "A Declaration in Defense of an Order of Court Made in May, 1637," in E. S. Morgan, ed., *Puritan Political Ideas* (Indianapolis, 1965), 144.

of contracting, with God, with one another, and with the government.[6]

While the charter dictated a form of government for the Massachusetts Bay Company, it did not prescribe what the government could or could not do except to forbid the making of laws contrary to the laws of England. It was thus possible to argue that the settlers had contracted, under the charter, to establish a government that would abide by the laws of God—which Charles I's government was manifestly failing to do in England. And while Winthrop thought that the Bible offered a sufficient guide to what the laws of God required both of rulers and of subjects, other Puritans felt that it was up to the people or the people's representatives to spell out the terms of the contract, the application of God's laws to their particular situation. Without having the terms before them, in what Englishmen would shortly be calling "fundamental constitutions," subjects would be unable to hold rulers to their proper task. As John Cotton put it, "it is therefore fit for every man to be studious of the bounds which the Lord hath set: and for the People, in whom fundamentally all power lyes, to give as much power as God in his word gives to men. . . . So let there be due bounds set."[7] The people's representatives accordingly drafted and enacted in 1641 a "Body of Liberties" setting due bounds in ninety-eight articles that specified what their government must and must not do in order to fulfill the contract to which (along with the king's charter) it owed its existence.[8] The leaders of Connecticut had already done the same for their government in the Fundamental Orders of 1639.

In Virginia and Maryland, the only early English colonies in North America outside New England, there were no comparable expressions of the popular origin and limitation of government, though during the interregnum in England both Virginia and Maryland were left pretty much to govern themselves. The restoration of Charles II and the renewal of divine right in England coincided with a renewed interest in colonies and colonization among the king's advisers and friends.

[6] On Winthrop's political ideas, see in general Stephen Foster, *Their Solitary Way* (New Haven, Conn., 1971), 67–98; Timothy H. Breen, *The Character of the Good Ruler* (New Haven, Conn., 1970), 35–86; and E. S. Morgan, *The Puritan Dilemma: The Story of John Winthrop* (Boston, 1958).

[7] Morgan, *Puritan Political Ideas*, 173–76.

[8] Ibid., 177–203.

The effects were twofold: first, the donation to highly placed courtiers of powers to found and govern new colonies in North America, not only in those areas wrested from the Dutch in 1664, but also in the Carolinas and Pennsylvania; and second, the tightening of English control over existing colonies. Neither move was calculated to advance sentiments of popular sovereignty in America, but despite the continued growth into the next century of mechanisms for royal control, the course of politics in England combined with conditions of colonization to produce widespread recognition of popular rights and popular power, and even affirmations of popular sovereignty.

The earlier colonies had begun at a time when England seemed to be overpopulated. For more than a century population had expanded more rapidly than the economy could provide new jobs, and the roads had been filled with the homeless. By the middle of the seventeenth century the population boom had ended and Englishmen were not so ready to pack themselves off to an unknown land across a perilous ocean. The courtiers to whom the king granted princely domains in America nevertheless expected to grow rich from the rent and sale of lands to settlers. In order to entice increasingly reluctant emigrants they had to offer "concessions and agreements" stipulating generous terms on which they would grant land and a share in government to the people they granted it to. They sought settlers not only in England but in New England too, where the Puritan population had heeded the command to "increase and multiply," and where people already enjoyed and expected a larger hand in government than was the case in England.[9]

New England settlers moving to northern New Jersey demanded their own representative assembly.[10] Although the proprietors refused to recognize this special claim, their Concessions and Agreements of 1664 guaranteed to all New Jersey settlers a representative assembly, to be elected by the freeholders, with power not only to levy all taxes but also to make "laws, acts and constitutions" for the province.[11] Since some of the same proprietors were among those to whom the

[9] On English population growth see E. A. Wrigley and R. S. Schofield, *The Population History of England, 1541–1871: A Reconstruction* (Cambridge, Mass., 1982). Evarts B. Greene and Virginia Harrington, *American Population Before the Federal Census of 1790* (New York, 1932) gives contemporary estimates for seventeenth-century New England.

[10] Andrews, *Colonial Period*, III, 138–50.

[11] Francis N. Thorpe, ed., *The Federal and State Constitutions, Colonial Charters, and Other Organic Laws* (Washington, D.C., 1906–9), 2535–44.

king granted the Carolinas, the same desire to attract New Englanders led them to issue an almost identical set of Concessions and Agreements there in 1665.[12]

But the bows to popular power made by the proprietors of Restoration colonies were not limited to the pragmatic concessions needed to attract settlers. By 1669 the principal proprietor of the Carolinas was Anthony Ashley Cooper, Baron Ashley, later the Earl of Shaftesbury and the leader of the Whig campaign to exclude the Duke of York from the throne. Ashley's secretary was John Locke, who seems at this time, like Ashley himself, to have been much taken with the ideas of James Harrington. In 1669 Locke drafted for the government of the Carolinas a set of "Fundamental Constitutions" modeled on Harrington's *Oceana*, to replace the Concessions and Agreements of 1665. As in *Oceana* the constitutions were to be established by decree, in this case the decree of the proprietors, but they provided for distribution of land and of corresponding political power on the Harringtonian model. Shaftesbury's brand of Harringtonianism, as already noticed, emphasized the role of the nobility, and the plan for the Carolinas gave two-fifths of the land in perpetuity to a set of outlandishly named hereditary aristocrats who would form the upper house of the legislature with the exclusive Harringtonian power of introducing legislation. The lower house, representing the other three-fifths of the colony's landowners, were to accept or reject the proposals of the upper house without alteration. The scheme as drafted, however republican in philosophy, was too cumbersome to work and proved unacceptable to the inhabitants because it gave not too much, but too little, power to the popular representative assembly.[13]

Another courtier whom Charles II favored with a huge colony of his own also endowed it at first with a Harringtonian government. It is perhaps unfair to call William Penn a courtier, for he was first and foremost a Quaker. But he was the son of an admiral in the navy and was himself a friend of Charles II and a close friend of the Duke of York. Penn never allowed his connections in high places to soften either his religious zeal or his equally ardent attachment to popular liberties. He first became interested in colonization when he and sev-

---

[12] Andrews, *Colonial Period*, III, 192–93; Craven, *Southern Colonies*, 318–19; Thorpe, *Federal and State Constitutions*, V, 2756–61.

[13] Thorpe, *Federal and State Constitutions*, V, 2772–86; M. E. Sirmans, *Colonial South Carolina: A Political History 1663–1763* (Chapel Hill, N.C., 1966), 6–16, 37, 67, 72–73.

eral other Quakers bought up the colony of West Jersey from other proprietors. Penn was presumably instrumental in drafting the new set of Concessions and Agreements which the group issued to prospective settlers in 1676. The terms, though later altered, offered the inhabitants more political and legal rights than most people enjoyed anywhere in the world then or now. West New Jersey's representative assembly was to be annually elected by all (presumably adult male) inhabitants. It was given complete and exclusive powers of legislation and taxation but forbidden to restrict trial by jury in either civil or criminal cases or to prescribe capital punishment for any crime other than murder or treason. Its meetings and those of all courts were to be open to the public and its members subject to instructions by their constituents.[14]

In 1681 when the king granted Penn a colony of his own, Penn created for it a government in which he or his deputy should hold the executive power; but he gave it a Harringtonian legislature, consisting of an upper house, with sole powers to initiate legislation, and a larger house of representatives to accept or reject it. Both houses would be elected by the landowners of the colony. Penn doubtless expected them to choose men of greater substance for the upper than for the lower house, but Pennsylvania would have no hereditary aristocracy of the kind attempted for the Carolinas. Even so, the lower house of representatives was not content with the limited functions assigned it. In the end Penn allowed the representatives to write their own constitution. In it they eliminated the upper house altogether and placed the whole legislative power, subject to executive veto, in themselves.[15]

The sovereignty of the people in England began and ended in the sovereignty of their representatives. The representative assemblies of the colonies showed the same tendency to magnify their own powers, but until they quarreled with England they did not claim everything. Englishmen in America continued to speak of England as home, and Englishmen in England spoke of the colonies as *their* colonies. No one inquired too closely what those words might mean, but it remained clear that colonial governments derived at least some of their author-

[14] William Penn, *The Papers of William Penn*, Mary Maples Dunn and Richard S. Dunn, eds. (Philadelphia, 1981–86), I, 387–410; E. S. Morgan, "The World and William Penn," American Philosophical Society, *Proceedings* 127 (1983), 291–315; John E. Pomfret, *The Province of West New Jersey* (Princeton, N.J., 1956), 86–101.

[15] Gary B. Nash, *Quakers and Politics, 1681–1726* (Princeton, N.J., 1968) contains the best discussion of political development in early Pennsylvania.

ity, not from the people they governed, but from England and specifically from England's king. And as the colonies grew in size and in economic importance, the English government's interest in exercising authority over them also grew.

That interest was expressed in the Navigation Acts, enacted by Parliament in 1660 and 1663, aimed at directing the growing colonial overseas trade to benefit England and England's merchants. Enforcement of the acts became the principal objective of English, and later British, colonial policy, an objective that was hampered by the autonomy which royal charters gave to colonial governments under private corporations and proprietors. Even as the king was inconsistently giving out new colonial charters with powers of government to his friends and favorites, including William Penn, his advisers were moving to place colonial governments more directly under his control, with governors of his appointing. New Hampshire, over which Massachusetts had assumed (or usurped) jurisdiction, got a royal governor in 1679. In later years the Carolinas, New Jersey, and New York (by virtue of the Duke of York's becoming king) came under royal government. But the biggest stumbling block to this extension of English control lay in the New England colonies and especially in Massachusetts.

When the Navigation Acts were passed, Massachusetts officials at first pretended that they had no application there, on the grounds that their charter from the king exempted them from laws not passed by their own legislature. When apprised otherwise by the king himself, they avoided direct confrontations but continued to go their own way until 1684 when an English court declared their charter void. At that point, as James II took the throne, the king's advisers put into operation a plan that seemed to realize bureaucratic dreams for centralized control of England's growing North American empire. It was called the Dominion of New England, and it provided a single government for the area embraced in present-day New England, New York, and New Jersey. This vast domain was to be ruled by a royally appointed governor and council, with complete powers of legislation and taxation, unencumbered by any representative assembly.[16]

---

[16] The classic account of the Dominion is Viola F. Barnes, *The Dominion of New England* (New Haven, Conn. 1923). On the events leading to it see G. L. Beer, *The Old Colonial System 1660–1688* (New York, 1913), I, 230–313; Michael G. Hall, *Edward Randolph and the American Colonies* (Chapel Hill, N.C., 1960); Richard R. Johnson, *Adjustment to Empire: The New England Colonies 1675–1715* (New Brunswick, N.J., 1981), 3–71; and J. M. Sosin, *English America and the Restoration Monarchy of Charles II* (Lincoln, Nebr., 1980).

Like so many schemes concocted by bureaucrats unfamiliar with
the people affected by them, this one ignored political realities. In
other words, it ignored the opinions on which government had hitherto rested in New England. New Englanders had lived for more than
fifty years under a government that satisfied them, however it may
have displeased the new architects of empire in London. They were
now told that whatever rights they may have enjoyed under the king's
charter had been withdrawn, that their ancestors had left behind in
England whatever rights they may have had simply as Englishmen,
so that "they did not differ much from slaves, and that the only difference was, that they were not bought and sold."[17]

The set of people to whom this message was delivered had not
hitherto shown themselves to be long-suffering, and they did not suffer long. Fortunately for them, James II's capacity for recognizing
political realities at home was no greater than that of his advisers for
assessing them in the colonies. James abdicated the throne rather than
face an army invading his country by invitation. And James's governor of the Dominion of New England, Sir Edmund Andros, while
prepared to fight for his master, found scarcely anyone ready to fight
beside him. He was easily and bloodlessly overpowered by the people
of Boston and shipped back to London.

Although England's new king held no brief for colonial autonomy,
neither he nor his immediate successors made the mistake of supposing that the colonists could be subjected to a government which they
had no share in choosing. In England William owed his title as king
largely, if not wholly, to a representative assembly; and it was understood, at first tacitly and later explicitly, that henceforth that assembly
would be the major and essential branch, indeed the center, of England's
government. At the time it was less clear what the king's relationship
to colonial governments would be (and not clear at all what relationship England's supreme Parliament would bear to the colonial representative assemblies). Later John Adams would argue that, as the people
of England, through Parliament, empowered William in a contract to
govern England, the people of Massachusetts made their own "original express contract" with him.[18]

That Adams could make such an argument was owing not only to

[17] *The Revolution in New England Justified* in W. H. Whitmore, ed., *The Andros Tracts*,
I, 82. Prince Society Publications, V (Boston, 1868); R. N. Toppan, ed., *Edward
Randolph*, II, 44. Prince Society Publications, XXV (Boston, 1898).
[18] "Novanglus," March 6, 1775, *Papers of John Adams*, Robert J. Taylor et al., eds.,
(Cambridge, Mass. 1977–), II, 321. The most searching scholarly discussion of

the royal charter that Massachusetts received in 1691, but also to the fact that William and his successors did govern the colonies through their respective representative assemblies. Despite continuing recommendations by the kind of bureaucrats who had devised the Dominion, there were no more blundering attempts (until the 1760s and 1770s) to impose English rule by decree. Although the campaign to strengthen and centralize English rule over the colonies continued after 1689, it was understood that the governors appointed to exercise control would have to do it within the framework of representative government.[19] And English policy-makers discovered that there could be advantages in doing so. In Virginia the exploitive regime of local magnates had pushed the colony to rebellion in 1676 and kept it close to rebellion for a long time thereafter. It therefore became a royal strategem, before as well as after 1689, to ally with the representative assembly against them.[20] When Pennsylvania and Maryland came temporarily under royal control as a result of the Revolution of 1688, the proprietors found after they got their provinces back, that their representative assemblies had acquired a considerably larger share of power under royal rule.[21]

In the early years of his reign William was too busy to give much attention to the colonies, and in 1695 Parliament was on the point of erecting a special administrative body to deal with them. Had Parliament done so, a confrontation between the sovereignty of the people's representatives in England and the people's representatives in the colonies might have come sooner than it did. But William forestalled Parliament's move by royal appointment of a Board of Trade and Plantations to formulate imperial policy, review colonial legislation, and draft the instructions through which royal governors would present the king's wishes to his American subjects. Throughout its existence the Board remained a royal agency and as such received little encouragement from a Parliament that had learned to be cautious about

the effects of the Revolution in America is David S. Lovejoy, *The Glorious Revolution in America* (New York, 1972). The best discussion of the impact on New England in particular is Johnson, *Adjustment to Empire*. Cf. J. M. Sosin, *English America and the Revolution of 1688* (Lincoln, Nebr., 1982).

[19] Cf. Stephen S. Webb, *The Governors-General: The English Army and the Definition of Empire* (Chapel Hill, N.C., 1979) and *1676: The End of American Independence* (New York, 1984).

[20] E. S. Morgan, *American Slavery American Freedom: The Ordeal of Colonial Virginia* (New York, 1975), 338–62.

[21] Nash, *Quakers and Politics;* Aubrey C. Land, *Colonial Maryland* (Millwood, N.Y., 1981), 119 and *passim.*

measures that might enhance the king's prerogative.[22]

The result was a situation in which the sovereignty of the people could be accepted as the basis of government in the colonies without anyone having to decide what people endowed whom with what powers. There might be a variety of opinions on the question, but they could be left unexpressed, the implications of them unexamined, as different elements within each colonial government vied with one another. In every colony three centers of power developed: the governor, the governor's council, and the house of representatives, but before the quarrel with England began in 1764, none of them challenged the authenticity or legitimacy of the others. Although their contests might be heated, they generally stopped short of the appeals to high principle that signalize the breakdown of peaceful politics.

The degree of royal authority and its exercise through governor and council varied from colony to colony. It was almost nonexistent in Connecticut and Rhode Island, where the king appointed none of the officers of government, and barely visible in Pennsylvania and Maryland, where proprietors resident in England continued to appoint the governor and the governor's council (though the king assumed that power in Pennsylvania from 1792 to 1794 and in Maryland from 1689 to 1715). In Massachusetts a new royal charter in 1691, while making the governor a royal appointee, allowed the House or Representatives, in conjunction with the preceding council, to elect the council annually. In all the other colonies the king appointed both the governor and the council, and in all the colonies except Pennsylvania the council served also as the upper house of the legislature.

That the king appointed both governor and council in most colonies (generally for lengthy terms if not for life) did not mean that governor and council were always allied in political contests. In the colonies as in England it was assumed that appointive offices of government must be conferred on persons whose social rank and worldly substance entitled them to the deference of the rest of the population. Although possession of office would enhance their prestige, their prestige would itself enhance the authority of the office.[23] In England over

---

[22] Andrews, *Colonial Period*, IV, 272–317; Ian K. Steele, *Politics of Colonial Policy: The Board of Trade in Colonial Administration* (Oxford, 1968); Johnson, *Adjustment to Empire*, 247–52.

[23] Such considerations could operate, though to a much lesser degree, even in the popular choice of representatives: a community might be better served in the legislature by someone who carried weight in his own right, than by someone who was unknown and unhonored.

the centuries the king had been troubled by overmighty subjects who threatened his rule, and in extending his government he had had to be careful to choose men who would be big enough to serve him but not big enough to rival him. In the colonies there were no men big enough to rival a king, and in most colonies there were only a few with the prestige necessary to lend weight to a governor's council. Such men, identified for him by his governors and by the Board of Trade, the king appointed. But in America, by virtue of the distance and differing circumstances, the big men of a particular colony might have developed interests peculiar to the locality, interests economically, religiously, or otherwise at odds with imperial policies that the governor was instructed to carry out, interests that would align them more with their lesser neighbors in the house of representatives than with the governor.

On the other hand, persons who were big enough to add weight to a governor's council might also be big enough to have interests that differed, simply by virtue of their magnitude, from those of the men likely to be elected to a representative assembly. Such men, while locally prominent, generally stood below those appointed to the governor's council. And where the unit of representation was small, as in New England, most representatives were ordinary persons of no great means at all.

The operation of colonial governments, therefore, was the product of a triad of forces, each of which might be pulling in a different direction from the others. In this three-way contest, any side might look for support outside the local government. There were two possible sources. The first was in England. A royal governor, of course, had the most direct access to avenues of power there, but his access was not exclusive. Since the government of England was divided not only into king, Lords, and Commons, but also into political parties and factions, it was possible for members of a governor's council or house of representatives to appeal for help to persons in positions of power or influence who were at odds with a policy devised by their political opponents and embodied in a governor's instructions. Beginning in the later seventeenth century the various colonial assemblies began employing agents on a regular basis to lobby in England for or against any measure affecting the colonies. The home government itself wanted colonial agents on hand to give information about local conditions, and the colonial agent became a recognized, if not quite official, colonial representative in London. A wise agent was one who knew where to seek support in the labyrinth of British politics and political institutions. Frequently the colonists made use of men who were not only knowledgeable but influential in their own right, members of Parliament, who could be expected to carry some weight in the quarters where British policy was made.[24]

In this way it was possible for a colonial assembly or a faction within it to mount a campaign of intrigue in England against a governor whose policies, dictated in England, they were opposing. Colonial governors were vulnerable to shifts in England's political climate. Governorships were political plums awarded to deserving friends or relatives of persons who had enough influence to get them named. Though the commission came from the king, the leading members of the party or faction that controlled a majority in Parliament could generally see that offices went to their adherents. But a party in power today would not be in power tomorrow. When a council or assembly found a particular governor obnoxious, they could lobby in England for his replacement by the party most likely to succeed the existing ministry. This tactic worked particularly well during the time, before 1715, when Whig and Tory succeeded each other rapidly in control of Parliament. As Alison Olson has described the process, the succession of one ministry by another "was often the signal for hostile colonists to begin a transatlantic campaign to unseat the governor. Letters complaining of his corruption, county resolutions opposing particular policies, unofficial protests against favoritism from a group of representatives in the provincial Assembly, petitions signed by prominent town dwellers, would flood Whitehall; ship captains going to London would be given information against the governor and sent to see the 'right people.' "[25]

After 1715 when the Tories (as alleged supporters of the Stuart pretenders to the throne) were excluded from office, it was no longer as easy to exploit English political divisions in the interest of colonial disputants. But appeals to England in colonial power struggles continued right up to the Revolution. In 1764, for example the Pennsylvania assembly, at odds with the governor appointed by the Penns, sent Benjamin Franklin to England to petition the king to withdraw the government of Pennsylvania from the Penn family and take it upon

[24] Michael G. Kammen, *A Rope of Sand: The Colonial Agents, British Politics, and The American Revolution* (Ithaca, N.Y., 1968); Ella Lonn, *Colonial Agents of the Southern Colonies* (Chapel Hill, N.C., 1945).

[25] Alison G. Olson, *Anglo-American Politics 1660–1775: The Relationship Between Politics in England and Colonial America* (Oxford, 1973), 91.

himself. The presumption was that royal government would strengthen the assembly. Given the ensuing quarrel of all the colonies with England, the assumption was dubious and the petition ill timed, but it suggests how representative assemblies might seek allies in improbable places.[26]

The other source of support outside the local government lay in the voters—one is tempted to say in the people. The voters in the colonies, probably a majority of adult males in all the colonies and a large majority in most, constituted a much greater proportion of the population than in England.[27] The fiction of representation was therefore somewhat closer to fact and public opinion the more influential. The means for influencing and shaping it were at hand in the ubiquitous colonial press. By the middle of the eighteenth century every sizeable colony had at least one newspaper, into which the issues debated in the assembly sometimes spilled over. The printer who published the newspaper was also available for pamphlets where any side of a question could be propounded at length. In 1754 a dispute over a proposed excise tax on rum in Massachusetts generated more pamphlets in that colony than the Sugar Act and the Stamp Act did a decade later.

It was possible to appeal to the public in other ways than the press. A governor could ingratiate himself by lavish entertainments open to all. He could hand out political favors to persons with wide family and business connections. But most governors were interested in making money from their jobs, not in spending it on entertainment, and in most colonies there were few lucrative political offices to hand out and fewer still within the governor's patronage.[28] The same was true in general of councillors. The members of a representative assembly, on the other hand, could claim to speak the voice of the people in their own persons. As we shall see, they might sometimes feel the need to manufacture evidence of popular support in petitions and instructions, and that course was open to their opponents as well. But governors and councillors could enlist popular support most effectively by trying to direct it toward the choice of suitable representatives.

[26]James H. Hutson, *Pennsylvania Politics 1746–1770: The Movement for Royal Government and its Consequences* (Princeton, N.J., 1972).

[27]Chilton Williamson, *American Suffrage: From Property to Democracy 1760–1860* (Princeton, N.J., 1960), 3–16; J. H. Plumb, "The Growth of the Electorate in England from 1600 to 1715," *Past and Present*, no. 45 (1969), 90–116.

[28]Bernard Bailyn, *The Origins of American Politics* (New York, 1968), 72–80.

Efforts aimed at influencing opinion on a particular issue would have no lasting benefit in contests within the government, but a pliant assembly could swing power in the direction of either the governor or the council or both for the assembly's duration.

Virginia politics in the late seventeenth and early eighteenth century furnish a good example of the way power within a government could be shifted by appeals for popular support on the one hand and by pulling strings in England on the other hand.[29] Francis Nicholson, Virginia's governor from 1690 to 1692 and again from 1698 to 1705, was a bluff army officer who played the power game with relish. In a continuing contest with his councillors he at first tried going over the heads of both the council and the House of Burgesses (the representative assembly) in direct attempts to build a popular following.

The councillors charged that he not only sought to gain "the good opinion of the Common people but allso to beget in them such jealousies and distrusts of the Council, as might render them incapable to withstand his arbitrary designs." The accusation was prompted by Nicholson's efforts to enlist a special militia ostensibly to protect the colony against French and Indian attack, but capable of more sinister uses. After Nicholson was thwarted in this attempt, he turned his attention to the House of Burgesses. While he had earlier been accused of wanting to "govern the Country without assemblies," he now campaigned successfully to get men favorably disposed to him elected to the House of Burgesses. Having done so, he had them pass a resolution condemning the allegations of the council against him.

The councillors countered with a successful campaign in England to secure Nicholson's recall, but they too had learned a lesson in popular politics. The next royal governor of Virginia, Alexander Spotswood, who held office from 1710 to 1723, found himself facing a House of Burgesses that seemed to him to be filled with "persons of mean figure and character." They catered, he said, to "a received opinion among them, that he is the best Patriot that most violently opposes all Overtures for raising money." Spotswood's response was to buy them out by persuading them to pass a tobacco inspection law, creating lucrative inspectorships to which he appointed twenty-five of their number. Thereafter they gave him no trouble. But at the next election the councillors campaigned so successfully against this "court Party"

[29] The following account is based on Morgan, *American Slavery American Freedom*, 351–62.

that the voters turned out all but seventeen of the old members (only two of the seventeen had accepted inspectorships). Spotswood complained that he had been "branded by Mr. Ludwell [a councillor] and his adherents (who set themselves up for Patriots of the People,) for endeavoring to oppress the people by extending the Prerogative of the Crown." But the councillors did not themselves neglect prerogative politics. Again one of them made a trip to England and was able to secure Spotswood's recall.

In New York, even more than in Virginia, contestants in the three-way pull for power played their trump cards in England, but here too governors commissioned by the king after 1689 made their obeisances to popular power. Although the New York council generally sided with the governor, their support was not enough to assure success against a small assembly whose members could usually match most of the councillors in rank and substance. Voters in New York, despite a wide franchise, regularly elected such men to represent them, but New York's elite was riddled with factional and family quarrels that often found expression in politics. It became a necessary objective of the royal governor to secure an assembly so far as possible composed of factions and families that would work with him. To that end he had to choose his candidates carefully and campaign for them among voters of every rank. Governor William Cosby and his adherents might complain that their opponents sought support from "the lowest Canaille of the People, of no Credit or Reputation, rak'd out of Bawdy-Houses and Kennels." But the charge was returned, that Cosby "became more familiar with the people and invited many of low rank to dine with him such as had never pretended or expected so much respect."[30]

In Pennsylvania the power triangle was given a peculiar twist when the governor appointed by aging William Penn in 1717, William Keith, allied himself with a popular party and outdid his opponents in rabble-rousing. Keith, it was said, appealed to the "very scum of mankind," and thereby was able to dominate Pennsylvania politics until his enemies finally got Penn's descendants in England to dismiss him in 1726. The ex-governor then proceeded to run for the assembly himself and made life difficult for the next governor by "perambulating our city and popping into the dramshops, tiff, and alehouses where he would find a great number of modern statesmen and some patriots

[30] Gary B. Nash, *The Urban Crucible: Social Change, Political Consciousness, and the Origins of the American Revolution* (Cambridge, Mass., 1979), 147.

settling affairs, cursing some, praising others, contriving lawes and swearing they will have them enacted cum multis aegis."[31]

The issues over which governors, councils, and assemblies contended varied from colony to colony and from time to time. Legislation affecting regional interests, land speculation, monetary policy, religious preferences, and other local concerns could be championed by one branch of government against another, as well as by one faction within the government against another. But whatever the immediate substantive issues, the most enduring source of conflict lay in the powers claimed by the representatives of the people in the lower houses of the assemblies. The lower houses saw themselves, not without reason, as the analogue of the House of Commons in England, and they claimed for themselves the powers and privileges that the Commons had won in the course of the seventeenth century. The most crucial of these was the power to tax, that is, the exclusive power to orginate all bills that proposed a tax and to bar the upper house from amending them. The representatives in every colony made good this claim, meeting with extended resistance from the council only in South Carolina.[32]

In England the power to tax had been the lever by which the House of Commons after the Restoration and the Revolution elevated themselves above the Lords and above the king. The colonial representatives were not quite as successful in using their power to elevate themselves above the king's governor and the governor's council. Although no English monarch after Queen Anne ventured to veto an act of Parliament, royal governors regularly vetoed colonial laws, which might also be subjected to royal veto even after acceptance by a governor. But the colonial representatives went a long way toward local supremacy in their emulation of the House of Commons. By withholding taxes, they could secure a governor's consent to measures he was instructed to veto. They used the power to control the expenditures of the moneys raised by taxes. They even invaded the executive administration of government in the supervision of public works and services and some military matters. By the middle of the eighteenth century, if they were not dominant over royal governors, they were clearly dominant over governors' councils.

The contests in which they had attained that position, unlike those

[31] Ibid., 148–54.

[32] Leonard W. Labaree, *Royal Government in America* (New Haven, Conn., 1930), 172–372; Jack P. Greene, *The Quest for Power* (Chapel Hill, N.C., 1963); Mary P. Clarke, *Parliamentary Privilege in the American Colonies* (New Haven, Conn., 1943).

that evoked the many affirmations of popular sovereignty in England in the 1640s, were not bloody. Even the overthrow of the Dominion of New England had been accomplished without bloodshed except briefly in New York, where internal social antagonisms surfaced. The colonial representative assemblies maneuvered to a dominant position within their respective governments by persistent bargaining with the other branches, a process that required no exploration of the problems and puzzles inherent in popular sovereignty that had troubled the English in the 1640s and continued to haunt them in 1689. Colonial representatives justified their claims to power by generalizing from the powers that the House of Commons already claimed in England, citing precedent rather than political theory. The colonists, they insisted, were Englishmen, with all the rights of Englishmen that the Constitution embodied in the House of Commons. They pointed to royal charters that recognized those rights. They even cited precedents in their own history, the way the House of Commons had so often done in its early contests with the king.[33]

The most extensive theoretical discussions of the popular origin of government came, as might be expected, from New England clergymen, who continued to exhibit the Puritan predilection for first principles. The clergy occupied a special place in the American social hierarchy and especially so in New England. Congregations there expected their ministers to exhibit a wisdom and erudition appropriate to their high calling. Although New Englanders carefully refrained from electing ministers to public office (lest the church be soiled by temporal corruption or temporal power be threatened by ecclesiastical usurpation), the clergy were expected to instruct their flocks not only in the intricacies of Puritan theology but in the political and social ramifications of that theology. Speaking as figures of authority they never tired of demonstrating that God was a god of order, an order that required keeping one's place in a hierarchical society, where men of learning and genteel employment, including themselves, stood near the top. The deference that inferiors owed superiors was the cement that held society together.

In the eighteenth century, as in the seventeenth, ministers paid their respects to the popular origin and limitation of government; and they might apply their lessons to current disputes, but they seem not to have applied them to the contests of representative assemblies against royal governors. In 1717 the Reverend John Wise of Ipswich, Massa-

---

[33] Greene, *Quest for Power*, 13–18 and *passim*.

chusetts, gave an explicitly detailed account of the beginnings of government among people in a state of nature. Following the scheme outlined by Samuel von Pufendorf's *De Jure Naturae et Gentium*, he distinguished three successive covenants that transformed a group of individuals into a society and subjected them to government. First, they must agree with one another to be bound by majority rule, then the majority must agree on a form of government, and finally "those on whom Sovereignty is conferred" must agree to guard "the Common Peace and Welfare. And the Subjects on the other hand, to yield them faithful Obedience." Wise was unequivocal in affirming that the powers of government conferred by the people could be withdrawn by them "when a Government so settled shall throw its self from its Foundations . . . or shall subvert or confound the Constitution." But Wise, though he had earlier suffered under the Dominion of New England, did not now suggest that the government of either England or New England was slipping from its foundations. What worried him was that the New England churches seemed to be slipping from theirs. His argument from popular sovereignty was directed not against royal governors or their councils but against a proposed ecclesiastical reform that would have enlarged the authority of clergymen like himself.[34]

Another New England clergyman, Elisha Williams, discussed first principles in a tract directed toward limiting the activities of government, but Williams too was more concerned with religion than with politics. In the wake of the Great Awakening, the widespread religious revival of 1741, the Connecticut assembly had passed acts restricting itinerant preachers and limiting the creation of new churches. Williams, following perhaps unwittingly in the footsteps of the Levellers and of his namesake Roger Williams, denied that government had authority to make laws limiting religious worship. Seventeenth-century arguments had generally proceeded from the premise that God did not endow the people with powers over religion, so that they could not confer any such powers on government. Williams, following John Locke, did not concern himself with what powers the people might not have, but focused on what they reserved to themselves when they left the state of nature to create government. They did not and could not confer powers to limit every man's natural right to worship

[34] John Wise, *A Vindication of the Government of New-England Churches* (Boston, 1717), 44–45, 65; Morgan, *Puritan Political Ideas*, 261–62.

according to his conscience. That right, he said, remained in the individual and was "so far from being given up by the Individuals of a Community that it cannot be given up by them if they should be so weak as to offer it."[35]

Williams's argument might well have been directed against some of the laws still on the statute books in England, but he did not apply it that way or to any of the contests within the colonies between royal governors and their assemblies. He was rebuking the representatives of the people in one of the colonies that had no royal officials.

Probably the boldest exposition of popular sovereignty before the Revolution was the famous sermon by Jonathan Mayhew, *A Discourse Concerning Unlimited Submission and Non-Resistance to the Higher Powers; With some Reflections on the Resistance made to King Charles I.* Preaching in Boston in 1750 on the anniversary of the regicide, Mayhew justified it more by biblical exegesis, in seventeenth-century terms, than by exposition of natural right and the social contract. He was not concerned to issue a warning to subsequent kings or to royal governors but to rebuke the Anglicans who celebrated Charles as a martyr and observed the anniversary of his death as a day of fasting and humiliation.[36]

Other New England ministers in sermons preached on election days expounded the doctrines of Locke and outlined the popular origin of government, without examining the implications their views might hold for the contests of representative assemblies with royal governors. The divine right of kings had never made much sense in the colonies, and even if it had, the king's governors would have been hard pressed to lay a plausible claim to it. By the eighteenth century, the sovereignty of the people was taken for granted. Its acceptance is attested to not only in the matter-of-fact expositions of it by New England ministers but also by the popularity throughout the colonies of the English writers who spoke for it, of Harrington, Sidney, and Locke and their eighteenth-century intellectual descendants, John Trenchard and Thomas Gordon and the other so-called eighteenth-century commonwealthmen. In 1752–53 a leading New York attorney, William Livingston, published a weekly periodical, *The Independent Reflector*, in imitation of Trenchard and Gordon's *Independent Whig*,

[35] Ibid., 277.

[36] Ibid., 304–30. Mayhew preached his sermon on "the Lord's Day after the 30th of January, 1749–50."

with similar affirmations of popular rights. *The Independent Reflector* did
not hesitate to reflect on local political controversies, but not in order
to challenge royal authority.[37]

It has been persuasively demonstrated that the ideas of the eighteenth-century commonwealthmen did profoundly affect the attitude
of colonial assemblies toward royal governors. The commonwealthmen emphasized the dangers to the sovereignty of the people from
ambitious executives: the people must be ever watchful against abuses
of power but especially of executive power. Colonial assemblies were
therefore suspicious to the point of paranoia of every move a governor
made, and their suspicions were heightened by the fact that royal
commissions and instructions seemed to convey to governors more
authority than any governor was able in practice to exercise.[38] But in
limiting its exercise through their own power of the purse, colonial
assemblies did not invoke the radical implications of popular sovereignty that would have challenged the authority itself. They were
certainly familiar with those implications and readily accepted popular sovereignty as the basis of government. They had none of the
squeamishness about it that the Civil Wars had induced in England
and that lingered there into the eighteenth century. But before the
quarrel with British authority began in the 1760s they were curiously
reticent about spelling out the popular basis of government as a way
of cutting royal governors down to size. In hindsight—the only kind
of sight that historians have—it is possible to suggest a number of
reasons why.

To begin with, the political system within which they operated,
despite its tensions, did work. Whatever disparity there may have
been between the interests of Great Britain and those of the colonists,
the benefits of empire outweighed them. Although British policy,
embodied in the Navigation Acts, was designed to subordinate colonial interests to British wherever they conflicted, the two were more
complementary than conflicting. The colonies, where land and resources
were abundant and labor scarce and dear by comparison with Britain,
engaged primarily in the production of raw materials, mainly agricultural. British policy simply reinforced that tendency. While the policy
required the colonies to purchase manufactured goods from the mother
country, the mother country furnished them more cheaply than the

---

[37] Alice Baldwin, *The New England Clergy and the American Revolution* (Durham, N.C.,
     1928); Clinton Rossiter, *Seedtime of the Republic* (New York, 1953), 139–47; *The Inde-
     pendent Reflector*, Milton M. Klein, ed. (Cambridge, Mass., 1963).

[38] Bailyn, *Origins of American Politics, passim*.

colonists could have done for themselves. Under this system the colonists prospered. Except for the slaves among them they enjoyed a higher standard of living than most of the rest of the world, higher too than they were to enjoy for some time after they became independent. Under this system too, Britain prospered equally or even more and grew to be the world's greatest power. While the two sides might dispute details in the contests between royal governors and assemblies, neither side was disposed to push the dispute too far—at least until Britain's Parliamentary politicians became imperial statesmen in the 1760s and 1770s and started both sides talking about rights.[39]

It would be hard to say if the relative absence of such talk in earlier contests resulted from a consciousness of where it could lead. With both sides recognizing the sovereignty of the people, any dispute that came to a showdown was likely to raise the question whether the colonists were a separate people from the British. As long as mother country and colonies were agreed on fundamentals and argued only about specific details, it was easy to assume that they were one people. Once they clashed on questions of right that assumption would inevitably come under examination, and some anticipation of the consequences may have inhibited a resort to first principles among all contestants.

As long as the system worked, both sides could and did take considerable pride in it and attributed its benefits to the operation of popular sovereignty in creating a government designed to protect the rights of the governed. The deficiencies that the commonwealthmen complained of lay in the government of Britain itself rather than its deployment in the colonies. The constitution which the people in their ancient wisdom had adopted was supposed to restrict the king within laws made by representatives of the people. But, as the commonwealthmen saw it, representation in England had grown into a travesty of the original. Archaic custom, venal voters, the rise of new towns and decline of others, combined with usurpations of power and influence both by monarchs and by other magnates, had produced a

---

[39] On colonial prosperity, see John J. McCusker and Russell R. Menard, *The Economy of British America 1607–1789* (Chapel Hill, N.C., 1985), 258–76; Alice Hanson Jones, *Wealth of a Nation To Be* (New York, 1980); Jackson Turner Main, *Society and Economy in Colonial Connecticut* (Princeton, N.J., 1985). The economic success of the system for both England and the colonists did not prevent English administrators from pressing for the kind of improvements that finally destroyed it. See Thomas C. Barrow, "The Old Colonial System from an English Point of View," in Alison G. Olson and Richard M. Brown, eds., *Anglo-American Political Relations 1675–1775* (New Brunswick, N.J., 1970), 125–39.

House of Commons remote from the people, unacquainted with their needs, and unwilling to heed their wishes. A handful of voters in a decayed village elected members, while thousands in busy cities elected none. The king's ministers could buy seats in Parliament outright for the sycophants whom they held in sway through the award of places of profit in government. The laws made by such a crowd offered no restrictions on an ambitious monarch or on the ministers who conducted his government. In order to reduce the expense of buying voters every three years, they had even replaced the triennial act with a septennial act that removed representatives further in time as well as place from the people they were supposed to represent and rendered them more pliant to the influences that could be brought to bear in London.

None of this had happened in the colonies. When a colonist read the commonwealthmen's pleas for reform, he could be shocked at the sad state of the British Parliament, but he knew that the king's deputy in his colony confronted a house of representatives much more closely identified with the people it represented than the House of Commons which the king's ministers had to deal with at Westminster. Although population in the colonies was growing much more rapidly than in England, the assignment of representation kept pace with movement into new areas much more closely than in England. It might lag behind, more in the colonies from Pennsylvania southward than in the North and East, but nowhere was it so out of proportion to the distribution of population as in England, where no new seats in Parliament were created (and none withdrawn) after 1675. While parliamentary representatives faced election only once in seven years, most colonial assemblies held the annual elections that English reformers had been demanding for more than a century as the supposed practice of the original ancient constitution. While the distribution of seats and restrictions on the suffrage excluded the majority of adult males in England from voting and enabled a small fraction of the voters to elect a major portion of the representatives, the majority of males in every colony and the great majority in many could vote. And while most colonies did not effectively exclude placeholders (holders of lucrative government offices) from their legislatures—another of the commonwealthmen's demands for England—there were too few placeholders in most colonies and the places they held of too little value to make them a menace to the quality of representation.

In short, most of the evils which the commonwealthmen denounced did not exist in the colonies; most of the remedies they proposed were already in practice there. The sovereignty of the people in the colonies, insofar as it was embodied in representation, had not departed so far from fact as to induce the kind of protest evoked in England. And the fact that the representatives in most colonies (all except Rhode Island and Connecticut) were engaged in controversies with governors whom the people had no hand in choosing served only to heighten the representatives' identity with the people who did choose *them*.

The most advanced development of popular sovereignty in England during the Civil Wars and interregnum had come when representatives assumed all power to themselves, had claimed to *be* the people. In that context, as always when the people's representatives push the fiction too far, it became necessary to differentiate the people from their representatives and to search for a way in which the people might act apart from them to limit and control them. In the colonies the need for such a differentiation did not appear as long as the representatives could not claim all power to themselves. Contending with royal governors, they retained their local, subject character as agents of the people to protect them from a governing authority that was something other, something beyond the people's choice. As long as the outside authority remained and as long as the protection they themselves offered was adequate, there was no need to turn to the ideas that had first been enunciated by the Levellers, no need to discuss the people's "real majesty" described by Lawson and urged in vain on the Convention Parliament of 1689.

The reluctance of that Convention to appeal to the people except as their legal representatives in Parliament can be attributed to a fear of renewing the popular ferments of the 1640s and 1650s. In retrospect at least, it appeared that in those days the social order had been inverted, with "the dregs of the people lording it over their betters and superiors."[40] The colonists had experienced no such inversions, except perhaps in Bacon's Rebellion of 1676 in Virginia. The social hierarchy in the colonies nowhere reached the exalted heights that it did in England, but a hierarchy nevertheless existed and persisted in every colony. The men whom the people elected to represent them in their assemblies, especially in the colonies to the south of New England, were generally those whose birth and wealth placed them a little or even a lot above their neighbors. Even in New England, where most

[40] Robert Eyre, 1695, quoted in J. P. Kenyon, *Revolution Principles: The Politics of Party 1689–1720* (Cambridge, Mass., 1977), 75.

seats were filled by comparatively ordinary men, those who stood highest socially and economically seem to have been deferred to by the other representatives and appointed to the committees that directed legislative action.[41] Such men, while identifying themselves with the people, had no more desire to subvert the social order than did the governors with whom they contended. Appeals to the people, in the colonies as in England, came from the top down.

In other words, popular sovereignty, in the colonies, as in England, became the prevailing fiction in a society where government was traditionally the province of a relatively small elite. Although the new fiction slowly widened popular participation in the governing process, those who made use of it generally belonged to that elite and employed it in contests with other members. In doing so they had to be cautious lest they invite a wider participation than they had bargained for. For that reason, in addition to any other, the contestants within a colonial government, while making their appeals to the people, were reluctant to spell out the implications of popular sovereignty until it became apparent that it was safe to do so. Although it never became entirely safe, the growth of ideas and institutions around it in the century or more after it came into play reduced the risk, as we shall see in ensuing chapters.

[41] Robert Zemsky, *Merchants, Farmers, and River Gods: An Essay on Eighteenth-century American Politics* (Boston, 1971), *passim.*

PART TWO

Useful Ambiguities

———◆———

BEFORE THE DIVINE RIGHT OF KINGS could be safely interred, the sovereignty of the people had to be tamed, its operation and meaning established in such a way as not to threaten the government of the few on the one hand or the rights of the many on the other. It had to be given a close enough resemblance to fact to permit the willing suspension of disbelief, but it must not be interpreted so literally as to invite subversion either of the social order or of the accompanying political authority it was designed to support. To state the problem in Hume's terms, the meaning of popular sovereignty had to be settled in opinions that would sustain government.

By Hume's own account that settlement had taken place in Great Britain within a half-century after 1689. Writing in 1741, he observed that by that time the divine right of kings had expired: "the mere name of *king*," he wrote, "commands little respect; and to talk of a king as GOD's vicegerent upon earth, or to give him any of those magnificent titles, which formerly dazzled mankind, would but excite laughter in everyone."[1] The developments that brought about this transformation and established the sovereignty of the people as the reigning fiction were many and complex. They took place in England's American colonies as much as in England itself, as we shall see, but they are more easily observed in England, where the fictions of popular sovereignty remained at a greater distance from fact than in the colonies and accordingly required more explanation, interpretation, and defense.

[1]"Whether the British government inclines more to Absolute Monarchy, or to a Republic," *Essays and Treatises on Several Subjects* (London, 1758), 35.

The history of popular sovereignty in both England and America after 1689 can be read as a history of the successive efforts of different generations to bring the facts into closer conformity with the fiction, efforts that have gradually transformed the very structure of society. But in the early stages of popular government the problem was to gain credence for the fiction without upsetting that structure, without threatening the patterns of deference which gave stability to society and enabled the few to dominate the many in all the transactions of daily life.

As we have already seen, the English gentlemen who first located the source of governmental authority in the people thought to place its exclusive exercise in themselves. The House of Commons in the 1640s apparently intended to speak for a sovereign but silent people much as the king had hitherto spoken for a sovereign but silent God. The people, however, had proved more vocal than anticipated, and the governing few who claimed to speak for them continued for a century and more to be nervous about what might happen if a substantial number of actual people undertook to speak for themselves.

The problem was to develop institutions and habits of thought that would recognize popular power but at the same time direct expression of it to the support of existing authority. Before inventing the sovereign people the House of Commons had found a way to restrain the king by exalting him above the rest of mankind. The exaltation of the people was susceptible to a similar reversal. Elevate the yeoman farmer as the embodiment of popular power, make obeisance to the voters in extravagant election campaigns, encourage constituents to give instructions to the persons they chose to represent them. In all these ways the governing few in both England and America gave recognition to popular power; and in each case the power was real, just as the power of the king had been real. But in each case the very exaltation of popular power furnished a means of directing and controlling it. The ensuing three chapters attempt to show how.

CHAPTER 7

The People in Arms:
The Invincible Yeoman

THE SOVEREIGNTY of the people is a much more complicated, one might say more fictional, fiction than the divine right of kings. A king, however dubious his divinity might seem, did not have to be imagined. He was a visible presence, wearing his crown and carrying his scepter. The people, on the other hand, are never visible as such. Before we ascribe sovereignty to the people we have to imagine that there is such a thing, something we personify as though it were a single body, capable of thinking, of acting, of making decisions and carrying them out, something quite apart from government, superior to government, and able to alter or remove a government at will, a collective entity more powerful and less fallible than a king or than any individual within it or than any group of individuals it singles out to govern it.

To sustain a fiction so palpably contrary to fact is not easy. And to begin with, it had to make its way in societies—England and England's colonies—where political authority was strongly linked with social class. The fact that it became the reigning fiction in such societies is not easily explained. But part of the explanation may lie in the operation of another fiction that accompanied and supported it. This was the notion that the ability of the people to exercise sovereignty and control their government rested on the righteousness, independence, and military might of the yeoman farmer, the man who owned his own land, made his living from it, and stood ready to defend it and his country by force of arms.

The notion existed at least as early as Aristotle, but it reappeared with new vigor in England and America during the seventeenth and eighteenth centuries. The germs of the idea, as it came to prevail in England, can be found even before the emergence of popular sovereignty there, at least as early as Sir John Fortescue in the fifteenth century and Niccolò Machiavelli in the sixteenth. Fortescue praised the laws of England because they protected the subject's property, and he contrasted the condition of ordinary Englishmen with that of the abject French peasantry, racked by arbitrary rents and taxes. The people of England, according to Fortescue, were "rich, abounding in gold and silver and all the necessaries of life." And as proof he offered a characteristically English piece of evidence: "They do not," he said, "drink water, except those who sometimes abstain from other drinks by way of devotional or penitential zeal." Englishmen ate well, drank well, lived well because their property was secure from arbitrary exactions. And property for Fortescue, despite the mention of gold and silver, surely meant land.[1]

It seems unlikely that Machiavelli had read Fortescue, but he entertained the same notion of Englishmen that Fortescue did, and he made his own invidious comparison of Englishmen to Frenchmen. "Quite lately," he wrote, sometime early in the sixteenth century, "the king of England attacked the kingdom of France, and employed for that purpose no other soldiers except his own subjects; and although his own kingdom had been for over thirty years in profound peace, so that he had at first neither soldiers nor captains who had seen any active military service, yet he did not hesitate with such troops to assail a kingdom that had many experienced commanders and good soldiers, who had been continually under arms in the Italian wars."[2]

Fortescue and Machiavelli between them contributed the basic elements for the concept of the invincible yeoman: England was a country filled with prosperous property owners, and they made good soldiers without previous experience. In 1622 Francis Bacon combined the two elements in his biography of Henry VII, giving Henry credit for keeping landed property widely spread through the population, by

[1] Sir John Fortescue, *De Laudibus Legum Angliae*, edited and translated by S. B. Chrimes (Cambridge, England, 1949), 80–91. Quotation at p. 87.
[2] Niccolò Machiavelli, *The Prince and the Discourses* (New York, 1950), 175. (Discourse No. 21.)

means of a statute forbidding alienation of land from farms of twenty acres or more. Henry thus perpetuated and increased the strength of the English yeomanry and prevented land-grabbing nobility and gentry from debasing them. By strengthening the yeomanry Henry made England strong, and to prove the point Bacon went on to the comparison with France, against which, he said, "England, though far less in territory and population, hath been (nevertheless) an overmatch; in regard the middle people of England make good soldiers, which the peasants of France do not."[3]

Even before Bacon's exposition of it, this view of the English yeoman had become standard fare in Parliamentary debates, and quite properly so, because the security of property that allegedly—and indeed actually—differentiated England from France was sustained by the exclusive authority of the English Parliament to levy taxes. European monarchs, including England's, had made use of parliaments in order to obtain grants of property in taxes, but except in England the grants had generally become perpetual. Englishmen had somehow managed to keep most of their grants temporary. Now, when the king, in need of revenue, threatened to levy a tax without the consent of Parliament, he would be warned against the national weakness that must ensue from reducing the security of the subject's property. The strength of the king, it was argued, came from the strength of his people, and the strength of the people came from the security of their property.[4]

That was before the 1640s, when Oliver Cromwell came upon the scene and demonstrated that the strength of the people could be used against the king as well as for him. England became a republic, and it remained only for James Harrington to give classic expression and a republican twist to the belief in the invincible yeoman. Harrington's version of the now familiar comparison of England with France differed only in emphasis from previous ones: "the true cause whence

[3] Francis Bacon, *Works*, James Spedding, R. L. Ellis, and D. D. Heath, eds., (London, 1857–74). VI, 94–95, 405–6, 446–47. Quotation at p. 447.

[4] See, for example, the eloquent speech by Thomas Hedley in the Parliament of 1610 (Elizabeth Foster, ed., *Proceedings in Parliament, 1610* [New Haven, Conn. 1966], II, 194–95): "So if the liberty of the subject be in this point impeached, that their lands and goods be any way in the king's absolute power to be taken from them, then they are (as hath been said) little better than the king's bondmen, which will so discourage them and so abase and deject their minds, that they will use little care or industry to get that which they cannot keep and so will grow both poor and base-minded like to the peasants in other countries, which be no soldiers nor will be ever made any, whereas every Englishman is as fit for a soldier as the gentleman elsewhere." Cf. Walter Raleigh, *Remains of Sir Walter Raleigh* (London, 1702), 226.

England hath been an overmatch in arms for France lay in the communication or distribution of property unto the lower sort." And for the same reason the lower sort had been an overmatch for their king. Quoting liberally from Bacon, Harrington showed how the steps taken by Henry VII to protect the land of the yeomanry had begun a process that little-by-little in the course of a century had reduced the property both of the crown and of the nobility while increasing that of the yeomanry and gentry. With less income from land the crown became more dependent on taxation, the province of the House of Commons. And so, concluded Harrington, "by these degrees came the house of commons to raise that head, which since hath been so high and formidable unto their princes that they have looked pale upon those assemblies." And Harrington went on to affirm not merely that English yeomen made better soldiers than French peasants but that an army built or bought by a king out of debased peasants or paupers would inevitably fall before an army of yeoman citizens, "wherefore an example of such an one [that is, an army of yeomen] overcome by the arms of a monarch, is not to be found in the world. . . ."[5]

Henceforth the tradition that began with Machiavelli and Fortescue, or perhaps earlier, flourished in England and America in Harrington's version. In that form it contained three or four distinct propositions:

1) That the freedom characteristic of popular governments depends on the independence of the voting population and their representatives, and that their independence in turn rests on the secure possession of sufficient property in land to support them and thus render them free of coercion by employers or landlords, a coercion to which landless men must yield or else lose their livelihood. The vulnerability of the landless made them unfit to be given the suffrage. The ability to vote independently made the yeomanry the political guardians of the internal freedom of a popular government.

2) That these independent yeomen, armed and embodied in a militia, are also a popular government's best protection against its enemies, whether they be aggressive foreign monarchs or scheming demagogues within the nation itself.

3) As a corollary to the second proposition, that standing armies

[5] James Harrington, *The Political Works of James Harrington*, J. G. A. Pocock, ed. (Cambridge, England, 1977), 198, 443, 688.

of professional soldiers are an internal threat to freedom and that popular governments must avoid them at all costs. A militia is the only safe form of military power that a popular government can employ; and because it is composed of the armed yeomanry, it will prevail over the mercenary professionals who man the armies of neighboring monarchs. The superiority of Englishmen to Frenchmen has become in Harrington the superiority of a militia to a professional army.

4) An additional proposition stressed by Aristotle was not so conspicuous in Harrington, but appealed strongly to Americans. The proposition was that farmers are somehow more virtuous than other people and the success of popular government must rest in part on their virtue as well as on their arms and property.

Harrington expounded, or rather buried, these ideas in his tiresome Utopian fantasy. But the fact that *Oceana* is virtually unreadable did not prevent the ideas in it from finding their way into popular tracts and gaining wide acceptance in both England and America in the seventeenth and eighteenth centuries.

Harrington's propositions could not have prevailed so widely without bearing some relation to fact. The English yeomanry did have something worth fighting for: they did, by definition, own land, and their ownership was protected by a government over which they at least had more control than the French peasantry had over theirs. They enjoyed, relatively speaking, a large degree of economic and political independence, and their counterparts in America, constituting a majority of the adult males there, had even more. On both sides of the water they prided themselves on the rights of Englishmen, of which none was more sacred than the security of their property.

Nevertheless, if Harrington's propositions rested on a substratum of reality, they were more fiction than fact. We should be warned from taking them as fact by the serious error into which Harrington himself was led by them. Writing in 1656, while England was a republic, he predicted that the widespread distribution of property among England's armed people, among its yeomanry, would make it impossible henceforth for England to be anything but a republic. Four years later the armed people submitted to their hereditary king.[6]

But this miscalculation aside, Harrington's propositions betray their fictional character when measured against the role that property-holding yeomen actually played in government and warfare in England

[6]Cf. David Hume, *Essays Moral and Political*, 3d ed. (London, 1748), 70–77.

and America. The yeoman's role in government did not rise much above the casting of votes for members of Parliament, and the way yeomen cast their votes discloses the narrow limits of their independence. Before the English revolution, during the Cromwellian republic, and after the restoration of the king, the yeomen never made a practice of electing their own kind. Through all the changes of government they used their votes, as they had traditionally always done, to man the House of Commons with untitled noblemen and higher gentry.

The enduring deference of the English yeomanry to their social superiors does not mean that they were reduced to the position that Englishmen attributed to the French. Eighteenth-century Englishmen still prided themselves on their standard of living, so much better than that of those peasants across the channel, who wore wooden shoes and fed on black bread and gruel. Liberty and property and no wooden shoes was the standard chant to put down any ministerial measures that seemed to threaten the security of property in England.[7] Yet we know that the House of Commons remained throughout the eighteenth century in the hands of an oligarchy that bullied or bought its way into office. And from whom did it buy the votes? Whom did it bully? Among others it bullied those very yeomen whose sturdy independence was supposed to be proof against bullies and bribes.

The independence in voting that the ownership of land was supposed to confer on the yeomanry rested on the assumption that a man of property would be less susceptible to bribery or coercion than one without. There may have been some validity in the assumption but not much. As we shall see, the limitation of the suffrage to property-holders did not in fact eliminate widespread coercion and corruption in eighteenth-century elections. Indeed it can be argued more convincingly that the limitation of suffrage to property-holders invited the most effective form of bribery. In English electoral contests it was less common for a candidate to buy his votes by outright purchase from individuals than by a promise to pay borough or county expenses, such as poor relief or the building of a bridge or market-house.[8] And who would benefit from such payments? Who but the property own-

---

[7] The association of wooden shoes with the supposed degradation of the French peasantry began early. See Henry Parker, *Some Few Observations* [London, 1642], 15; *Vox Pacifica* (London, 1644), 11.

[8] Edward and Annie G. Porritt, *The Unreformed House of Commons: Parliamentary Representation before 1832* (Cambridge, England, 1903), I, 151–203.

ers, the landowners, the yeomanry, who would otherwise be taxed for the purpose. The very ownership of property thus became the means by which voters could be bribed in a body. Property was the handle by which they could be twisted this way or that, perhaps as readily as any laborer could have been twisted by threats to his livelihood had he been able to vote. A bought vote was no more an independent vote than a coerced vote, and yeomen, it appears, were quite willing to be bought en masse.

But bribery was seldom necessary, because voters were seldom offered a choice of candidates. In order to avoid the expense of an election contest the big families in a county increasingly agreed in advance on a single set of candidates to stand for the local seats. And since contests were so expensive when they could not be avoided, the members of the House of Commons in 1716 minimized the number of them by extending the interval between elections from three to seven years. The desire to save their own property thus warped the gentlemen candidates as much as the yeomen voters. There were, of course, Englishmen who decried septennial elections as betrayals of popular liberty. But the yeomanry themselves seem to have accepted the state of affairs without serious resistance, unless we count as resistance the abortive attempts to return the Stuarts to the throne, and it requires a certain degree of eccentricity to interpret the Jacobite movement as a thrust for popular government.[9] The sturdy yeomanry of the eighteenth century even allowed themselves to be disarmed by the laws which their representatives passed in order to preserve game for the hunting pleasure of nobility and gentry.[10]

The case was a little different in the American colonies, where the ownership of land and of arms was much more widespread than in England and where uncontested elections seem to have been less common. The power and independence of the yeomanry were accordingly more in evidence, especially in New England, where yeoman farmers did elect men of their own kind to represent them. In the political contests of the middle and southern colonies, however, we can see the same use as in England of property ownership as the han-

[9] But it is possible to make a powerful argument that the Tories were the political radicals of the eighteenth century before Wilkes. See Linda Colley, "Eigteenth-Century English Radicalism before Wilkes," Royal Historical Society *Transactions* 31 (1981), 1–19. See also Colley, *In Defiance of Oligarchy: The Tory Party 1714–60* (Cambridge, England, 1982).

[10] C. H. Kirby, "The English Game Law System," *American Historical Review* 38 (1932–33), 240–62.

dle by which to move voters in one direction or another. Candidates
would obtain election by agreeing to oppose taxes and also by agreeing
to serve without pay,[11] a form of bribery not possible in England,
where representatives were unpaid anyhow and sought election for
the prestige and profits that attached to their office. Candidates also
resorted to more direct forms of bribery, common in England too, by
treating the voters to dinners and drink in staggering quantities. And
in the southern colonies, the site of the most ardent advocates of the
independent yeoman farmer, candidates were not above outright
intimidation of voters who preferred a different candidate.[12] But that
is part of the next chapter. Suffice to say that even in the colonies the
supposed independence and virtue of the yeoman farmer as a voter
scarcely squares with the facts.

Equally at odds with fact is that cherished tenet of the yeomanry
in arms, embodied in the militia, as the best and only safe form of
military protection for a republic. What was the actual wartime record
of those wonderful English yeomen who could allegedly dispose so
easily of the debased peasantry or mercenaries in the armies of France?
It is true that England was able to mount effective forces against France
in the age of the longbow, before Machiavelli offered his flattering
analysis of English strength. But for a century and a half after Machiavelli wrote, until the 1690s, when England created a permanent
professional army, England mounted no formidable land force against
France or any other country.[13] It was not because England remained
at peace with the world during those years. She went to war repeatedly with Spain, with France, and with the Netherlands. And she did
build a powerful navy. But her soldiers, her land forces, proved an
overmatch for nobody. English seamen might singe the king of Spain's
beard, but the only land forces sent to the continent were feeble and

---

[11] Alexander Spotswood, *The Official Letters of Alexander Spotswood*, R. A. Brock, ed.
(Richmond, 1882–85, Virginia Historical Society *Collections*, n.s. I–II), I, 140, II,
1–2; H. R. McIlwaine, ed., *Journals of the House of Burgesses of Virginia 1752–1755,
1756–1758* (Richmond, 1909), 360–61.

[12] See below, pp. 184–189.

[13] For a differing view of the English military, see Stephen Saunders Webb, *The Governors-General: The English Army and the Definition of the Empire, 1569–1681* (Chapel
Hill, N.C., 1969); and *1676: The End of American Independence* (New York, 1984).
Cf. Richard R. Johnson, "The Imperial Webb: The Thesis of Garrison Government in Early America Considered," *William and Mary Quarterly*, third series, vol.
43 (1986), 408–30; and Webb, "The Data and Theory of Restoration Empire,"
ibid., 431–59.

ineffectual, composed mainly of the country's paupers and ne'er-do-wells, rather than the valued yeomanry. We will never know whether the yeoman would have done any better, because they stayed comfortably by their firesides. England did defeat France in the long series of wars that ended with the Peace of Paris in 1763, but that was after England had established a professional army. The eighteenth-century wars were fought on both sides by professional armies, and in their ranks yeomen were conspicuous by their absence. England's yeomen remained invincible, to foreign foes at least, by virtue of not having to fight.

In England's American colonies yeoman militia did prove sufficient in the sporadic, guerilla-type warfare that the first settlers carried on with the Indians. But the colonists' success owed much to the mere fact of their possessing firearms. And though the Indians quickly acquired firearms too, they did not have the skills or the equipment to keep them in repair or to make ammunition for them. Moreover, their social organization and culture were even less well adapted to sustained military operations than was the militia system that the colonists relied on. It was a different story when the Indians were organized and supplied by the French. In the final contest for the continent, the so-called French and Indian War that lasted from 1754 to 1763, the victory was not one of colonial militia over Indians but of British professionals, assisted by colonists, over French professionals, assisted by the Indians.[14]

The colonists chafed over the subordinate position assigned them in that war and may have nourished illusions about their own military skills. In 1775, when they challenged the professionals who had so recently defeated the French, their initial successes at Concord and Bunker Hill gave new support to the notion of the invincibility of amateurs and impeded the creation of a professional American army. The Continental Congress was all too ready to believe that stout-hearted American farmers, enlisted for a short stretch, would win the war quickly against the hired mercenaries of George III.[15] But George

[14] Douglas E. Leach, *Roots of Conflict: British Armed Forces and Colonial Americans 1677–1763* (Chapel Hill, N.C., 1986), 176–233; Fred Anderson, *A People's Army: Massachusetts Soldiers and Society in the Seven Years War* (Chapel Hill, N.C., 1984).

[15] Charles Royster, *A Revolutionary People at War: The Continental Army and American Character 1775–1783* (Chapel Hill, N.C., 1979); E. Wayne Carp, *To Starve the Army at Pleasure: Continental Army Administration and American Political Culture* (Chapel Hill, N.C., 1984).

Washington did not make that mistake. Even before the professionals trounced him in the Battle of Long Island, he knew that he needed professionals to beat them. In the end he got his professionals: in the end he was allowed to enlist a small number of men for long enough periods to make professionals of them. But these were mostly men who did not have property that they wanted to stay home to look after. In the words of Commissary General Jeremiah Wadsworth, the Continental army was ultimately constituted of "very idle and very worthless fellows, which did not hinder them from doing their duty."[16] They did their duty because they could be made to do it, because there was no fireside waiting to shelter them from the stern discipline an army required. And in the eyes of their contemporaries they earned no credit for their submission to that discipline.

Popular hostility to a standing army grew not only out of the danger it posed to republican government but also out of contempt for the persons who would subject themselves to the tyranny of military discipline. "Can a friend to liberty," asked one pamphleteer, "entertain a tender regard for men, who without any motive but a dislike to labour, have relinquished voluntarily the blessings of freedom, for a state in which they are arbitrarily beaten like slaves?" Regular soldiers were "a species of animals, wholly at the disposal of government." They were "the dregs of the people;" and what made them "fit instruments of tyranny and oppression" was "the severity of discipline" by which they were themselves reduced "to a degree of slavery."[17]

It may be argued whether the men of the Continental army were moved by a dislike of labor or by patriotism, but statistical studies do confirm the fact that they were generally drawn from the lowest ranks of society, from the poor and landless.[18] The trouble was that there were never enough of these "idle fellows" in America, the land of the

[16] *The Debates and Proceedings of the Congress of the United States.* Third Congress, first session, (Washington, D.C., 1855) (*Annals of Congress*, III), 162 Jan. 6, 1794. Cf. ibid., II, 796.

[17] Alexander Smyth, *The Third and Last Letter from Alexander Smyth to Francis Preston* (n.p. 1796), 15. Herbert J. Storing, ed., *The Complete Anti-Federalist* (Chicago, 1981), III, 202; V, 181. John Steele, representative from North Carolina in congressional debate in January 1793, giving yeoman militia credit for winning the revolutionary war, argued that "Such men will not enlist in regular armies, nor will any one who has the disposition or the constitution of a freeman." (*Annals of Congress*, II, 796.)

[18] The question of motivation is discussed in Robert Middlekauff, "Why Men Fought in the American Revolution," in D. D. Hall, J. M. Murrin, and T. W. Tate, eds., *Saints and Revolutionaries* (New York, 1984), 318–31, and in Royster, *A Revolutionary People at War*, 373–78, where the relevant statistical studies are cited.

yeoman farmer. The French king's despised peasants, drilled into a regular army at their monarch's command, contributed as much to the final American victory at Yorktown as the freeborn Americans did at the behest of their popular governments. Cornwallis surrendered to Washington, but Washington's forces at Yorktown, if we include the indispensable naval forces, numbered more French than Americans.

It would be difficult to demonstrate that militia either in England or America have prevailed in any sustained contest with professionals. What made them ineffective was the very quality that Bacon and Harrington and others saw as the source of the militia's alleged superiority, namely the independent spirit that went with their possession of property. After England came to rely on a professional army, a knowledgeable member of Parliament explained why it was not and should not be composed of men with property. "Battles," he said, "are not won by fury, but by discipline." Independent yeomen might show a certain fury against the enemy for a short time—their independent spirit—but it was too hard to discipline an army made up of such men. And he explained with unusual candor: "The last man I desire to have the command of, is the substantial tenant or freeholder . . . it were an ungracious business to bring a constituent to the halberds, or too bitterly to animadvert on *him* for getting drunk, whom courteously I entreated, and invited by example, to do the same but yesterday."[19]

In America, George Washington expressed a similar opinion. As a general it was the bane of his existence that he had so often to rely on militia to supply deficiencies in his Continental army. "Men just dragged from the tender Scenes of domestick life; unaccustomed to the din of Arms" he found worse than useless on the battlefield. Their impatience to be back home again made them desert in droves, and it was all but impossible to bring them to discipline. "Men," he observed, "accustomed to unbounded freedom, and no control, cannot brook the Restraint which is indispensably necessary to the good order and Government of an Army; without which, licentiousness, and every kind of disorder triumphantly reign." Reliance on militia, in Washington's view, was the way to lose a war. Militia simply could not stand up against regular troops.[20]

[19] Sir George Savile, *An Argument Concerning the Militia* (London, 1762), 15–16.
[20] George Washington, *Writings*, John C. Fitzpatrick, ed., (Washington, D.C., 1931–44), VI, 110–11. Cf. ibid., IV, 124; VI, 5.

If we turn to the question of domestic safety, of militia not endangering popular liberties in the way that a professional army does or can, the fiction is again betrayed by the facts. At first glance it would appear that the militia, by virtue of their very ineffectiveness, could not have been a serious threat to anything. Moreover, militia did sometimes seem to support liberty by joining a popular protest they had been called out to suppress. The people, as so often stated, would not be likely to oppress themselves. The very independence that made militia unreliable in battle would lead them to refuse the orders of a government that wished to use them against their fellow citizens.[21]

But the actual record, while it does contain instances of this kind, is just as replete with cases where the government did use militia successfully to suppress popular dissent. In England during the sixteenth and seventeenth centuries the government underwent a number of abrupt and radical shifts that provoked resistance and rebellion from subjects adversely affected. To suppress resistance, the government, whatever its current complexion, relied heavily on militia. When the government went Catholic under Mary Tudor, the militia suppressed Protestants. When it went Protestant under Elizabeth, militia disarmed Catholics. Although the militia failed Charles I, it was under circumstances that ultimately required the formation of a professional army. And when Charles II reclaimed the throne, it was again the militia that put down those who opposed the Restoration or were suspected of opposing it. Militia disarmed the die-hard Puritans, hanged them, deported them, levelled the fortifications of their towns, and broke up the conventicles in which they carried on their Sunday worship.[22]

In the colonies, as in sixteenth- and seventeenth-century England, the militia was the principal, indeed the only, method of forcibly suppressing discontent, not only the discontent of slaves, but the discontent of the free as well. Granted, in the largest colonial rebellion before the American Revolution, that of Nathaniel Bacon in 1676, the militia were at first completely without effect (most of them were with Bacon) and England dispatched an expeditionary force to uphold Virginia's

[21] John Trenchard and Walter Moyle, *An Argument Showing, that a Standing Army is Inconsistent with a Free Government.* (London, 1697), 20; E. S. and H. M. Morgan, *The Stamp Act Crisis* (Chapel Hill, N.C., 1953), 124, 131, 197–98.

[22] J. R. Western, *The English Militia in the Eighteenth Century: The Story of a Political Issue 1660–1802* (London, 1965), Chapters 1 and 2, *passim*; John Miller, "The Militia and the Army in the Reign of James II," *The Historical Journal* 16 (1973), 659–79.

government. Before it arrived, however, the rebellion had subsided, and Governor Berkeley with a handful of loyal militia had regained control. Against most other American rebels militia proved adequate: against the North Carolina Regulators at Allamance in 1771, against Shays's Rebellion in Massachusetts in 1787, against the Whiskey Rebellion in Pennsylvania in 1794. In every instance militia enabled the established government to ignore grievances that had moved people to take up arms. And the people so readily suppressed by the yeoman militia were not urban mobs, not proletariat, but other yeoman farmers.

In sum, it appears that in both England and America actual experience was at odds with the beliefs that elevated the yeoman to so high a place in the folklore of popular government. We are left with the question why. If yeoman farmers were vulnerable to bribery and intimidation in politics, why did people insist that they were independent and virtuous upholders of civil liberty? If as militia they were neither effective in warfare nor a bulwark against tyranny and oppression, why did people keep insisting that they were? Did the political and military exaltation of the yeoman contribute to popular government in ways that do not appear in the repeated but undeserved eulogies of the armed people? If we say yes, if we go on the assumption, as I think we must, that the persistence of a set of beliefs in apparent defiance of facts must have served some not so apparent social and political purpose, a couple of possibilities suggest themselves.

The first relates only to the notion that the militia make a mightier force than a professional army. Obviously this notion was viable only where a country's security was not seriously threatened by aggressive neighbors. It could thrive in England and America because the English Channel in the one case and the colonists' superior technology in the other made it possible to do without a professional army for more than a century. During that time the prevalence of the idea of a mighty militia made it possible for government to eliminate what is always the largest element in any country's budget. The mighty militia offered a cheap rhetorical substitute for an expense that might otherwise have placed a heavy and unnecessary drain on the economy. It helped to prevent the government from burdening the people with taxes to pay for an army at times when an army was not needed.

That in itself was enough to make the fiction attractive, but relief from taxes may also point to the intricate way in which this particular fiction shaped reality and helped to mold a society in which the larger fiction of popular sovereignty could flourish. By relieving the yeoman of the taxes that arbitrary governments levied in support of their expensive armies, the fiction of the mighty militia enabled him to keep his land, to enlarge his acreage, free of mortages and free of rents, free of seizure for taxes. And it gave to larger and larger numbers the disposable income to acquire land and become yeomen. Thus the fiction of the mighty militia, by nourishing the economic independence of the yeoman farmer, helped to create a factual base on which the fiction could rest. It is not, perhaps, a coincidence that the rise of popular sovereignty in England and America was accompanied for so long by reliance on militia and by acceptance of the notion, however dubious, that English yeomen could fight better than French peasants and that militia could overpower professional armies.

But the magnification of the militia was only one of the ways in which the fictional glorification of the yeoman may have contributed to the success of popular sovereignty. The notion of the independent yeoman as the bulwark of civil liberty, we have seen, was equally persistent in defiance of fact. In this case we may find a clue to the persistence of the notion and to the purpose it served if we ask what the seventeenth- and eighteenth-century champions of the yeoman wanted him to be independent of and what sort of liberty they conceived him to be guardian of. It was independence, not of his lordly neighbors, but of the king and his court and of anyone else who might threaten the security of landed property. Spokesmen for the Country party in England, while extolling the yeomanry, urged the gentry to wield over them and over all their inferiors "that Influence which their Family and Fortune procure them."[23] They had, they were told, "a Right to interfere in those elections that are carrying on round about you."[24] The liberty that the yeoman must guard was the liberty to follow his local superiors in defying the influence of the court and its minions.

In the seventeenth century Harrington, though down on hereditary kings, had been no enemy of aristocracy. And the neo-Harring-

[23] *Common Sense*, July 19, 1740; *Gentleman's Magazine* 10 (1740), 346.

[24] *A Serious Exhortation to the Electors of Great Britain* (London, 1741), 51–53. Cf. the statement by Thomas Carew, *Parliamentary History* 13, 1061, that "If elections were allowed to go in their natural course [i.e., without court influence] such men only [i.e., gentlemen of substance] would be chosen." This was a point regularly made in debate on place-bills and on bills to repeal the Septennial Act. See for example ibid., vol. 9, 430–31, 448.

tonians of the eighteenth century emphasized the necessity of the landholding aristocracy as well as the landholding yeomanry for the maintenance of popular liberty.[25] The danger, as they saw it, was that an ambitious king would seek arbitrary power through a standing army and a venal commercial aristocracy. The way to head off royal thrusts of this kind was through the yeomanry, embodied in a militia, on the one hand, and through the landed aristocracy, embodied in Parliament, on the other. The two were closely linked: the landed aristocracy were the natural leaders of the landed yeomanry. Accordingly the neo-Harringtonians, the Englishmen who were most vociferous in idolizing the independent yeomen, showed no concern to keep the yeomen independent of the big country gentlemen and county families that had traditionally commanded their votes and led their militia. And the yeomen, secure in their idealized independence, showed no concern to strike out on an independent unfamiliar political course of their own.

In other words, the glorification of the yeoman farmer in England and America during the eighteenth century functioned as an expression of solidarity among landowners, large and small, against the changing but continuous threats to the security of their property. Or perhaps it would be fairer to say that it was an exhortation by large landowners to stand behind them against the protean political dangers that threatened them both.

In England the greatest threat still came from the court, but backed now by the rise of a money power, a commercial and financial class against which large and small landowners must stand together. The villains in England were the corrupt ministry surrounding the king and the stockjobbers and financiers, who were hand-in-glove with the ministry in schemes for getting rich out of the pockets of both yeomen and gentlemen by means of financial manipulations. We may recall that Trenchard and Gordon's famous *Cato's Letters* began in 1720 in the *London Journal* as an attack on the South Sea bubble as well as on the ministry that permitted stockjobbers to fleece the public.[26]

The colonists in America, avid readers of Trenchard and Gordon,

---

[25] J. G. A. Pocock, "Machiavelli, Harrington and English Political Ideologies in the Eighteenth Century," *William and Mary Quarterly*, third series, vol. 22 (1965), 549–83.

[26] John Trenchard and Thomas Gordon, *Cato's Letters; or Essays on Liberty, Civil and Religious, and Other Important Subjects* (London, 1723). Isaac Kramnick, *Bolingbroke and his Circle: The Politics of Nostalgia in the Age of Walpole* (Cambridge, Mass., 1968).

feared the spread of ministerial schemes across the water and after establishing independence in the Revolution remained alert for any similar danger in their new nation. They found it in the programs of Alexander Hamilton. In the 1790s when Madison and Jefferson sought to organize the yeoman farmers of America in what became the Republican party, they worked against the money power, against the unnatural aristocracy created and nurtured by Hamilton—not against America's natural aristocracy, not against men like themselves who had traditionally, since the beginning of settlement, furnished the country with leaders. Those leaders, whatever their personal faults, had demonstrated in the Revolution their vigilance against threats to the colonists' property rights. With independence won, their vigilance was needed more than ever to fend off new and more insidious threats. For the voters to be bullied or bought by their natural leaders, the proven protectors of their property, was no cause for alarm. What the voters, indeed the whole country, needed protection from was the sinister and hidden influence of the "paper aristocracy" that Hamilton seemed to be fabricating.

A distinct but related threat to property, greater in England than in America, came from the poor. The glorification of the yeoman had begun with a denigration of the peasant and carried on with a denigration of paupers and landless laborers, who spent their earnings on drink and went on relief when the jobs gave out, people whom landowners had to support with taxes that ate away at their property.[27] Nor did glorification of the yeoman involve much sympathy with the slaves who manned the American plantations of the South. When Thomas Jefferson talked about those who labored in the earth being the chosen people of God, he did not mean slaves. Englishmen and Americans in the eighteenth century regarded slaves, paupers, and destitute laborers as an ever-present danger to liberty as well as property. From the poor an ambitious monarch or executive might forge an army and impose a tyranny. And they were also the material out of which the new capitalists would recruit workers for their factories. If they were allowed to vote, their employers might march them to the polls to vote down the independent yeomen. The best way for the yeoman to deal with the danger was to line up behind his big neighbor, who had the experience, the resources, and the political clout to defend the land and the liberty of both of them.

[27] I have discussed the association of these ideas in *American Slavery American Freedom: the Ordeal of Colonial Virginia* (New York, 1975), 316–87.

In other words, the glorification of the yeoman in the seventeenth and eighteenth centuries, which seemed to elevate the ordinary man, served paradoxically as the central ideological tenet of deferential politics, (especially for the so-called country parties whether in England or America). The paradox appears only from our modern perspective. We assume too easily that popular sovereignty was the product of popular demand, a rising of the many against the few. It was not. It was a question of some of the few enlisting the many against the rest of the few. Yeomen did not declare their own independence. Their lordly neighbors declared it, in an appeal for support against those other few whom they feared and distrusted as enemies to liberty and to the security of property—against irresponsible kings, against courtiers and bankers, stockjobbers and speculators—and against that unsafe portion of the many whom they also feared and distrusted for the same reason: paupers and laborers who held no land.

In the last resort the yeomen might have to be bullied or bought, along with other voters; but just as the fictional exaltation of the king could be a means of controlling him, so the fictional exaltation of the yeomen could be a means of controlling them. Landed gentlemen, those who touted themselves as "the country" against "the court," proclaimed the yeoman's independence—and claimed his vote as the proper exercise of that independence. They were the "natural" superiors the yeoman would defer to, if his independence were not subverted by the wiles of courtiers and court politicians (even if those courtiers were themselves landed gentlemen). In their common ownership of land, yeomen and gentlemen could make common cause and join hands, in election time at least, in a curious combination of camaraderie and condescension on the part of the big men and of deference and self-respect on the part of the small.[28]

Another look at the militia will reveal that the military glorification of the yeoman could serve similarly as a prop for deferential politics. The militia, besides suppressing revolts, were also a means of forestalling them and of fostering consent to government, not by force but by instruction. Service in the militia was a school of subordination, where the structure of society was most visibly displayed, especially on the annual or semiannual or even monthly training days. Officers of the militia in sixteenth- and seventeenth-century England and in seventeenth- and eighteenth-century America were selected, not for

[28] See below, pp. 197–200.

their military skill but for their social position. There are recorded instances not only in Elizabethan England but in revolutionary America of militia refusing or objecting to serve under officers with insufficient social standing.[29] High social position helped officers to secure obedience to their commands, and conversely, subordination to an officer in uniform helped to secure subordination to him out of uniform. In some colonies militia officers were popularly elected and their men therefore the more devoted to them. The officers they elected were generally men whom they recognized as their social superiors.[30]

In the absence of titles of honor, which no colonial government had authority to confer and which of course were formally forbidden by both the Articles of Confederation and the Constitution, military titles were the most important designation of social status in America, and they were seldom attained except by large landholders, who also held the lion's share of political offices. Contests for captaincies or colonelcies in the militia were often more bitter than those for political office.[31] And the winners were correspondingly more proud of their military titles than of those that might attach to political office. John Leverett, who was governor of Massachusetts from 1673 to 1679, continued for the rest of his life to be addressed, not as Governor Leverett but as Captain Leverett, the rank he had held in the militia.[32] And George Washington himself continued to be referred to most commonly as General Washington, even after he became president.

Training days for the militia were much alike throughout the colonies. The officers put the men through their paces, and then they all got drunk together, at the officers' expense.[33] There was that same strange combination of camaraderie and condescension, of deference

[29] Lindsay Boynton, *The Elizabethan Militia 1558–1638* (London, 1967), 101–9; *Archives of Maryland*, XI, 350–51.

[30] Timothy H. Breen, *Puritans and Adventurers: Change and Persistence in Early America* (New York, 1980), 25–45; Robert Gross, *The Minutemen and Their World* (New York, 1976), 70–74, 156–59; Ronald L. Boucher, "The Colonial Militia as a Social Institution: Salem Massachusetts 1764–1775," *Military Affairs* 37 (1973) 125–28; John K. Rowland, "Origins of the Second Amendment: The Creation of the Constitutional Rights of Militia and of Keeping and Bearing Arms." (Ph.D. dissertation, The Ohio State University, 1978), p 335.

[31] See for example the account of the riots in Mifflin County, Pa., in 1791, raised by disgruntled candidates for commissions. *The Universal Asylum and Columbian Magazine for September, 1791* (Philadelphia, 1791), 214–15.

[32] Norman Dawes, "Titles as Symbols of Prestige in Seventeenth-Century New England," *William and Mary Quarterly*, third series, vol 6 (1949), 69–83, at p. 79.

[33] *Essex Gazette*, Jan. 29–31, 1769.

and conviviality that bound high and low together politically. It was a time for showing both the structure and the tone of society. And those who thought that the structure needed tightening and the tone needed elevating would accordingly call for a tightening of discipline in the militia. Timothy Pickering, for example, an ardent conservative, argued in 1769 that a better disciplined militia would "in a great measure prevent *domestic* jars, by promoting good *Order*, and *a just Sense of the Subordination, necessary not only to the Well-Being but to the very* Existence, *of Society;* as one Act of Obedience and Respect leads to another; and Acts repeated grow into Habit."[34] And in 1788 another New England conservative, Jonathan Jackson, arguing for a stronger militia, insisted that "the most important thing to be learned [from militia service] and for which alone the institution would be wise, is— that discipline of the mind—subordination."[35]

But most Americans were content with the festivity and the easier, looser variety of subordination that went with training days, when the soldiers delighted in surrounding a pretty girl and firing their muskets in the air, while officers dashed about in glittering uniforms that bespoke social rank more than military prowess.[36] The subordination taught in the militia was not the kind that deprived a man of his independence and made a professional army effective, not a forced subordination or a blind subordination but a willing social subordination, the kind of subordination that made orderly government possible. It was subordination to one's large landholding neighbors, men whom one knew and might with confidence elect to government office. It was not the kind of subordination that George Washington wanted in the Continental army or Alexander Hamilton in the Army of the United States, but a considered deference of free men to their acknowledged superiors, a kind of subordination that did not violate the yeoman's independent spirit.

Patrick Henry, as governor of Virginia, was brought up short along with his legislature, when he and they momentarily ignored the social function of the militia. George Washington, fresh from his disappointments with militia performance in the revolutionary war, recommended to Henry in 1784 that the state militia be strengthened by

[34] Ibid., Feb. 14–21, 1769.

[35] Jonathan Jackson, *Thoughts Upon the Political Situation* (Worcester, Mass., 1788).

[36] *Essex Gazette*, Jan. 29–31, 1769; *Connecticut Gazette*, May 8, 1762; John Sullivan, *General Sullivan's Address to the Freemen of New Hampshire* (Portsmouth, N.H., 1785), 7.

the replacement of existing officers with former Continental army officers, adding only the caution "so far as can be done without creating uneasiness and jealousy." The Virginia legislature obliged the general with an act authorizing the change but left it up to the governor to do the job. Henry tried to move cautiously by consulting "respectable characters" in different counties for nominations, but many of them refused to have anything to do with so wild a scheme and refused to make recommendations. When Henry went ahead and made appointments, he met with a political storm. Prominent citizens were furious at being displaced from positions on which their prestige and local influence had in part rested; and the rank and file were furious at the prospect of being treated like regular soldiers. The next year the legislature repealed the act and restored the old officers to their commands and the militia to its military incompetence and its social and political effectiveness.[37]

In teaching the yeoman his place in the social order the militia performed an undesignated but crucial political function as well as a social function and performed both more successfully than its military function. In the American Revolution, as John Shy has shown us, the militia, however lacking in armed prowess, was a formidable means of lining up indifferent citizens on the side of the gentlemen who led the popular opposition to England and created popular governments in America.[38] But the militia's most valuable service during the seventeenth and eighteenth centuries was in reconciling the incongruity of popular sovereignty with a hierarchical society. The willing deference of men to their officers, in or out of uniform, was of particular importance in America, because militia office generally went hand-in-hand with political office and because the American militia included all able-bodied free men, most of whom were voters, conditioned by their militia service to support their officers.

Throughout the colonial period in America the formal presence of militia was not uncommon at political ceremonies and elections. And after the Revolution, when politics took on a new character with the development of political parties, the militia for a time was the obvious organizing unit at the local level. Militia officers made campaign speeches at musters and sometimes marched their companies to the polls. In

[37] Harrison M. Ethridge, "Governor Patrick Henry and the Reorganization of the Virginia Militia 1784–1786," *Virginia Magazine of History and Biography* 85 (1977) 427–39.
[38] *A People Numerous and Armed* (New York, 1976), 195–224.

Maryland in the 1790s, the state militia organization formed an interlocking directorate with the Republican party.[39] And in South Carolina a grand jury complained in 1800 that "There is nothing more common, than for a militia officer to have a place appointed for his men to meet him, or some other influential character that he may appoint, in order to prepare their votes for such person or persons as he may think proper; indeed, some of them have the assurance to march them in a body to the very election, and others to march at their head even into the house to give their votes."[40] In the early years of the republic the militia thus continued to function as a prop for deferential politics, and the politicians in Congress and the state governments thwarted every effort to turn it into an effective military organization.

To sum up, then, the fiction of popular sovereignty, conceived by gentlemen contending with an irresponsible king, had to be buttressed by other fictions that would leave the hegemony of gentlemen intact. The imaginary invincible yeoman served that purpose admirably. He was not really needed either for valor in battle or independence at the hustings, he was needed as an ideological shield against arbitrary monarchs and conniving courtiers on the one hand and against scheming demagogues and pliant paupers on the other. And his ingrained deference to his big neighbors was needed to reconcile popular sovereignty with a social hierarchy that was too deeply entrenched to be overthrown, even had there been a widespread desire to overthrow it. The fiction of the invincible yeoman thus embodied the same ambiguities as the larger fiction it supported: it sustained the government of the many by the few, even while it elevated and glorified the many.

[39] Frank A. Cassell, *Merchant Congressman in the Young Republic: Samuel Smith of Maryland* (Madison, Wis., 1971), 71, 87–89, 92.

[40] *City Gazette and Daily Advertiser* (Charleston, S.C.), Dec. 23, 1800. I owe this reference to Professor Rachel Klein.

CHAPTER 8

The People's Choice:
Elections and Electioneering

I N ELECTIONS the fiction of popular sovereignty makes its strongest
approach to reality, as actual people ostensibly go about selecting
from among themselves the few to whose government they consent. In many elections the ostensible comes close to the actual,
the fiction momentarily approaches the fact, and our belief in the sovereignty of the people—or our willingness to suspend disbelief—is
heightened. But not always. When we look closely at some elections,
whether in our own times or earlier, we find ourselves in the midst of
transactions that seem to have little to do with the will of the people,
transactions where popular choice becomes a charade and issues are
reduced to triviality. Such elections, we might reasonably presume,
would weaken the belief in popular sovereignty instead of supporting
it; and yet these travesties may generate more popular participation
and enthusiasm than elections where the choice appears to be genuine
and the fiction visibly gains credibility. It would almost seem that the
activities of the campaign preceding some elections may matter more
than the outcome, may satisfy some deeper need than the designation
of one person or another to be governor or legislator.

In the preceding chapter we have seen that the deference at the
polls of yeoman landholders to their social superiors went hand-in-
hand with the affirmation of the yeoman's political independence. And
we have also seen that this affirmation, in apparent defiance of fact,
nevertheless served a social and political purpose. But something still

more can be learned about the consent of the governed from a closer look at the way in which the voters were bullied or bought or simply talked into choosing their betters to govern them. Recent studies of the electoral process in America have disclosed that the deference of voters was a more complex matter than might at first sight appear,[1] that the many who cast their votes for the few were larger in number and more demanding of a quid pro quo than historians had once assumed.

The size of the electorate in the colonies, it now appears, included the great majority of free adult males.[2] In England it amounted to a quarter or perhaps even a third of the adult males in the early seventeenth century and perhaps no fewer in the eighteenth century.[3] One historian estimates that between 700,000 and 800,000 men voted in one election or another in England between 1702 and 1722.[4] Another has shown that seemingly uncontested elections in English counties were often preceded by a spirited contest that ended just short of the polls when a thorough canvass of the votes showed one of the contestants that he would lose.[5] Even the distribution of representation in England before the great reform of 1832 has been shown to be less bizarre than has generally been supposed.[6]

Elections in England, as in England's colonies, it now appears, involved not only too many voters but also voters of too demanding a disposition to be dismissed simply as the willing tools of their social

[1] John B. Kirby, "Early American Politics—The Search for Ideology: An Historical Analysis and Critique of the Concept of 'Deference.' " *Journal of Politics* 32 (1970), 808–38; Alan Tully, "Constituent-Representative Relationships in Early America," *Canadian Journal of History* 11 (1976), 139–54; Joy B. and Robert B. Gilsdorf, "Elites and Electorates: Some Plain Truths for Historians of Colonial America," in David D. Hall, John M. Murrin, and Thad W. Tate, eds., *Saints and Revolutionaries* (New York, 1984), 207–44.

[2] Robert E. Brown, *Middle-Class Democracy and the Revolution in Massachusetts, 1691–1780* (Ithaca, N.Y., 1955); Robert E. and B. Katherine Brown, *Virginia 1705–1786: Aristocracy or Democracy?* (East Lansing, Mich., 1964); Chilton Williamson, *American Suffrage from Property to Democracy 1760–1860* (Princeton, N.J., 1960); Robert J. Dinkin, *Voting in Provincial America* (Westport, Conn., 1977); J. R. Pole, *Political Representation in England and the Origins of the American Republic* (New York, 1966).

[3] Derek Hirst, *The Representative of the People? Voters and Voting in England Under the Early Stuarts* (Cambridge, England, 1975).

[4] Geoffrey Holmes, *The Electorate and the National Will in the First Age of Party. An Inaugural Lecture* (Lancaster, England, 1976), 24.

[5] R. W. Smith, "Political Organization and Canvassing: Yorkshire Before the Reform Bill," *American Historical Review* 74 (1969), 1538–60.

[6] Holmes, *The Electorate and the National Will.*

superiors or as the unwilling tools of landlords and employers who simply marched them to the polls. There are examples of landlords threatening to evict uncompliant tenants, of gentlemen threatening to withdraw their patronage from uncompliant tradesmen, and of government officials threatening to dismiss subordinates who voted the wrong way, but recent studies suggest that such tactics were rare and often counterproductive. Even in boroughs with a small electorate, persuasion rather than coercion,the carrot rather than the stick, was the usual pattern.[7]

To be sure, persuasion commonly took the form of bribery. It might consist simply in treating the voters to food and drink in heroic quantities, but it could involve more solid rewards, individually or collectively, to the constituents. Often, as noted earlier, a candidate bought his seat by offering to pay for some civic benefit: paving the streets, erecting a town hall or school or market, paying the town's public debt or its bill for poor relief.[8] Bribery in this form begins to take on political functions not usually associated with it. And the complexity of the process increases when we find parties of voters forming in populous boroughs for what amounts to collective bargaining to extract the maximum payoff from an election. Such combinations might have constructive objectives like the "Market House Society" in Taunton (Somerset), formed in 1763 "to prevent the evils and dunkenness of a contested election" by channelling the largesse of the candidates into municipal improvements.[9] Others, like the club "of the lower kind of burgesses" in Shrewsbury, or the "Malt-house Club" in Arundel (Sussex), had no more in view than raising the ante.[10] The *English Chronicle*

[7] Roy Carroll, "Yorkshire Parliamentary Boroughs in the Seventeenth Century," *Northern History* 3 (1968), 71–104; Frank O'Gorman, "Electoral Deference in Unreformed England: 1760–1852," *Journal of Modern History* 56 (1984), 391–429; Nicholas Rogers, "Aristocratic Clientage, Trade and Independency: Popular Politics in pre-Radical Westminster," *Past and Present*, no. 61 (Nov. 1973), 70–106. Norma Landau, "Independence, Deference, and Voter Participation: The Behavior of the Electorate in Early Eighteenth-Century Kent," *The Historical Journal* 22 (1979), 561–83.

[8] Edward and Annie G. Porritt, *The Unreformed House of Commons* (Cambridge, England, 1903), I, 151–203.

[9] Lewis Namier and John Brooke, *The House of Commons 1754–1790* (New York, 1964), I, 372. Hereafter cited as Namier and Brooke.

[10] Namier and Brooke, I, 364. Cf. the report in 1761 from Seaford, one of the Cinque Ports, that "the lowest class of the people, especially the fishermen, are very desirous of having an opposition [i.e., a contested election] in order to get money . . . and have entered into an association to stand by each other." Namier and Brooke, I, 454.

reported the proceedings when Percy Charles Wyndham offered himself to the Malt-House Club in the 1780 election.

The chairman of the club gave him to understand that as he was a gentleman
of the neighbourhood and recommended by the Earl of Surrey they would
give him the preference to any other candidate, provided he would speak so
as for them to *understand him;* Mr. Wyndham told them he was an independent man and meant to remain so, that if they did him the honour to elect
him their Member he would serve them faithfully and honestly to the best
of his abilities. This was not the species of elocution adapted to the organs of
the chairman, and he informed the hon. candidate that he might as well have
said nothing. Sir Patrick Crauford was then called in, and he, with a much
keener perception of the peculiar style of oratory that would produce the
best effect, told the Club that if they would honour him with their suffrages
he would return the favour with a present of thirty guineas to each voter. Sir
Patrick was given to understand that he spoke to the purpose, and the chairman pledged himself to the body to get another candidate . . . who would
speak in a language equally intelligible and convincing.[11]

What are we to make of such clubs? Should we consider them
prototypes of trade unions or of political parties or of both? In any
case they may remind us that the political process and the political
fictions on which it depends seldom work in one direction only. Candidates bought their way into government by payments to the governed and then rewarded themselves from public funds extracted from —
among others—the people to whom they had paid their bribes. We
may be reminded also that demands for reform of this system were
not likely to come from the bottom up. The poorer inhabitants of
parliamentary boroughs were not interested in doing away with a system that brought them periodic outpourings of food, drink, and money.
What they got, especially when the election was contested, might be
substantial. The thirty guineas promised by Sir Patrick Crauford at
Arundel was a good deal more than an agricultural laborer could expect
to earn in a year. In very large constituencies votes might sell for £2
or £3 apiece, but in smaller ones a candidate might pay as much as
£300 for one.[12]

The total redistribution of wealth at an election could thus be substantial. In the Arundel election just referred to, 167 persons voted

[11] Namier and Brooke, I, 389. Italics in original.
[12] Romney Sedgwick, *The House of Commons 1715–1754* (New York, 1970), I, 264.
Hereafter cited as Sedgwick.

for Crauford. [13] If he paid each of them the stipulated price, the total would have been 5,010 guineas or £5,261. This was not an excessive amount to pay for a seat in Parliament. Even where there was no contest an election in a relatively small borough could cost half that much. In the larger constituencies, though the number of voters might prohibit the expense of outright purchase, the costs of treating and other less direct forms of bribery could run into many thousands of pounds. At the most costly election of the eighteenth century, the famous "spendthrift election" in Northamptonshire in 1768, the three contestants are said to have spent over £100,000 apiece. [14]

The recipients of this largesse were not, for the most part, already rich. The qualifications for voting in the counties required only the possession in freehold of land that brought in forty shillings a year. This meant that virtually the only landholders excluded were those whose property was exclusively in leasehold or copyhold. In the boroughs the suffrage was determined by custom. In some the vote might be confined to the governing corporation (often a self-perpetuating body of fifteen or twenty persons); in others it was open to all adult male inhabitants not receiving alms, or to all freemen paying scot and lot (an archaic tax levied on virtually everyone not receiving alms) or to all holders of "burgages" (an archaic form of municipal land tenure). The persons thus favored were for the most part small artisans and tradesmen who welcomed and even promoted contests because of the supplement to their incomes from the sale of their votes. Where the vote was denied to persons receiving alms, that is, poor relief, the prohibition could itself be a means of keeping them off relief. It was charged, at least, that potential voters were sometimes offered more for their votes than they could expect from public or private charity, thereby "deterring them from resorting to parochial relief, not from an honest spirit of independence, but that they might keep up the market price of votes in the borough. . . ."[15] The persons elected to Parliament might be always of the elite, but the voters themselves can hardly be called so.

That the voters did defer to their superiors seems undeniable, but it is equally apparent that they did not defer automatically to any

[13] Namier and Brooke, I, 388.

[14] Joseph Grego, *A History of Parliamentary Elections and Electioneering in the Old Days* (London, 1886), 226–28.

[15] George Lipscomb, *The History and Antiquities of the County of Buckingham* (London, 1847), II, 24.

particular candidate. It was frequently stated and understood that a particular nobleman owned a borough or indeed a number of them. And it might be that all or most of the voters were his tenants. But commonly a patron was said to have an "interest" in a borough, by which it was meant that he could in some way control or influence a number of votes. An essential ingredient in the formation or continuation of an interest was usually economic power in some form, the power of landlord over tenant, of customer over tradesman, or simply of pounds over pence, the power of the rich over the poor. But mere wealth, if necessary, was not in itself sufficient. An interest generally involved some personal bond, some favor done, greeting given, hand extended, some charm exercised that went beyond the cash nexus. Even when a man owned all the land in a village and all the voters were his tenants, he had to win their votes. If he took them for granted and neglected to show a concern for their welfare, they might set up a candidate of their own and elect him, as Sir George Downing's tenants did at Dunwich (Suffolk). According to the son of the man who ousted one of Sir George's candidates,

Sir George Downing either residing at too great a distance or for want of an heir had not thought it worth his while to pay that attention to the freemen that they thought they deserved, and though he possessed all the land and houses, still he was obliged to give way to the wishes of the freemen and my father was elected with himself in the year 1747.[16]

This touchiness of voters who might seem to be in a patron's pocket was often remarked on. A man might momentarily swallow his pride for a sufficient sum, but votes bought without recognition of the voter's feelings could endanger the long-run survival of an interest. The Bruce family, which had gained control of the corporation at Marlborough, paid £50 to each of the members to vote as ordered in the 1740s, but Henry Pelham, an experienced politician, noted that the sum "failed . . . of giving them the same satisfaction that it might have afforded, if there had been any kind of civility or solicitation mixed with the order, which was generally too peremptory."[17]

It was sometimes possible for a talented politician to establish an interest with no clear economic basis at all. The Marquis of Rock-

[16] Sedgwick, I, 324. CF. ibid., I, 317, and Howard S. Reinmuth, Jr., "A Mysterious Dispute Demystified," *The Historical Journal* 27 (1984), 289–307, for similar situations.

[17] Sedgwick, I, 350.

ingham gained a commanding interest at York, one of the largest boroughs in England, simply by personal charm and attention to the
voters.[18] And Lord Granby allegedly began an interest in Scarbor-
ough (Yorkshire) in 1768 "by getting drunk with the mayor and corporation." He cemented the interest with the favors he was able to
obtain for people in the borough by virtue of his position in the Chatham
government. His son, inheriting the father's interest, was unable or
unwilling to maintain it by the bibulous means under which it began
and so acknowledged that his interest was an "artificial" one, "nourished in the hotbed of Government favour, without any natural
warmth," while his rivals in the borough, who lived in the vicinity,
had "those constant means of cultivating a good intercourse with the
inhabitants which must ever of itself establish a member."[19]

Several persons might have an interest in a single borough or county;
and they might sell their interest or trade it or bequeath it to their heirs
as though it were a piece of property. Frequently, of course, it might
accompany the inheritance or sale of property, but in itself it was
highly perishable. An interest had to be cultivated or, like an untended
garden, it could go to seed. And given the political fictions that prevailed in England after the Civil Wars, the cultivation of an interest
required some kind of acknowledgment of the voters' independence
and power. In practical terms this meant that a patron must not be
dictatorial, must not push too hard. It was unusual for him to dictate
the choice of both members for a borough. Since most constituencies
elected two members, the voter was free to give—or sell—his other
vote to whomever he chose, and thus belong to more than one interest.[20]

In short, the political process in unreformed England was not quite
as one-sided as once supposed. The number who could vote was not
few, nor did they simply give their votes at the beck and call of their
social superiors. They had to be wheedled, flattered, cajoled, and
caressed. They had to be paid substantial amounts, whether in direct
bribes or in the form of civic improvements, and they were capable of
organizing to make the most of their collective bargaining power.

In England's American colonies the pattern of interests and of large-
scale bribery was much less developed. Elective offices in the colonies
were frequently more of a burden than a benefit. And even when an

[18] Namier and Brooke, I, 441.
[19] Namier and Brooke, I, 440.
[20] O'Gorman, "Electoral Deference."

office carried benefits, it could seldom be attained through bribery, direct or indirect, because the size of the electorate was too large to make bribery practicable. In the colonies the fiction of popular sovereignty was already closer to the fact than in the mother country.[21]

Nevertheless, when we have recognized all the ways in which elections, whether in England or America, gave to a large number of men some opportunity to share in the selection of their governors, we will have to admit that the share was not large. When we have shown that the distribution of seats in Parliament was not quite as bizarre as it seems, we must still acknowledge the irrationality that reformers had condemned from the time that Parliament first asserted its supremacy in the 1640s. And when we have established that voters were less dependent on patrons than previously supposed, we must still acknowledge that a much smaller number of persons than the actual voters determined the outcome of elections in virtually every English constituency, that indeed the choice of candidates was made before the election in most cases, that even where the voters were given a choice between candidates, the outcome was often determined by the last-minute manufacture of voters through purchase of burgages or through the creation of new, usually nonresident, freemen. We must acknowledge too that one candidate might prevail over another by hiring thugs to prevent the other's followers from voting, or by getting the returning officer or the House of Commons itself to declare the loser to be the winner.

In the face of such inescapable facts, was the insistence of the voters on being properly bribed or cajoled sufficient to sustain the fiction of popular sovereignty? Obviously the fiction was sustained, but it seems doubtful that the contribution of actual independent voting can be given all the credit. The question arises whether something more than the actual exercise of choice was at work in an election, something in the political process that would sustain the fiction in ways that may not be immediately apparent.

To answer the question we may first look at some contested elections at their worst in both England and America, elections in which, though there was a contest, the free exercise of choice seems to have been flagrantly violated. We begin with the notorious election of 1784 in Westminster, where three candidates, Charles James Fox, Sir Cecil Wray, and Admiral Samuel Hood contended for the borough's two

[21] Richard Bushman, *King and People in Provincial Massachusetts* (Chapel Hill, N.C., 1985), 74–85.

seats. We can observe the scene through the eyes of Elkanah Watson, a New Englander visiting London.

It was [says Watson] a spectacle of the deepest excitement and interest; but disgraceful, in the outrages and violence constantly attending it. I occupied a position near the hustings, upon a temporary stage, which afforded me a view of every occurrence. The candidates, with their immediate friends, were stationed in front of a small church, the hustings being enclosed within a railway. From my elevated station, looking upon the sea of faces, I judged there were assembled within the square, at the windows commanding a view of it, and in the adjacent streets, twenty thousand spectators, to witness *free-men* giving in their suffrages. The contest had already continued several weeks. Instead of the silent dignity that usually characterizes an American election, here all was confusion and conflict; bloody noses and broken heads, intimidation and corruption. In the midst of the canvass, two self-created armies were seen entering the square, at different points; the one headed by a son of Lord Hood (a captain in the navy,) consisting of sailors, and armed with bludgeons; the other led by a champion of Fox, composed principally of hardy Irish chairmen. They bore banners inscribed with the names of their respective candidates.

The purpose of each party was to secure to its friends access to the polls. These zealous and *intelligent* champions of British liberty and *free* elections, met with a rude shock exactly in front of the hustings. A violent conflict ensued; each party made great efforts to prostrate the standard of its opponents. They fought with proverbial English ferocity. The excitement instantly spread in every direction; and clubs, fists, and canes were in brisk motion throughout the crowd. Such a scene I had never witnessed. Victory soon declared for the sailors; the chairmen were scudding through every avenue, with the sailors in brisk pursuit.

The poll was in consequence open exclusively to the friends of Hood and Wray. Within two hours, the chairmen, strongly reinforced, returned, and a new conflict ensued. I saw Fox, in front of the hustings, clapping his hands, and shouting with the utmost engagedness. The sailors, in turn, were compelled to fly, leaving many of both parties mangled and bloody, who were borne into the adjacent houses. A French gentleman at my elbow, justly exclaimed, 'If this is liberty, Heaven deliver my country from it.'[22]

In other English constituencies it was technically illegal for members of the armed forces to be present in the vicinity of the polls, but Westminster, because it was the residence of the king, was exempt from this ruling. Candidates favored by the court made the most of the exception, mobilizing both soldiers and sailors to intimidate their opponents, who responded by enlisting Irish chairmen with clubs and

[22] Elkanah Watson, *Men and Times of the Revolution* (New York, 1856), 217–18.

butchers armed with meat cleavers and marrow bones. Voters at a
Westminster election—and candidates too—often had to brave a bar-
rage of sticks, brickbats, bottles, cutlery, and flowerpots, not to mention dead cats and dogs.[23] The scene that Watson described was merely
one episode of an election in which the polls were open for seven
weeks, during which the people of Westminster did little else but crowd
about the hustings and take part in the fray.

Violence was endemic in Westminster elections but was by no
means exceptional elsewhere. In many constituencies, riots were a
regular component of elections and sometimes prolonged the voting
through several days or weeks. At Coventry in 1780, two of the candidates reported that "Before the opening of the poll on Saturday, the
freemen in our interest (a few excepted) were forcibly kept back from
the booth; many of them stripped naked and their clothes torn to pieces
by a mob of colliers hired for that purpose; others cruelly beaten and
shamefully treated." As a result in eight days of polling only ninety-
seven votes were cast before the sheriff gave up the attempt. A month
later he opened the polls again, and it required twenty-five more days
to complete the election.[24]

Violence could develop not only at the election itself but also in
the canvassing and treating that preceded it and in the "chairing" of
the winning candidates afterwards, as Hogarth records in his famous
series, inspired by the Oxfordshire elections of 1754. In Northampton, after the election of 1774, it was reported that the winning candidates "gave not any treat or liquors after their chairing, for which
their own mob broke their windows for them."[25] And in York at the
same election a candidate who seemed to be winning at the polls was
threatened with being pelted himself at his chairing if he did not provide more drink.[26]

Elkanah Watson, the pious New Englander, was shocked by the
violence he observed at Westminster, which he compared to the "silent
dignity" of an American election. But like many New Englanders,
when Watson used the word "American" he really meant New England.
And it is true that in New England, where a secret ballot generally
prevailed, elections were pretty tame affairs. But Watson himself had

[23] Rogers, "Aristocratic Clientage, Trade and Independency;" *A True Account of the Election for Members of Parliament for the City and Liberties of Westminster* (London, 1741), 21.
[24] Namier and Brooke, I, 400–402.
[25] Ibid., I, 345.
[26] Ibid., I, 443.

184 USEFUL AMBIGUITIES

travelled in the southern colonies and states and had witnessed elections there that in many respects resembled English elections. At Hanover courthouse in Virginia he found the crowd at the polling place engaged in various fist fights and narrowly escaped being caught in one himself.[27]

Elections in the South were viva voce, as in England. The electioneering that preceded them usually lasted no more than four or five weeks, but it included the same kind of treating with the same results: barbecued oxen, kegs of rum, and everybody roaring drunk. Candidates made speeches extolling their own virtue both before and during the election and travelled about the county to solicit votes personally just as their English counterparts did. There was also the same effort to line up influential persons who might swing other votes, a landlord perhaps, or a big planter who bought and sold the produce of smaller planters, a merchant with debtors—anyone, in short, who had an advantage over someone else.

The actual election took place at the county courthouse, the point of convergence for people trooping in from all over the countryside. According to a French observer the crowds at Virginia elections spent the day in debauchery and brawling; and the candidates' friends, including numbers of women, circulated among the crowd soliciting votes from high and low.[28] Elections in South Carolina were much the same. Edward Hooker, a visitor from Connecticut, described one he witnessed at Greenville as a "scene of noise, blab, and confusion. . . . much drinking, swearing, cursing, and threatening. . . . clamor and confusion and disgrace." The streets were thronged with hundreds of people, including a troop of cavalry. One candidate dispensed whiskey from a bench in the middle of the street, "standing behind it like a shop boy behind his counter," and all the candidates could be seen "distributing whiskey, giving dinners, talking, and haranguing, their friends at the same time making similar exertions for them."[29]

[27] Watson, *Men and Times*, 71–72.

[28] Ferdinand M. Bayard, *Voyage dans l'Intérieur des États-Unis . . . Pendant l'Été de 1791.*, seconde édition (Paris, 1797), 125–26.

[29] "Diary of Edward Hooker," J. F. Jameson, ed., American Historical Association, *Annual Report for the Year 1896*, 900–901. I am indebted to Professor Rachel Klein for this reference. The lubrication of elections with free whiskey continued through the nineteenth century. See D. J. Whitner, *Prohibition in North Carolina 1715–1945* (Chapel Hill, N.C., 1945), 36–38; H. G. Crowgey, *Kentucky Bourbon: The Early Years of Whiskeymaking* (Lexington, Ky., 1971), 67–69. I am indebted to Professor David Courtwright for these references.

In the South while the polls were open, the candidates, if not out in the street drumming up votes, might be seated on a platform at the courthouse. In Virginia every voter had to ascend the platform, to be called by name by the sheriff and to announce his vote. The candidate to whom he gave it then thanked him personally. The election did not ordinarily last more than one day, and there was no chairing of the winner. But another barbecue treat usually followed, with the winner footing the bill.[30]

In most colonial Virginia elections, as in most English ones, although there were virtually no issues other than the personal popularity of the candidates, feelings often ran high, with violence not uncommon. For example, in 1742 in Orange County the sheriff managed to keep order only by posting deputies with drawn swords at the courthouse door. In spite of this precaution, one voter managed to hurl a deputy headlong out the door and seized his sword. Bystanders rescued the deputy and he regained his post, but towards evening the crowd surged in anyhow, according to the sheriff "in a drunken riotous Manner, one of them jumping upon the Clerk's Table, and dancing among the Papers, so that the sheriff was unable to clear the Bar, or the Clerks to take the Poll."[31] In Caroline County in 1736 Jonathan Gibson got elected by having twenty-six of his friends beat up anyone who proposed to vote for his opponent, John Martin. When Martin later sued for assault and battery in their behalf, the jury refused to award any damages.[32]

Although the coming of independence brought many political changes to Americans it did not alter the character of elections in the South. In Maryland at the election of the state convention that ratified the Constitution, the voters of Baltimore participated in a brawl comparable to a Westminster election. According to one report a pro-Federalist mob, including "a body of sailors . . . and a very large number of persons not entitled to vote . . . took possession of the polls, at the

[30]George Wythe Munford, *The Two Parsons* . . . (Richmond, 1884), 207–11; Martha von Briesen, ed., *The Letters of Elijah Fletcher* (Charlottesville, N.C., 1965), 52–53; John Cook Wyllie, "Observations Made During a Short Residence in Virginia," *Virginia Magazine of History and Biography* 76 (1968), 408; Robert Munford, *The Candidates*, Jay B. Hubbell and Douglass Adair, eds., *William and Mary Quarterly*, third series, vol. 5 (1948), 217–57; Charles S. Sydnor, *Gentlemen Freeholders* (Chapel Hill, N.C., 1952), 14–26 and *passim*.

[31]H. R. McIlwaine, *Journals of the House of Burgesses of Virginia 1742–1747, 1748–1749* (Richmond, 1909), 50–51.

[32]T. E. Campbell, *Colonial Carolina* (Richmond, 1954), 83–88, 461.

hour appointed for taking the votes, and kept possession the whole day, and ALL ACCESS TO THE HUSTINGS DEPENDED ON THEIR PLEASURE." The next day the Antifederalists seized control for a time "but were forced from their station by violence, and many of them were beat, and grossly abused, by persons *not voters*, encouraged and assisted by others." Federalists claimed that their opponents were equally violent but nevertheless contended "that they never saw a contested election conducted with more peace, order and decorum,"—a significant comment on what usually transpired at contested elections in the South.[33]

The adoption of the Constitution did not effect a reform. Elections to the new federal government closely resembled those that had taken place under the old colonial governments. The South Carolina candidates described by Edward Hooker at that scene of noise, blab, and confusion had been competing, not for state or local office, but for a seat in the United States House of Representatives. And the records of the House of Representatives contain the most detailed and illuminating account of southern election practices. It may be found in the report of a congressional committee investigating Francis Preston's election to the United States House of Representatives in 1794 from the Virginia district embracing the counties of Montgomery, Washington, and Lee.[34] Preston's opponent, Abram Trigg, had petitioned the House on the grounds that many of his supporters had been intimidated and violently prevented from voting.

The congressional committee on elections heard the evidence and made a recommendation to the House, in which they set forth the facts, which do not seem to have been the subject of any serious challenge. Francis Preston had been elected by a majority of only ten votes. And Preston's brother William, a captain in the federal military establishment, had attended the election at the Montgomery County courthouse with sixty or seventy troops under his command. Trigg showed that Captain Preston had marched his troops three times around the courthouse and then paraded them up and down in front of it, where they threatened those who proposed to vote for Trigg. Trigg contended and the committee, after sifting the evidence, agreed that the soldiers, following Preston's instructions, had behaved toward the

[33] *Maryland Gazette* (Annapolis) Oct. 16 and 30, 1788. Italics in original.
[34] *Debates and Proceedings in the Congress of the United States 1789–1824 [Annals of Congress]* (Washington, D.C., 1855), III, 598–600. 608–13. Several documents concerning the election are in the Preston Papers, Virginia Historical Society.

voters in a manner that affected the outcome of the election. Specifically the committee found:

that some of them threatened to beat any person who should vote in favor of the petitioner; that one of the soldiers struck and knocked known a magistrate who was attending at the said election; that three soldiers stood at the door of the court-house, and refused to admit a voter because he declared he would vote for the petitioner; that many of the country people were dissatisfied with the conduct of the soldiers, which produced altercations at the election between the soldiers and the country people, the former being generally for the sitting member, and the latter for the petitioner, and terminated in a violent affray between them after the poll was closed; that some of the soldiers being afterwards interrogated why they said they would beat any man who voted for Trigg, replied, "they who are bound must obey." That, though it is doubtful whether any of the soldiers were armed at the court-house, yet it appears that, at the time of the affray, after the election, Captain Preston had a sword and dagger; and that, when the soldiers being overpowered by the country people, retreated to their barracks, some guns were fired by the soldiers towards the country people.

All this the committee felt was established as fact, and they went on to make what seems to be a reasonable recommendation, namely "that the election was unduly and unfairly biassed by the turbulent and menacing conduct of the military; and that the petitioner, who only lost his election by a majority of ten votes, has not had that fair opportunity of obtaining the suffrages of the people of that district, to which every candidate is entitled."

The congressmen's response to the committee's report is one of the more illuminating passages in the early record of debates in the United States House of Representatives. The first man up was Thomas Scott of Pennsylvania. He said "He could not, for his soul, discover the smallest pretence to set aside the election of Mr. Preston, nor could he comprehend or conceive upon what ground so strange a notion had been started." The behavior of Mr. Preston's brother, the captain, he pronounced "that of a sage." As for the soldiers, "They had a right to be there, for they were equally entitled with other American citizens to give their votes in the choice of a Representative." Nathaniel Macon of North Carolina agreed with Scott. He could not see that any law had been violated.

When William Smith of South Carolina attempted to defend the committee's report, he was immediately answered by Samuel Smith of Maryland, who expressed his astonishment that William Smith should be so upset by an election riot. Samuel Smith had examined the evidence and found nothing unusual. "Much had been said," he complained, "about the enormity of knocking down a Justice of the Peace; and in the report of the affair, it was stated as if the Magistrate had been at the Court-house in his official capacity. . . . He was there drunk, sir; and he gave the first blow, sir, to the man who knocked him down." And "as to the menace of the soldiers, [saying] that they could knock down one of Colonel Trigg's voters, this was very different from asserting that they would do it. Were a man to have come up to Mr. S. in the street, and say, 'I *will* knock you down sir,' Mr. S. would be for striking that man; but were he only to say 'I *can* knock you down, sir,' the expression would be quite different."

In short, Samuel Smith "declared that he had never known an election in the Southern States where there was so little mischief. He was sorry, for the honor of his part of the country, to give this account of it to the Eastern members [i.e., New Englanders], but in point of common justice to Mr. Preston, they ought to be informed that a Southern election is quite a different sort of transaction from one of theirs." This was not the end of the lesson in southern politics. In the evidence before the House, it had been stated that one person was seen at the courthouse with a club under his coat. "But, sir," said Samuel Smith to Willian Smith,

I suppose that five hundred of my constituents had clubs under their coats; so that if this be sufficient for putting an end to an election, the Committee may begin by dissolving mine. If the Committee are to break up every election where persons were seen drunk, they will have a great deal of work upon hand, sir. In what way were elections for Southern members carried on? A man of influence came to the place of election at the head of two or three hundred of his friends, and to be sure they would not, if they could help it, suffer anybody on the other side to give a vote, as long as they were there. It was certainly a very bad custom, and must very much surprise an Eastern member; but it was the custom, and perfectly known to be so; and therefore it was very injurious to hold up the conduct of Captain Preston as a pretence for dissolving the election.

But the ultimate riposte to William Smith and the report he had tried to defend came from Alexander Gillon, another member from South Carolina, who revealed that there was a riot at William Smith's own election, "and in his own favor. . . . Mr. Gillon saw, therefore, no reason, why there should be such a noise about this election in particular, when others were just as bad, or a great deal worse." There were a number of other speeches, but the recorder of the proceedings found them too tedious to include. When the question was finally called, the petition of Abram Trigg and the committee recommendation on it were rejected without a division. Francis Preston kept his seat.

In none of these eighteenth-century elections, whether in England or America, did the contest depend much on principle. Abram Trigg and Francis Preston came from the two most prominent families in Montgomery County, and they had no serious disagreements in politics. At the time of the election dispute in 1794 James Madison and Thomas Jefferson were organizing the Republican opposition to the Federalists in Congress. Francis Preston supported them in that effort. In a later election when Trigg at last succeeded in winning Preston's seat, Trigg too supported the Republicans.[35]

Not all election contests were so devoid of substantive issues. When landed gentlemen campaigned against courtiers or against candidates backed by commercial and financial giants, there might be something more at stake than a choice between Tweedledum and Tweedledee. But more often one candidate's views of what would be good for the country or the county looked much like the other's. Indeed in many cases the candidates scarcely made their views known, if they had any. To return to our question, then, what was going on in these elections besides the choice of Tweedledum over Tweedledee?

The answer takes us back to the nature of the "interests" arrayed against each other. An interest, as we have seen, was a collection of voters held together by various ties to some patron or friend, ties that might be labelled economic, social, emotional, customary; or ties that might be hard to label at all. They were ties that bound the patron as well as the patronized, ties that might easily wither away if not nurtured between elections but which had to be cultivated to the utmost and be put to the test at election time. The canvass by aspiring candidates before the election was at once a means of measuring the current size of the interest and of strengthening and expanding it. In a canvass the candidate or his friends went from house to house asking for votes, accompanied by all the members of his interest whom he could persuade to join the procession. The hope was to win adherents

---

[35] *Biographical Directory of the American Congress* (Washington, D.C., 1961), 1480, 1727; Francis Preston, *Address to the People of the Congressional District Composed of the Counties of Wythe, Washington, Montgomery, Greenbrier, Kanhawa, Greyson, Russell, and Lee* (Philadelphia, 1796); Preston Papers, Virginia Historical Society.

from the bandwagon effect as well as from personal flattery, promises, gifts, or condescension. The size of the procession could be crucial to its success.[36]

If the canvass was unsuccessful, if it showed that a candidate's interest or the collection of interests put together in his behalf would probably be insufficient to carry the election, he might withdraw and leave the field uncontested to his opponents. If he went ahead with the contest, he must be prepared to step up the wheedling, caressing, and treating and to get help from any of his friends who could influence votes that might be beyond the candidate's own reach. An election became a test of influence, of the ability of one person to affect another.

The clash of interests at an election, as it was a test of influence, was thus in some measure a test of political talent, an exhibition of the political process in its most elemental form. And the opportunities it offered for the exercise of political talent went beyond those who won or lost official position in the poll. The controlling interest in an election often lay in the hands of someone who was not a candidate but who directed his followers toward one side or the other. Peers of the realm could not sit in the House of Commons, but many of them held powerful interests in more than one constituency. Peers, of course, also held political power in their own right anyhow in the House of Lords; what is more to the point is the exercise of political talent by those who did not or could not hold political office, the sharing of power by those who could not officially aspire to it at all.

In this connection the role played by women in eighteenth-century elections is instructive.[37] Women, of course, could neither vote nor hold office. In the ordinary operation of government they had no public role whatever, unless the accident of birth made one of them queen. But women were publicly and openly active at the foundation level of politics in managing interests and in the electioneering that such management required. Sarah, Duchess of Marlborough, had

[36] Donald R. McAdam, "Electioneering Techniques in Popular Constituencies 1784–96," *Studies in Burke and His Time* 14 (1972), 23–54; R. W. Smith, "Political Organization and Canvassing."

[37] The evidence for the seventeenth century is less abundant, but George Wither, in urging reform of parliamentary elections in 1645, complained of the subservience of voters who chose a candidate merely out of fear of "the Lords and Ladies displeasure who sollicited for him." *Letters of Advice Touching the Choice of Knights and Burgesses for the Parliament* (London, 1645), 5.

interests in both Oxfordshire and Hertfordshire which she held from the time of her husband's death in 1722 until her own death in 1744. Dorothy Luttrell managed the family interest at Minehead (Somerset) and was generally able to determine the choice of at least one member.[38] Lady Bute inherited her father's interest in the borough of Bossiney (Cornwall) at his death in 1761 and kept it for the next twenty-three years.[39] Lady Orford possessed interests in two Cornwall and Devonshire boroughs in the 1750s and 1760s. She made over her interest in the Devonshire borough to her son in 1767, but continued to exert an influence in the Cornwall one until her death in 1781.[40] Lady Frances Irwin, inheriting from her husband a commanding interest in Horsham (Sussex) in 1778, maintained control of the borough until her death in 1807, despite the efforts of the Duke of Norfolk to wrest it from her (he spent more than £70,000 in the attempt.)[41]

Other women were active in electioneering for their borough candidates even when they did not themselves have an interest. When the third Duke of Marlborough undertook to sponsor two candidates in the Oxfordshire election of 1754, Lady Susan Keck became virtually a campaign manager for him. Susan Keck was the wife of Anthony Keck, whom Marlborough was having elected from the borough of Woodstock, in which Marlborough had the sole interest. She did not have to campaign for her husband, but she had a taste and a talent for politics, and for a year before the election she rode all over Oxfordshire lining up votes for Marlborough's county candidates.[42] In the Suffolk election of 1767 Lady Sarah Bunbury canvassed one part of the county for her husband while he took care of another part. One observer calculated that "the other day she alone secured 94 out of 100 voters," and went on, "I am only surprised how those remaining six could withstand so charming a solicitress."[43]

In the Whig against Tory contests at the opening of the eighteenth

---

[38] Sedgwick, I, 262, 302, 304, 316.

[39] Namier and Brooke, I, 224–25.

[40] Ibid., I, 225–26, 249–50.

[41] William Albery, *A Parliamentary History of the Ancient Borough of Horsham, 1295–1885* (London, 1927), 114–243.

[42] R. J. Robson, *The Oxfordshire Election of 1754* (Oxford, 1949), 22–23, 34–35, and *passim*.

[43] Historical Manuscripts Commission, Fifteenth Report, Appendix, Part VI, *The Manuscripts of the Earl of Carlisle* (London, 1897), 221.

century the ladies of the Tory Verney family were active in behalf of their husbands and encountered equally active feminine opponents.[44] One Yorkshire gentlewoman, Jane Osbaldeston, was so active in the county elections of 1807 that when her candidates won, the inhabitants of Malton, according to the *York Herald*, "carried her in a triumphal procession around the town, preceded by an excellent band of music, with gold fringed colors waving before them, amidst the ringing of bells and a thousand acclamations from the victorious party."[45]

Although female electioneering was probably not general, it was certainly not uncommon, even in the larger constituencies. At the Westminster election of 1774 the Duchess of Northumberland harangued the Covent Garden mob daily to vote for her son, who was at that point with the British army in Boston. She succeeded in securing his election, in spite of the support given his opponents by the notorious and almost invincible John Wilkes.[46] At the Westminster election observed by Elkanah Watson in 1784, the Duchess of Devonshire, a famous beauty, was the principal campaigner for Charles James Fox. Fox's opponents complained that "she is the candidate to all intents and purposes." And throughout the seven weeks of the election she could be seen daily parading from shop to shop, soliciting votes from tradesmen and allegedly paying them ten times value for their goods as well as favoring them with kisses or something more than kisses. The duchess was aided by her sister, Lady Duncannon, and a host of other noble ladies, while the opposing candidates' female supporters were led by Mrs. Albinia Hobart, familiarly known as Madam Blubber, whose enormous size and weight made her favors rather less effective than those of the duchess.[47]

The duchess also took a hand in a less known contest in the same year at St. Albans (Hertfordshire), where her mother, Lady Spencer, was managing the campaign of one candidate against an opponent sponsored by another noble lady. With the assistance of the duchess,

[44] Margaret Maria Lady Verney, *Verney Letters of the Eighteenth Century from the Mss. at Claydon House* (London, 1930), I, 159, 318.

[45] E. A. Smith, "The Yorkshire Elections of 1806 and 1807," *Northern History* 2 (1967), 62–90, at p. 80.

[46] W. S. Lewis et al., eds., *Horace Walpole's Correspondence with Sir Horace Mann*, (New Haven, Conn. 1967), VIII (Oct. 22, 1774).

[47] *History of the Westminster Election* (London, 1784), 254, 309, and *passim*; F. G. Stephens and M. D. George, eds., *Catalogue of Personal and Political Satires Preserved in the Department of Prints and Drawings in the British Museum* (London, 1870–1954), VI, 96, 105, and *passim*.

Lady Spencer's candidate won, as Fox did at Westminster.[48]

In America too women were active political campaigners. In 1732 when Andrew Galbraith was running for a seat in the Pennsylvania assembly from Lancaster County, his wife, according to a contemporary account, "mounted her favorite mare, Nelly, a spur she fastened to her ankle, and away she went, her red cloak flowing in the wind, to scour the county for Andrew." And in the same county in 1742 a defeated candidate bemoaned the fact that Susannah Wright had opposed him so effectively. "Could any one believe," he asked, "that Susy could act so unbecoming and unfemale a part as to be employ'd in copying such infamous stuff [that is, campaign propaganda] and to take her stand as she did at Lancaster in an Upper Room in a publick House and to have a Ladder erected to the window and there distribute Lies and Tickets all day of the election."[49]

Elkanah Watson, who described the riotous Westminster election of 1784, gives us an amusing example of a woman campaigner in North Carolina. Watson was visiting Warrenton on election day 1786, and was observing the crowd milling around the courthouse when an Irishman he had met shortly before asked him, "have you seen the sight?" "What sight?" asked Watson. "Follow me," said the Irishman. And Watson was shown an American Mrs. Hobart:

We pressed through the mob, intermixed with some respectable planters, and a few females. "There!" says he, "did you ever look upon the like?" pointing to the most obese woman I ever had seen; and, what was more striking, she appeared to be an active leader at the polls.

Watson, bemused by the sight, showed it to a local gentleman, who made no comment on it but invited him to dine the next day at his plantation. There Watson was mortified to discover the obese lady presiding over the occasion. She was the mother of his host and quickly put him at ease. "I never met," he said, "with a more sensible, spirited old lady. She was a great politician; and I was assured, that she had more political influence, and exerted it with greater effect, than any man in her county."[50]

The women who involved themselves so conspicuously in elections in America as in England were probably all upper-class, and the social rank they assimilated from their husbands or fathers probably

[48] Namier and Brooke, I, 307–10.
[49] Robert J. Dinkin, *Voting in Provincial America* (Westport, Conn., 1977), 101.
[50] Watson, *Men and Times*, 287–88.

contributed to the influence they exercised. Nevertheless, something else was involved, some kind of talent that transcended class or gender. Not all women had it or wanted it. And the same was true of men. The ability to sway votes went beyond class. Someone who did not have social prestige or economic power or even the right to vote might possess an eloquence, whether in print or in speech, a capacity for intrigue or flattery or whatever goes into political talent. For a time, during an election, such a person could enjoy an influence not otherwise possible in the station he or she ordinarily occupied.

While an election thus energized the political talents of men and women other than the candidates for office, it also drew into the political process larger numbers of people who were supposedly excluded from the "political nation" of voters. It is difficult to determine the extent to which electioneering affected those who were denied the vote, but once again the role of women is suggestive. In English political prints of the eighteenth century, women appear not only as campaigners or as members of crowds at the hustings but as direct recipients of the canvassers' and candidates' attentions. A 1734 print attributed to Hogarth shows Sir Robert Fagg, candidate for Steyning (Sussex) offering a bribe to a woman.[51] In another print of the same year, "The Humours of a Country Election," one of the candidates is offering a woman a large bag, marked "50" [pounds], which she takes into her apron. In another part of the same print a candidate pays court to a pregnant women and offers to stand as godfather to her child. And in another section the candidates are feasting the voters and their wives and offering presents to the wives and children.[52]

That bribes were actually offered to women is borne out by the testimony given in cases of disputed elections before the House of Commons[53] and by the records candidates kept of election expenses. For example, in a list labelled "Money paid at Wendover [Buckinghamshire] on Monday the 13th of October 1740 when Mr. Hampden

[51] Stephens and George, *Personal and Political Satires*, III, Part I, 11.

[52] Ibid., III, Part I, 23–24; cf. *The Daily Gazetteer*, Feb. 2, 1741. in which a supporter of the government complains that the opposition have used "all the methods of influence which can be imagined, even to that of treating the wives of Electors, that they may be henpecked into Patriotism."

[53] Thomas Carew, *An Historical Account of the Rights of Elections of the Several Counties, Cities, and Boroughs of Great Britain* (London, 1755), Part I, 20, 53, 122, 148, 149, 161, 203. *Journals of the House of Commons*, Vol. XI (London, 1883), 63.

went round the town to ask votes," among the eighteen persons paid
were three women. Presumably they were paid in order to obtain the
votes of their husbands, but some may have been paid because they
could influence other votes.[54] In the Ellesmere Papers at the Huntington Library is the record of a canvass of Amersham (Buckinghamshire) in which voters are listed along with their preferences among
three candidates. On the back of the record is another brief list headed
"Influences" with fourteen names of persons supposed to have an
influence, together with the names, ranging from one to six persons,
of those influenced. One of the fourteen is "Windfields wife," who is
credited with being able to influence William Oakley and William
Hobbes.[55]

Voters and those who could influence voters were the principal
beneficiaries of elections. But candidates and their sponsors could not
afford to confine their condescension within narrow limits. In the 1784
election, while the Duchess of Devonshire was bestowing her favors
throughout Westminster, the candidates for Buckinghamshire were
canvassing that county in the same wholesale fashion. William Cowper, the poet, who had no vote in the county and in his own view no
influence, recorded the visitation of one of the candidates in a well-
known passage:

> We were sitting yesterday after dinner, the two ladies and myself, very com-
> posedly, and without the least apprehension of any such intrusion in our
> snug parlor, one lady knitting, and the other netting, and the gentlemen
> winding worsted, when to our unspeakable surprise a mob appeared before
> the window. . . . In a minute the yard, the kitchen, and the parlour were
> filled. Mr. Grenville advancing toward me shook me by the hand with a
> degree of cordiality that was extremely seducing. . . . I told him I had no
> vote, for which he readily gave me credit. I assured him I had no influence,
> which he was not equally inclined to believe, and the less no doubt, because
> Mr. Ashburner, the draper, addressing himself to me at this moment, informed
> me that I had a great deal. Supposing that I could not be possessed of such a
> treasure without knowing it, I ventured to confirm my first assertion by say-
> ing, that if I had any I was utterly at a loss to imagine where it could be, or
> wherein it consisted. Thus ended the conference. Mr. Grenville squeezed
> me by the hand again, kissed the ladies, and withdrew. He kissed likewise

[54] T. A. Hume, "Buckinghamshire and Parliament," *Records of Buckinghamshire* 16 (1953–60), 95–98.
[55] Ellesmere Mss. 10745.

the maid in the kitchen, and seemed upon the whole a most loving, kissing, kind-hearted gentlemen.[56]

Mr. Grenville showed his kindheartedness not only in kissing the ladies but in treating the voters throughout the county. The bills he paid show that while he feasted the freeholders at various public houses, with prodigious charges for wine and beer, he also paid smaller sums for "ale to the populous," and "for Beer given to Stowe and Dadford lads at time of Election." On the opening day of the actual election a mob destroyed the hustings and polling places, and Grenville's bills included £3 19s for "Bread & cheese gave to the mob," as well as £84.5.6 1/2 "for erecting the Hustings & Booth for the Election and for rebuilding the Booths after the Riot." Two years later he was still paying for the eighty temporary constables, sworn in after the riot, who policed the polls for the next two weeks and were themselves "poor men and most of them not a penny to support themselves."[57]

The treating which made elections so expensive for the candidates was expressly forbidden by law as was every form of bribery, but the laws had the effect of extending it more widely. Defeated candidates generally petitioned the House of Commons to declare an election invalid. If it could be shown that the winning candidate bribed the electors, he might be in trouble, especially if his friends did not command a majority in the House of Commons. Among the ways of evading the law was to treat all comers. Before the writs for an election were issued, it was legal to treat voters alone, for the election was not yet legally announced. After the writs were issued it was still legal to treat if the generosity was not limited to voters.[58] And having treated indiscriminately a candidate might encourage his beneficiaries to vote, whether they were qualified or not. In every contest each side was likely to claim that the voters on the other side included a crucial number of unqualified voters.

In these ways the excitement of an election spread through the populace at large. Riots and mobs, as already noted, were a common accompaniment of elections. But they must often have taken on a festive air, for another item that turns up regularly in the papers of can-

[56] Thomas Wright, ed., *The Correspondence of William Cowper* (London, 1904), II, 182–83.

[57] Stowe Paper, Huntington Library STG. Elections, Box 1, folders 11, 18; Box 2, folders 2, 5, and *passim*.

[58] McAdams, "Electioneering Techniques," 37–38.

didates is payments to "ringers," as well as to trumpeters, drummers, fiddlers, and even to morris dancers. Each side distributed ribbons and "favours" to its supporters. And at the 1713 election in Buckinghamshire, in what may well have been a common practice, two of the candidates (and perhaps the other two) gave outright £5 "to the poor of Aylesbury," where the election was held.[59]

The festivities at American elections were probably less extensive than those in an English contest, but here too the fun extended beyond the actual voters. Those who joined in the barbecues and reached out for the free whiskey were not asked to show their credentials. At the first election for United States congressmen in one Virginia county in 1789 an observer reported that "ther Could not a ben less than 2 or 3 Thousand persons men women Children and negrows" who crowded around for a taste of the roasted oxen.[60]

In one way or another, then, an election could draw in the mass of people in a community. It could also split a whole community vertically down the middle and turn everyday social relations topsy turvy. It enabled like-minded persons of all ranks to oppose, denounce, and even attack persons of all ranks on the other side. And it exerted a temporary equalizing influence within the ranks of each side. It gave a boost to the ego, a possibility of hobnobbing with the great, that anyone might enjoy simply by espousing one side or the other. And the spectrum of those who did take sides in an election contest whether as voters or merely as boosters was broad indeed. As one observer put it, "Great men and the stewards of great men, men of property and men without property, men of honour and men of no honour, women of gaiety and women of gallantry, women of rigid virtue and women of easy virtue, all, all engage in the same common cause."[61]

An election was a time when ordinary men found themselves the center of attention. The frantic solicitation of their votes elevated them to a position of importance they could not dream of at other times and it broke up the patterns of social deference that normally bound them. In England, as we have seen, the cultivation of an interest in any constituency required the personal attention of the patron and of those he or she might sponsor. It was considered an insult for a candidate

[59] Ellesmere Mss., Huntington Library, 10729, 10734, 10741; Verney, *Verney Letters*, I, 302.

[60] Merrill Jensen, Gordon Den Boer, et al., *The Documentary History of the First Federal Elections* (Madison, 1976–), II, 198.

[61] *History of the Westminster Election*, 330.

or one of his close associates not to meet individually with each voter and ask for his vote.[62] The candidates' wives were supposed to get into the act too, and behave like their husbands, as though every voter were their social equal. Thus, for example, a newspaper piece at the time of one election depicted a typical freeholder as saying that the candidates scarcely knew him before the campaign but "now . . . tis, Dear Billy! give me your hand and interest . . . Make my house your home . . . bring your friends with you. . . . The Lady courtesies . . . Sir bows . . . The footmen scrape and fawn." Another newspaper item quoted the wife of one of the candidates bemoaning the liberties she had to allow to one of the more unkempt voters: "nothing would serve him," she said, "but he must kiss me, which I was obliged to submit to for fear of losing his vote and interest."[63]

For the candidates and their most influential backers election campaigns were a paroxysm of condescension and conviviality. A gentleman had to go about shaking hands and soliciting the approval of people who normally had to solicit his approval. To win votes a man had to prostrate himself before the voters, take off his hat to people whom he would not recognize when the election was over. He had to dine with them, chat with them, and above all get them drunk and get drunk with them. John Trusler, a playwright, depicted it in a farce called *The County Election*. In it one of a candidate's supporters commiserates with him because he must be "Up night and day for weeks together, fawning on, kissing and flattering the women, all day, smoking, boozing, and licking the very spittle of the men, all night." To which the candidate adds in reply, "Twould be well enough at particular times, and with particular persons, but, to be obliged to do it with all ranks and degrees of people, and so long together; Taylors, Barbers, Shoemakers, Tinkers and Blacksmiths; and to be forced to be obsequious to those, whom you hate the sight of."[64] Such complaints were often voiced by actual candidates and by the aristocratic friends who campaigned for them, as when some of the Duke of Newcastle's supporters told him that voters were not content to be solicited by his servants "but expected to be waited on by persons of a superior

[62] *Jackson's Oxford Journal*. See the advertisement by Viscount Parker and Sir Edward Turner, carried from June 1753 onward, and a piece signed "A Freeholder," July 28, 1753. See also Sedgwick, I, 303 and E. A. Smith, "The Election Agent in English Politics," *English Historical Review* 84 (1969), 12–35, at p. 13.

[63] R. J. Robson, *The Oxfordshire Election of 1754*, 22n, 54–55.

[64] (London, 1768), 37. I am indebted to Professor Ann Withington for this reference.

rank," for every freeholder looked "upon himself as a gentleman at this time and a man of very great consequence."[65] Similarly David Hartley, an experienced campaigner, observed in 1784 that during an election the populace "must be at least treated as equals—and *pro hac vice* as superiors. The hearty shake and the familiar bit of conversation must be attended to."[66]

It could be a strenuous business. When Henry Savile became a candidate for election in the small town of Newark in Nottinghamshire in 1685, he arrived in town to find it rumored that he had supported a bill in the previous Parliament to limit election entertainments. He hastened to deny so damaging a charge, but it took him four days of treating, in which he swallowed, as he reported to his brother, "more good ale and ill sack than one would have thought a country town could have held." He had not only to supply the drink but to join in the drinking until he was sick as a dog.[67] Gilbert Spencer made a comparable sacrifice for Henry Sidney at Bramber, reporting to his principal that "You would have laughed to see how pleased I seemed to be in kissing of old women, and drinking wine with handfulls of sugar, and great glasses of burnt brandy, three things much against the stomach, yet with a very good will, to serve him I most honoured."[68] The people whom Savile and Spencer drank with of course knew that this fraternization with them was temporary. There was a make-believe quality to it, a temporary pretending that people were equal when everybody knew they were not.

The reversal of roles, the spectacle of the great paying court to the small, was comical and gave each side the opportunity to make satirical thrusts at the other. A favorite theme was that of the lowly but solid citizen who encouraged the candidate to humble himself in false comradeship and then declared he would not vote for someone who so demeaned himself.[69] But such stories only served to point up the fact that electioneering normally required demeaning conduct. It was part of the game to charge the other side with it, even while your own side went about it in the same way. The campaigning by aristocratic

[65] Quoted in E. A. Smith, "The Election Agent," 13.

[66] Ibid.

[67] W. D. Cooper, ed., "Savile Correspondence: Letters to and from Henry Savile," Camden Society, *Publications* 71 (London, 1858), 43–44.

[68] R. W. Blencowe, ed., *Diary of the Times of Charles the Second by the Honourable Henry Sidney* (London, 1843), I, 119.

[69] For example, *History of the Westminster Election*, 319, 332–34.

women offered even larger opportunities for satirical play on role reversal. The lady who went campaigning invited mockery not only for her condescension to the lowly but also for taking on a man's role. Lady Susan Keck, galloping about the country in search of votes for Marlborough's candidates, was greeted with ribald verses that hailed her as Lord Sue and warned her "how such Exercise will peel your Bum and your Complexion."[70]

Ribaldry was part of the game and often carried to an excess that defied all conventions. At an election in Nottingham in 1803 the winning candidate was preceded at his chairing by a number of young women discribed as "lascivious wantons," one of them "in a state of entire nudity."[71] The cartoons portraying the Duchess of Devonshire and Charles James Fox in 1784 indulged in obscenities that left nothing to the imagination.[72] Newspaper squibs were only slightly more restrained. It was said that Fox's ladies "finding the arts hitherto practised of kissing, coaxing, etc., less efficacious than usual, are come to a resolution of canvassing in *buff*."[73] Fox was described as "singing and drinking with forty half-naked whores," while the duchess "was squeezing and fingering the butchers."[74] She was said "to call frequently at a B[awd]y house" in an effort to win the proprietor, who declared he would vote only if escorted by her in her own carriage.[75] And there was a great deal of punning on the fondness of the ladies for their favorite member. The suggestions of sexual license, however gross, were what every electioneering woman had to expect. When noble ladies stepped out of the roles normally assigned their sex, there was no telling where they would stop—or so at least their opponents liked to infer, especially when they could not muster comparable female support of their own.

The charges that each side flung at the other in an election were expected to be extravagant. Things were said and done that would not be permitted at another time, and it was bad form to take serious offense at them, though occasionally someone did. At a Maryland

[70] *The Oxfordshire Contest* (London, 1753), 43, 52ff.

[71] *Coke and Birch: The Paper War Carried On At The Nottingham Election* (Nottingham, 1803), 12.

[72] See for example the cartoons described in Stephens and George, *Personal and Political Satires*, VI, nos. 6520, 6526, 6527, 6533, 6541, 6544, 6546, 6561, 6564, 6572.

[73] *History of the Westminster Election*, 246.

[74] Ibld., 277.

[75] Ibid., 246.

election in 1786 one candidate found the other's denunciation of him so offensive that he challenged him to a duel afterwards. The challenge was accepted, but the person challenged expressed his surprise "that a man should be called out for anything that passed at an election."[76] Everybody was supposed to know that electioneering invective was not for real.

Even the violence at the polls, while real enough to intimidate, had something of a ritual quality about it and was not to be held against a man when the election was over. We have already noticed the refusal of a Caroline County jury in Virginia to award damages for the assault made by one candidate's supporters against men who wanted to vote for the other candidate. After another Virginia election in 1736, when a defeated candidate charged his opponent with intimidating an elector, his neighbors criticized him for making "such frivolous Complaints."[77] The expectations of southerners about elections are evident also in the complacency of southern congressmen toward the violence of the soldiers at the Montgomery County election of Francis Preston in 1794 and in the testimony of one of the witnesses examined in the case. He had stated that the soldiers intimidated people and prevented them from voting for Trigg. But when asked if one group had not behaved riotously, he answered, that "they came in lively but I remember no particular matter more than usual in Elections."[78] Even in the extraordinarily violent Westminster election of 1784, when some of the principal rioters were brought before a magistrate, he dismissed them with an admonition, because "a serious prosecution might only create ill blood and widen differences."[79] And when a constable died from the blow of a club, a jury found no one guilty, the presiding judge having virtually instructed them to that effect.[80] Fighting to kill was not part of the script. Seldom do we find any mention of firearms in the accounts of violence. There might be clubs and cleavers but not guns, there might be bruises and blood, but no dead bodies. If anyone was dangerously injured it was by acci-

[76] James Lloyd, *Address of General James Lloyd, to the Citizens of Kent and Queen Anne's Counties* (Annapolis [1794]), 4.

[77] Thomas Jones to Mrs. Jones, Sept. 17, 1736, *Virginia Magazine of History and Biography* 26 (1918), 180–81.

[78] Deposition of James Charlton, June 26, 1793. Preston Papers. Virginia Historical Society.

[79] *History of the Westminster Election*, 113.

[80] Ibid., 379–409.

dent. Hence the reluctance of the courts to punish those at fault; election brawls were not to be taken seriously once the election was over.

From all the evidence it seems clear that brawling, violence, and intimidation were an accepted and expected part of an election and that it was understood they would end when the election ended. The violence of the election was a temporary, one-time thing and was probably not in fact as violent as it seems from the extravagant charges and countercharges that the two sides flung at each other. It was not quite for keeps. It was partly mock violence, partly make-believe, a routine that engaged the participants only temporarily and ended abruptly when the election was over.

If I am correct in perceiving a kind of make-believe quality in eighteenth-century elections, as noticeable in the egalitarian fraternization as in the extravagant partisanship that characterized them, it may be that we can reach some further understanding of their political and social function by considering other occasions in which a society has indulged in collective make-believe and exaggerated partisanship or emotion or behavior outside the bounds of everyday life.

In some ways sports competitions offer a parallel. People can become extraordinarily partisan and boisterous in support of one team against another in baseball, football, soccer, or whatever. Cheering for the side they favor, people of all classes are brought briefly into a kind of fraternization. Although the outcome of the competition affects their daily lives not at all, the fans may even go after one another with fists and clubs. And the winners enjoy a brief triumph not unlike that of an electoral victory. The parallel was apparent even in the eighteenth century. In 1791 the historian of Derby, England, in denouncing football matches, could think of no more disgraceful transaction to compare them with than an election. "I have seen," he said, "this coarse sport carried to the barbarous height of an election contest."[81]

There were other parallels in contemporary English country life, in the fairs, "wakes," and local festivals that punctuated the seasons, where sexual restraints were loosened and class barriers briefly broken in a "rough and ready social equality."[82] But these were simply milder versions of what may be the most instructive parallel to an eighteenth-century election, namely the carnival—not the travelling amusement park familiar in America, but the festivities that preceded Lent in

[81] R. W. Malcolmson, *Popular Recreations in English Society 1700–1850*, (Cambridge, England, 1973), 85.
[82] Ibid., 75–88.

Catholic countries. The pre-Lenten carnival still survives in many places and still occupies an important place in community life, but it has assumed quite different functions from the earlier festivals.[83] It is the older carnivals, before the nineteenth century, that will bear comparison with eighteenth-century elections.

The carnival of the medieval or early modern period elicited from a community far more outrageous behavior and detailed ritual than did the elections that concern us.[84] But the carnival's embellishments emphasize rather than obscure the fact that make-believe was the carnival's basic characteristic and that carnival make-believe, like election make-believe, involved role reversal by the participants. In a carnival, people threw off the roles they played in everyday life and assumed new ones for the duration of the festivities. They donned masks and costumes to emphasize the fact. They engaged in frivolous contests conducted in seeming earnestness, a footrace, the pursuit of an animal, or a mock battle. Everybody got drunk. A great many fantastic things went on, full of symbolic meanings related to fertility, purification, and rites of passage. But the core of the festivities was the violation of everything that was customary and restrained in everyday life, a reduction of order to chaos, a deliberate outrageousness.

Carnival behavior equaled or exceeded the worst libels concocted in election campaigns. Women bared their breasts in public, men lifted women's skirts, rowdies rushed about insulting their betters, calling names that would land them in jail at any other season. It was a time for the mouse to eat the cat, the sheep to eat the wolf, the rabbit to shoot the hunter (favorite themes in popular woodcuts). It was a time to turn the world upside down and most particularly in social relations. The plowman acted the noble lord and the noble lord bowed to him. Regular government was replaced by misgovernment. A king or lord of misrule was chosen, with a court of fools dressed in fool's costume as his council of state. The poor demanded and received trib-

---

[83] On the social functions of modern pre-Lenten carnivals see Nancie L. Gonzalez, "Social Functions of Carnival in a Dominican City," *Southwestern Journal of Anthropology* 26 (1970), 328–42; and Phyllis H. Raabe, "Status and Its Impact: New Orleans' Carnival, The Social Upper Class and Upper-Class Power" (Ph.D. dissertation, Penn. State University, 1973).

[84] See in general Natalie Z. Davis, *Society and Culture in Early Modern France*, (Stanford, Calif., 1975), 97–123; Emmanuel Le Roy Ladurie, *Carnival in Romans* (New York, 1979); Peter Weidkuhn, "Carnival in Basle: Playing History in Reverse," *Cultures* 3 (1976), 29–53; Peter Burke, *Popular Culture in Early Modern Europe* (New York, 1978), 178–204.

ute from those who exploited them during the rest of the year. Children spanked their parents. Everything had to be the reverse of what it usually was, and the more outrageous the inversion the more fun it was. Every town and village had its own special ways of doing it, of mocking the order that everyone would return to a week later.

This kind of play has exercised a fascination for people in many different societies. Brief suspension of a king's reign with the substitution of a lowly person as temporary king or other more elaborate role-reversal rituals can be found today in some Asian and African villages.[85] The European carnival, though it probably had pagan origins of some kind, presumably developed within the Christian world as an episode of merriment before a community entered the austerity of Lent. But as in the role-reversal rituals of other societies, it served social purposes that went deeper than merriment. At the most elementary level it allowed people to escape for a time from the restraints of the social order and to act as though they had powers and capacities that were in fact denied them in their real lives. Fifty years ago Robert Briffault, in describing festivities of the carnival type, noted that "The temporary obliteration of class distinctions . . . the transitory illusion of affluence and luxury afforded by largess to the populace, the relaxation of rigid sexual codes, all operate as powerful elements in the appeal of chartered festivities and serve at the same time as safety valves against the dangerous effects of continuous restraint."[86] The same thought has occurred to most students of the phenomenon. Keith Thomas, for example, sees the role reversals in festivals as "explicable only in terms of the periodic release necessary in a rigidly hierarchical society."[87]

Le Roy Ladurie carries the idea a step farther when he observes that "If men exchanged roles during Carnival it was only to reaffirm the strength and permanence of the social hierarchy."[88] It was not simply the release from continuous restraint that helped reaffirm the social hierarchy, it was also the delineation of what was right by the vivid exhibition of its opposite. By turning the world obviously and

[85] J. G. Frazer, *The Golden Bough*, 3d ed. (London, 1911), IV, 148–59; Victor Turner, *The Ritual Process* (Chicago, 1969).

[86] Robert Briffault, "Festivals," E. R. A. Seligman and Alvin Johnson, eds., *Encyclopedia of the Social Sciences*, V, 198–201.

[87] Keith Thomas, "Work and Leisure in pre-Industrial Society," *Past and Present* 29 (1964), 53–54.

[88] Le Roy Ladurie, *Carnival in Romans*, 192.

deliberately upside down for a time, the carnival gave everybody the opportunity to recognize and accept what was rightside up when the festivities were over. Mice do not really eat cats. Sheep do not really eat wolves. And plowmen, if they know what is good for them, do not try for more than a day to act as though they were noble lords.

To be sure, the lesson in social order did not always work. Where social tensions ran too high the carnival might become the occasion for putting a real scare into the cats and wolves of the community. There was always a cutting edge to the reversal of roles and to the seemingly frivolous competition. And when a society was ripe for revolt, the carnival activated it, as Le Roy Ladurie has shown in his account of the carnival at Romans in 1580. But normally a community went its way with the structure of power reinforced by its survival of the carnival's make-believe challenge.

To put this idea in another way, one might say that the carnival provided society with a means of renewing consent to government, of annually legitimizing (in a loose sense of the word) the existing structure of power. Those who enacted the reversal of roles, by terminating the act accepted the validity of the order that they had ritually defied. By *not* carrying the make-believe forward into rebellion, they demonstrated their consent. By defying the social order only ritually they endorsed it.

In weighing the plausibility of this line of reasoning we should not forget the ubiquity of religious festivals involving role reversal nor the indisputable connection of such festivals with religious and magical efforts to bring prosperity to the society that engaged in them. In a religious context the purpose of role reversals was renewal. The order of the universe was violated, reduced to chaos by every kind of license, in order that it might then be restored in a reenactment of the creation. In this way the society purged itself and began life anew, with its order freshly established.[89] Although the frenzied European carnival was probably a pale descendant of some more frenzied pagan ancestor, it retained a degree of power, nonetheless. It renewed the commitment of men to God and of subjects to rulers.

The underlying similitude of an eighteenth-century election to a carnival is by now apparent. The two resembled each other not only in obvious outward manifestations—in the reversal of roles, in the make-believe quality of the contests, in the extravagance of the parti-

[89] Roger Caillois, *Man and the Sacred* (Glencoe, Ill., 1959), 97–127.

sanship of artificial causes, in the outrageous behavior and language, in the drunkenness, the mob violence, even in the loosening of sexual restraints—not only in all these external attributes but also in an identity of social function. An election too was a safety valve, an interlude when the humble could feel a power otherwise denied them, a power that was only half illusory. And it was also a legitimizing ritual, a rite by which the populace renewed their consent to an oligarchical power structure.

Hence the insistence that the candidate himself or someone of the same rank solicit the votes of the humble. The election would not fully serve its purpose unless the truly great became for a time humble. Nor would it serve its purpose if the humble did not for a time put on a show of greatness, not giving their votes automatically to those who would ordinarily command their deference. Hence too the involvement of the whole populace in one way or another, if not in the voting or soliciting of votes, then in the tumults and riots, in the drinking and feasting, in the music and morris dancing.

It would be too much to say that the election was a substitute for a carnival. It will not do to push the analogy too far. The carnival was embedded deeply in folk culture, and its functions were probably more magical and religious than, overtly at least, political. An election, on the other hand, was almost exclusively a political affair. It had no magical overtones; it was not connected with any religious calendar.[90] Nor did it always exhibit the wild excesses of a carnival; and when it did, it was surely not because the local oligarchy felt that this would renew their authority. They would generally have preferred to preserve "the peace of the country" by avoiding the contests that engaged them so hotly and cost them so much when they occurred. Moreover, the reversal of roles did not go anywhere near as far as in a carnival. In an election, along with the fraternization and condescension, there could be a great deal of direct pressure brought by the mighty on those who stood below them, with no pretense of reversing roles.

The resemblance to a carnival nevertheless remains striking. Is it wholly coincidence that there were no carnivals in Protestant England and her colonies where these carnival-like elections took place, and that in countries where carnivals did prevail elections were moribund or nonexistent? Is it too much to say that the important part of an

---

[90] But it could be a rite of passage for the candidate, who suffered an ordeal of popular ridicule before passing from a local status to a more distant one at the center of government. I owe this observation to Professor Linda Colley.

eighteenth-century election contest in England and in the southern colonies and states was the contest itself, not the outcome of it? Is it too much to say that the temporary engagement of the population in a ritual, half-serious, half-comic battle was a mode of consent to government that filled a deeper popular need than the selection of one candidate over another by a process that in many ways denied voters the free choice ostensibly offered to them? Is it too much to say that the choice the voters made was not so much a choice of candidates as it was a choice to participate in the charade and act out the fiction of their own power, renewing their submission by accepting the ritual homage of those who sought their votes?

If these observations have any validity, they open a perspective on the early history of popular government that may require some readjustment of conventional views. Colonial New England has often been held up as the cradle of American democracy, and it must be admitted that New Englanders enjoyed a much greater degree of social, political, and economic equality than can be found either in the southern colonies or in eighteenth-century England. Elections there, except in Rhode Island, displayed none of the violence, none of the campaigning, none of the corruption—and none of the excitement—to be found in the South. It is tempting to say that there was less need for a carnival-type election in societies where the fiction of popular power was closer to reality, where representative assemblies were filled with ordinary men who had not campaigned for the position and sat there, often reluctantly, as a civic duty.

This may well have been the case, but it heightens what is already an irony in the history of American popular government. The turnout of voters in egalitarian New England's sober elections was smaller than in the aristocratic South's drunken ones. The number of qualified voters probably comprised a majority of adult males in both regions; but in New England, without the campaigning and corruption, fewer of them bothered to vote, and there was no one interested in rounding up the unqualified in an attempt to pass them off as qualified. The actual participation of the general public in the political process, at least in elections, was less in New England than in the South.

The irony is compounded when we consider the political posture of the two regions in the first years of the national government. New England became the stronghold of the Federalist party and of the conservative semi-aristocratic measures that it fostered; the South became the center of the democratic Republican opposition. While that opposition marched under the banner of equality and raised the cry of corruption and aristocracy against the Federalists, it was led by aristocrats, by slaveholders.

I have argued elsewhere that the leadership of slaveholders in a party dedicated to equality was no accident, that in a slaveholding society freedom and whiteness made it possible for patrician and plebeian to meet and fraternize on common ground.[91] And elections were the chosen meeting place. In the hubbub of eighteenth-century elections southerners served an apprenticeship in the kind of politicking that was to prevail, albeit in much subdued form, in American national politics. New England may have been the cradle of American democracy, but if elections and election campaigns give plausibility to the fiction of popular government, southerners knew a good deal more about engaging the public in elections than New Englanders did. Southerners were aristocrats and oligarchs, but they had already learned something about political leadership in the make-believe world of elections, where men are equal. And in the last analysis, in a popular government, persuading the many to submit to the few is a matter of leadership, a subject to which we shall turn in the final chapter.

[91] E. S. Morgan, *American Slavery American Freedom: The Ordeal of Colonial Virginia* (New York, 1975).

CHAPTER 9

The People's Voice: Instructions, Petitions, Associations

WHEN THE English Parliament affirmed or invented the sovereignty of the people in the 1640s, the members intended to assimilate to themselves the power they ascribed to the people. If they were not themselves the people, as they liked to claim, they were at least the representatives of the people, authorized to act for them. And the fiction was already established that every man, woman, and child in England was present in Parliament through these representatives.

The plausibility of the fiction had been enhanced by the imaginary history of ancient days when the people themselves had assembled in person, whether at the summons of a king or on their own initiative, to conduct public business. This mythical assemblage had supposedly given way to an assembly of representatives when the numbers of people and the extent of territory where they lived had grown too large for them conveniently to gather in person. The supposed origin of representation thus emphasized its expedience: the people made use of representatives only when it was impracticable for them to meet in person. William Penn, the founder of Pennsylvania, was fond of dipping into ancient records and professed to have found a meeting of the whole kingdom still functioning under King Ina in the eighth century, consisting of the "generality of the Free-men of the Kingdom; for all might come that pleased. . . . But as . . . the number of Free-men encreased, there was a Necessity for a Representative."[1]

Even before the rise of popular sovereignty it had become accepted as history that representation originated in this way. James I, the great exponent of the king's divine right, envisioned representative assemblies in his time as a convenience, whether for himself or for his subjects. In one of the little lectures in which he periodically instructed the House of Commons about who and what they were, he told them that because the numbers were too great "for all the gentlemen and burgesses [of the kingdom] to be present at every parliament therefore a certain number is selected and chosen out of that great body, serving only for that parliament where their persons are the representation of that body."[2] James regarded these assemblies of substitutes as instruments of royal rule. But when the sovereignty of the people displaced the sovereignty of God's lieutenant, the notion persisted that the representatives who exercised the people's sovereignty did so only in default of the people's ability to assemble in person. Thus William Ball, in 1645, denying that the king could thwart the actions of a parliament elected by the people, thought it proper to add parenthetically, "if the people without confusion or disorder could assemble together, there were no need of such election."[3]

In America, as we have seen vividly illustrated in the first Maryland assemblies, the primitive gathering of the whole people, or at least of the free men, actually took place and gave force to the notion of representatives as a mere convenience. After American representative assemblies had taken control of government in the Revolution, it remained a truism, as one member of the federal convention of 1787 put it, that representation was "an expedient by which an assembly of certain individuals chosen by the people is substituted in place of the inconvenient meeting of the people themselves."[4] In the first Congress under the Constitution John Page of Virginia asserted that "If it

[1] *A Collection of the Works of William Penn*, [Joseph Besse, ed.] (London, 1726), I, 684. Cf. *An Address to the Electors of Great Britain* (Edinburgh, 1740), 27: "It appears then, that, among our Ancestors, the whole People had a Right to assemble to give their Opinion, Advice and Consent in Councils; that, in the earliest Times They executed this by themselves, and, in subsequent Ages, by their Deputies."

[2] William Cobbett, *Cobbett's Parliamentary History of England* (London, 1811), I, 1060.

[3] William Ball, *Tractatus de Jure Regnandi et Regni* ([London], 1645), 11.

[4] Max Farrand, ed., *The Records of the Federal Convention of 1787* (New Haven, Conn., 1911, 1937), I, 561.

were consistent with the peace and tranquility of the inhabitants, every freeman would have a right to come and give his vote."[5]

The notion that the people, but for the inconvenience and impediments of assembling in large numbers, could act for themselves, was a necessary ingredient of popular sovereignty. It helped to give verisimilitude to the transfer of powers to representatives in elections and thus helped to sustain the authority of the few. But it invited popular activities that might limit or even threaten that authority. The members of the Long Parliament, even while elevating themselves as agents of the people, had been embarrassed by suggestions that the people might dispense with them. Richard Overton, speaking, he said, for "Many Thousand Citizens, and other Free-born People of England," told the House of Commons in 1646, that they were there "to deliver us from all kind of Bondage, and to preserve the Commonwealth in Peace and Happiness: For effecting whereof we possessed you with the same Power that was in our selves, to have done the same; For wee might justly have done it our selves without you, if we had thought it Convenient."[6]

Although it was not only inconvenient but virtually impossible to assemble the whole people of a country the size of England, it was not impossible or even inconvenient, for the voters of a borough or county to come together for the purpose of electing a representative. If they could meet together for an election, could they not meet also in order to instruct their representative, their deputy, as to how he should act for them on particular questions when he joined the deputies of other constituencies in a representative assembly? As elections contributed an infusion of reality to popular sovereignty, so did the instruction of representatives by their constituents.

The use of instructions, like elections, was no novelty of popular sovereignty. Since the local, subject character of the representative was as old as representation itself and originally predominated over his national character as part of the government, it was apparently common from an early period for constituents to instruct their representatives at the time of their election. Before the 1640s such instructions were normally confined to local matters, calling upon the

[5] *The Debates and Proceedings of the Congress of the United States* (Washington, D.C., 1855) (*Annals of Congress*), I, 744.

[6] William Haller, ed., *Tracts on Liberty in the Puritan Revolution* (New York, 1934), III, 353.

representative to secure from the government some favor for the locality—deepening a riverbed, locating a lighthouse, lessening local taxes.
But instructions on matters of national policy were not unknown, and
with the summoning of the Long Parliament, as more people became
concerned about creeping Catholicism and as Parliament took a larger
view of its authority, instructions to members were more often directed
to national matters. With no general election held in England from
1641 to 1653, some constituencies, or what purported to be constituencies, issued instructions to members already at Westminster.[7]

The practice did not cease with the revival of divine right at the
Restoration. During the Exclusion Crisis of 1679–81 members of Parliament were deluged with instructions to vote for excluding the Duke
of York from the throne. After the Revolution of 1688 various political
crises produced instructions from boroughs and counties all over the
kingdom: in favor of the Hanoverian succession in 1701, against the
excise tax in 1733, against an agreement with Spain in 1739, against
the naturalization of Jews in 1754, in favor of John Wilkes in 1769.[8]

In the colonies too the instruction of members was common both
at and between elections. The town of Boston issued instructions to
its representatives in the Massachusetts assembly on at least eighteen
occasions before 1689. From the beginning instructions by New
England towns often touched on matters of colony-wide concern, such
as legal procedures and the electoral franchise. In the eighteenth century the attempt of the Massachusetts royal governor to get the assembly to vote him a permanent salary brought out a host of instructions
from towns telling their deputies to do no such thing; and in 1754 an
excise tax prompted another colony-wide set of instructions. Outside
New England, where representation was usually by county and it was
difficult to assemble the voters, instructions were less common, but
in 1652 Northampton County, Virginia, instructed its representatives
in the House of Burgesses to secure the county an abatement of taxes.
And in Westchester County, New York, Lewis Morris took the lead

[7]Edward and Annie G. Porritt, *The Unreformed House of Commons: Parliamentary Representation before 1832* (Cambridge, England, 1903), I, 263–71; Hirst, *Representative of
the People*, 161–66, 181–86.

[8]Cecil S. Emden, *The People and the Constitution* (Oxford, 1956), 12–22; Lucy S. Suth-
erland, "Edmund Burke and the Relations Between Members of Parliament and
their Constituents," *Studies in Burke and His Time* 10 (1968), 1005–21. James Burgh,
Political Disquisitions (London, 1775), I, 186–205, cites numerous examples of
instructions in arguing the novelty of the rising view that representatives, once elected,
were not the agents of, or responsible to, their constituents.

in a move to draw up instructions for the county's representative in the New York assembly.[9]

With the onset of the quarrel with England and the growing assertiveness of the colonial assemblies, both counties and towns all over the colonies began instructing their representatives in formulations of colonial rights. Boston led the way in May 1764 when Samuel Adams opened his public career as a revolutionary by drafting instructions for the Boston representatives, denouncing the levying of taxes on the colonies by Parliament.[10] John Adams also entered the arena by drafting instructions for Braintree's representatives. At least forty-nine Massachusetts towns instructed their representatives to oppose the execution of the Stamp Act, to let the world know, as John Adams put it, that "we never can be slaves."[11] Thereafter, throughout the revolutionary period, Americans instructed representatives whenever major issues came before the state legislatures.[12]

State constitutions encouraged the practice. The Massachusetts constitution of 1780, for example, stated specifically that "All power residing originally in the people, and being derived from them, the several magistrates and officers of government, vested with authority, whether legislative, executive, or judicial, are their substitutes and agents and are at all times accountable to them." What was meant by accountable was further specified in an article providing that "The people have a right, in an orderly and peaceable manner, to assemble to consult upon the common good" and to "give instructions to their representatives."[13] Similar provisions were included in the constitutions of New Hampshire, Vermont, Pennsylvania, and North Carolina.[14]

The instructions given to both English and American representatives frequently contained little homilies on popular sovereignty. Sometimes they were couched in respectful terms, simply explaining

[9]Kenneth Colegrove, "New England Town Mandates," Colonial Society of Massachusetts, *Publications* 21 (1919), 411–49.

[10]*A Report of the Record Commissioners of the City of Boston, containing the Boston Town Records, 1768 to 1769* (Boston, 1886), 119–22; William V. Wells, *The Life and Public Services of Samuel Adams* (Boston, 1865), I, 46–48.

[11]John Adams, *Papers*, I, 129–44.

[12]Colegrove, "New England Town Mandates," 436–39.

[13]Thorpe, *Federal and State Constitutions*, III, 1890, 1892.

[14]Ibid., III, 1686–87; IV, 2453–54, 2457–74; V, 2787–88, 3082–84; VI, 3762–64; VII, 3812–14.

the rights of constituents to instruct representatives. Often they were hortatory in tone, imploring the representative to save the country by securing the passage of measures he was instructed to favor. And sometimes they were issued as commands. The city of Bristol, England, in 1701 prefaced its message with the assertion that "it is no doubt to us that we have a right to direct our Representatives," and the instructions that followed ("we do direct and require you") were printed along with several from other constituencies to their members (calling for support of the Protestant succession to the throne) in a pamphlet reminding every member that "the power with which he is intrusted, must be larger and fuller in the People who chuse and give him that Trust, than it can be in Him, their Delegate and Substitute."[15]

The implication was that the representative, being a mere agent or deputy, was obliged to act as his constituents directed, regardless of his own views. Members of Parliament receiving instructions frequently replied with due humility: "We thankfully acknowledge your Commands, and with Joy receive your Renewal of a Fundamental Right."[16] "I shall never," said a representative from Coventry, "think myself at Liberty to act contrary to your Representations."[17] Thomas Gage, a member of the House of Commons from Tewkesbury, in voting to bar placeholders under the crown from sitting in Parliament in 1740, averred that he did so because "I am required so by my constituents, who, I think have a right to direct those that represent them."[18] The Levellers of the seventeenth century could have asked for no more, and indeed the passage from Richard Overton previously quoted had just been reprinted approvingly in *The Gentlemen's Magazine* at the time when Gage spoke.[19]

The idea that popular sovereignty required representatives to follow the instructions of constituents reached its high point in England at the election of 1774, when radical Whigs in London and Westminster sought to exact pledges from candidates to obey any instructions

[15]*The Electors Right Asserted with the Advices and Charges of Several Counties, Cities and Burroughs in England to their Respective Members of Parliament* (London, 1601), 2, 13.

[16]*Great Britain's Memorial. Collections of the Instructions, Representations etc. of the Freeholders and other Electors of Great Britain to their Representatives in Parliament, for these Two Years past* (London, 1741–42), II, 60.

[17]Ibid., II, 92.

[18]*Parliamentary History*, XI, 380.

[19]*The Gentleman's Magazine* 9 (1739), 536–37

given them. Only a handful of candidates agreed, and outside London
the movement to make instructions binding failed completely.[20] Despite
statements like Gage's, which can be found at all periods, representatives in England and America have never been legally or constitutionally bound to follow the instructions, advice, or expressed wishes of
their constituents. From the time when the king first summoned representatives to Parliament and required them to come with full powers
of attorney, these attorneys of the people have been free to act without
attention to any directives their principals might give or send them. If
the people had a right to instruct their representatives, whether in
England or England's colonies or the independent United States, the
representative had an equal right to disregard their instructions.

It does not quite follow that instructions were mere ritual or rhetoric. Like elections they were an expression of the local, subject character of representation, emphasizing the identification of the
representative with the people of a particular locality. But representatives, especially after they assumed the dominant position in government, had to balance their local with their national character, their
position as subjects of government with their position *in* government.
Whenever a representative professed himself, like Gage, to be bound
by instructions, he was likely to be answered by other representatives
with a reminder of his obligation to make decisions for, and exercise
authority over, the whole people. In 1681, when several members of
the House of Commons argued for exclusion of the Duke of York on
the grounds of instructions by their constituents, Sir Thomas Little-
ton warned them that instructions were "uncertain things" and "of
dangerous consequence," and Sir Francis Winnington, while affirming the desirability of consulting constituents "upon any weighty affair,"
felt obliged to add, "I am not subjected to what my country [i.e.,
county] does propose. I have my Trust to serve them here as well as
I can."[21]

In 1734 John Willes, the attorney general, was more direct: "After
we are chosen, and have our seats in this House," he said, "we have
no longer any dependence on our electors so far as regards our behav-
iour here. Their whole power is then devolved upon us, to regard only
the public good in general. . . ." Although Sir John Barnard, a for-

[20]Ian Christie, "The Wilkites and the General Election of 1774," in Christie, *Myth and Reality* (London, 1970), 244–60.

[21]Grey, *Debates*, VIII, 309–22.

midable member of the Country party, rebuked this declaration as "something very new," Sir William Yonge found it "so far from being a doctrine very extraordinary, or altogether new, that I wish every gentleman in this House would make it a standing rule for his conduct."[22] And as the eighteenth century wore on, and gentlemen became more and more outspoken in support of popular sovereignty, more and more of them expressed their adherence to this interpretation of it. The 1774 campaign to make instructions binding on members of Parliament through pledges by candidates to observe them was notable principally for prompting Burke's classic refusal. In the past Bristol, as we have seen, had sometimes given peremptory orders to its representatives, and Burke's running mate in the election of 1774 offered to abide by whatever instructions the town might give him. Burke, in stating why he could not make such a pledge, explained that election for Bristol made him a governor of England. Parliament, he said,

> is not a *congress* of ambassadors from different and hostile interests, which interests each must maintain, as an agent and advocate; but parliament is a *deliberative* assembly of *one* nation, with *one* interest, that of the whole. . . . You choose a member, indeed; but when you have chosen him, he is not a member of Bristol, but he is a member of *Parliament*.[23]

Even in the American colonies, where the local, subject character of representation generally outweighed its other character, representatives often declined to serve constituents as simply "their dapple-gray" to haul messages to the assembly.[24] In 1754 the Massachusetts assembly, in which the members from the farming towns of the interior constituted a majority, laid an excise tax on rum consumed in households. It was a soak-the-rich or soak-the-East tax, for rum was drunk mainly in eastern towns, and the tax affected only large-scale consumption (in lots of thirty gallons) in private households. The farmers of the interior drank cider of their own making and would be virtually untouched by the tax. The governor of the colony, who thought the East was already bearing too heavy a share of the tax

[22] *Parliamentary History*, IX, 435, 443–46, 450. Eleven years later, in reiterating the point, Yonge suggested that a representative was the attorney, not of his constituents but of the whole people, "in the same manner as an elective king or chief magistrate is the servant of the people." Ibid., XIII, 1078.

[23] *Works*, (Boston, 1866), II, 96.

[24] The phrase is from a "Dialogue between Sylvester and Philarchias" in the *Connecticut Courant*, Oct. 2, 1770.

burden, refused to sign the measure until the representatives had consulted their constituents.[25]

The bill was printed and distributed to the towns, and pamphlets poured from the Boston presses denouncing the tax as an unconstitutional violation of the rights of Englishmen, an invasion of the privacy of the home, a threat to the virtue of every woman, who would henceforth be at the mercy of the excise collector. Town meetings assembled, especially in the East, and gave instructions to their representatives against this monster of monsters, as one pamphlet called it. When the Massachusetts assembly reconvened, the members had before them a large body of instructions, which had been specifically requested for the guidance of the legislators. The great majority of the instructions apparently were against the tax, though it seems likely that few western towns had bothered to meet on the matter (there are records of twenty-four instructions against the excise and six in favor).[26] On the second day of its new session the assembly entertained a motion to consider the instructions. After "a large debate thereon" the substance of which was not recorded, the question was put and the motion failed. In other words, the assemblymen refused to consider the instructions given them. The next day they ordered one of the pamphlets against the tax (namely *The Monster of Monsters*) to be burned by the common hangman and the publisher of it to be jailed. Two weeks later they repassed the tax, and the governor reluctantly signed it.[27]

The decision to ignore instructions was not produced by pliant tools of a corrupt court. While the majority of members in the Massachusetts assembly were generally content to follow the lead of the eastern members, usually merchants and lawyers, with whom they filled the key committees, the merchants and lawyers along with the governor opposed the excise tax. Its passage seems to have been the result of a rank-and-file action by members who did not ordinarily take much of a hand in assembly proceedings. These members evidently believed that they spoke the voice of the people more clearly than instructions from the constituencies could. One of the more articulate of them explained what they were doing: "the business of a

---

[25] A good account of the whole episode is in Robert Zemsky, *Merchants, Farmers, and River Gods*, 276–81.

[26] Colegrove, "New England Town Mandates," 535; Zemsky, *Merchants, Farmers, and River Gods*, 277n–278n.

[27] *Journals of the House of Representatives of Massachusetts* 31, 1754–55 (Boston, 1956), 60, 63, 101.

representative," he said, "is to consult the good of the whole body, and to take particular care that the town he represents, does not pay a greater proportion of the charges of government than it ought to do . . . I take [this] to be the proper business of a representative, and not to follow the humor of his constituents, when it is evidently contrary to the good of the community."[28]

Not so very different, that, from what Edmund Burke told the electors of Bristol twenty years later. "Certainly, Gentlemen," said Burke, "it ought to be the happiness and glory of a representative to live in the strictest union, the closest correspondence, and the most unreserved communication with his constituents. Their wishes ought to have great weight with him; their opinions high respect; their business unremitted attention. . . . But his unbiased opinion, his mature judgment, his enlightened conscience, he ought not to sacrifice to you, to any man, or to any set of men living. . . . Your representative owes you, not his industry only, but his judgment; and betrays, instead of serving you, if he sacrifices it to your opinion."[29]

Burke's views were eminently rational and mediating, recognizing some sort of obligation on the part of a representative to heed the wishes of his constituents but refusing to surrender his judgment to them. David Hume had offered equally rational observations in a controversy over instructions in 1739–41, the controversy which generated Gage's announcement that he felt bound by them. The controversy, Hume insisted,

is a very frivolous one, and can never be brought to any Decision, as it is managed by both parties. The country-party pretend not, that a member is absolutely bound to follow instructions, as an ambassador or general is confined by his orders, and that his vote is not to be received in the house, but so far as it is conformable to them. The court-party again, pretend not, that the sentiments of the people ought to have no weight with each member; much less that he ought to despise the sentiments of those whom he represents, and with whom he is more particularly concerned.[30]

Hume at this time was pondering the mystery with which this book began, the ease with which the few were able to govern the many, which he traced to the force of opinion. Opinion now placed sovereignty in the people and accordingly assigned to the House of

[28]Quoted in Zemsky, *Merchants, Farmers, and River Gods*, 280.
[29]*Works*, II, 95.
[30]*Essays and Treatises on Several Subjects* (London, 1758), 22.

Commons a power "so great, that it absolutely commands all the other parts of the government." Given the prevalence of such an opinion, the only thing that prevented England from becoming a republic was, by Hume's reasoning, the independence of representatives in the House of Commons from the binding power of instructions by their constituents. The crown was able by influencing elections ("we may . . . give to this influence what name we please; we may call it by the invidious appellations of *corruption* and *dependence*") to maintain a considerable power within the House of Commons. But "were the members of the house obliged to receive instructions from their constituents like the Dutch deputies, this would entirely alter the case." The crown could afford the expense of exerting its influence in elections every seven years. But if influence (buying votes) had to be employed "in bringing over the people to every vote, it would soon be wasted" and England reduced to a republic, an outcome that Hume contemplated with horror.[31]

Hume's reasoning, if more devious than Burke's, was also more pragmatic. But neither Hume nor Burke, though they both recognized the dual character of representation, suggested the function that *non*-binding instructions could play in forming the public opinion to which Hume ascribed the crucial role in reconciling the many to the government of the few. The House of Commons in Hume's day was certainly as powerful as he alleges, and its power rested on the sovereignty of the people. If the influence of the monarch was preserved by the members' freedom from binding instructions, the members themselves discovered in instructions a means of affecting public opinion and bringing it to bear on legislative decisions.

Ostensibly instructions came from the bottom up (from the people to their representatives) and gained whatever force they had from that supposition. They could come, of course, from only a part of the people, the part that chose the particular representative to whom they were addressed; and one reason for not making them binding was that a part should not dictate to the whole. But instructions, especially those offered between elections, might bear only a tenuous relationship to the views even of that part of the people they purported to come from. There was no formal way for voters to register assent to or dissent from a particular set of instructions. Where the number of voters was small, it might be possible to assemble them to draft

[31]Ibid., 22, 31–32.

instructions and to vote on them, as was the case in instructions from New England towns. But the quorum required for adopting instructions at a town meeting could not have been large. Where representation was by county, it would have been impossible to gather many of the voters except at election time (and instructions from a county were normally offered simply by the county's grand jury). But there was nothing official about any set of instructions and nothing to prevent any group of people from volunteering them in the name of the constituency. Since they were not binding anyhow, there was no attempt in either England or America to establish their authority by due process of law.

Because any collection of people in a constituency could hold a meeting and send instructions to the representative, the possibility of organizing such meetings as a means of influencing, rather than simply expressing, public opinion presented itself at an early date. With the development of popular sovereignty in the 1640s, various members of Parliament opened communications with constituents to gain popular support for Parliamentary measures directed against the king.[32] It is not clear whether these resulted in instructions coming back to them according to their own prescription, but on several later occasions when Parliament was flooded with instructions, the similarity of wording suggests not only that they were inspired from above but that they originated in a single source. Such, for example, was the case in the instructions on excluding the Duke of York in 1681, probably inspired by the Earl of Shaftesbury and his supporters in Parliament.[33]

As it happens, one case of inspired instructions that can be voluminously documented was the one that prompted the observations by Hume noted above. In the year 1739 Sir Robert Walpole, by a narrow margin, won acceptance in Parliament of an agreement with Spain that seemed to sacrifice English pride and English commercial interests. Opposition newspapers and pamphlets denouncing the agreement charged that it had been ratified by the venal votes of representatives who held places of profit under the crown and thus under the influence of the ministry. Soon meetings purporting to speak

[32]Hirst, *Representative of the People*, 182–83; Valerie Pearl, *London and the Outbreak of the Puritan Revolution* (Oxford, 1961), 210–36.

[33]M. Dorothy George, "Elections and Electioneering, 1679–81," *English Historical Review* 45 (1930), 552–78; Grey, *Debates* 8, 309–32.

from various constituencies were sending instructions to their representatives to secure various reforms that the "Country party" had long contended for and especially legislation limiting the number of seats in Parliament that could be occupied by placeholders. By 1742 after a general election Walpole lost his majority in Parliament. He was obliged to resign, and a bill against placeholders finally got through Parliament.

It would be difficult to assess precisely what role instructions played in the unseating of Walpole or the passage of the bill, but it is not impossible to assess the validity of the ministry's charge that the instructions had been originated, not by the constituencies but by the members who were instructed. The whole thing, the ministry charged, was "a mere juggle . . . the Member first transmits his Notions to his Creatures, and then they, under the name of his Constituents, instruct him, as he first instructed them."[34] When the opposition replied that instructions, however originated, were still the voice of the people, the ministry answered, "that tho' the Voice be Isaac's the Hands are Esau's. It is the People that speak but the Malecontents dictate. A gross piece of State Mummery, wherein A instructs B how B shall instruct A."[35]

That this charge was pretty close to the facts can be demonstrated from surviving correspondence. The mummery was orchestrated by four noble lords: Bolingbroke, Chesterfield, Stair, and Marchmont, leaders of the Country party. None was a member of the House of Commons, and only Chesterfield was a member of the House of Lords, Stair and Marchmont being Scottish and Bolingbroke having been barred long before for his support of the Pretender. But they were able to operate through Country party representatives in Parliament and through gentlemen of influence in the constituencies. Stair and Chesterfield exchanged drafts of what the instructions should say, along lines suggested to them by Bolingbroke in a letter from France. Chesterfield hoped to get simultaneous instructions from "almost every county and borough in England," and to that end he distributed his plan to all the county members and to other influential persons all over the country. His draft was formulated in general terms that could be "differently worded according to the disposition of the respective

---

[34]*A Letter to a Member of Parliament Concerning the Present State of Affairs* (London, 1740), 6.
[35]*Daily Gazetteer*, Feb. 6, 1740.

counties or boroughs that send them."[36] In the end Chesterfield got nowhere near a majority of English constituencies to comply, but the Scots were more successful, and altogether there were enough to keep the newspapers printing a succession of instructions, variously worded but sufficiently alike to betray their common origin. Later, they were gathered together and published in two slim volumes grandly titled *Great Britain's Memorial*.[37]

Those from London, delivered early in the game before the plan was matured, were the most demanding and went beyond what had been intended. They required the London members to make the passage of a place bill the condition of passing any money bill. The procedure envisaged was to tack a place bill as a rider on the first money bill that came along. The Earl of Stair was enthusiastic about this tactic and proposed that they make it a part of all the instructions, but Chesterfield, after consulting other opposition leaders, dissuaded him: "I find that will not do," he said, "because, to tell you the plain truth, many of the Opposition do not in their hearts greatly relish the place-bill itself, which they think might prove a clog upon their own Administration."[38] In other words, the opposition smelled power coming their way. Once they succeeded in unseating Walpole they hoped to hold on to parliamentary majorities in the same way that Walpole had, through doling out places to their supporters. They wanted instructions from the people that would be strong enough to embarrass the ministry but not strong enough to embarrass themselves once they took over. Subsequent instructions were softened accordingly. And in fact, though a place bill finally became law, it did not have enough teeth to embarrass anyone.

It is apparent, then, that while the opposition campaign of 1739–41 produced some strong pronouncements of the people's right to dictate to their representatives, the dictates that the people ostensibly gave were drafted by a few members of the nobility and were adapted to the needs of a parliamentary faction in search of power. We may dismiss the whole business, in the ministry's terms, as a bit of mummery. But we have to ask why it was undertaken. Why did represen-

[36]Chesterfield to Stair, March 30, 1740, J. M. Graham, ed., *Annals and Correspondence of the Viscount and the First and Second Earl of Stair* (Edinburgh and London, 1875), II, 260.

[37]See above, note 16.

[38]*Great Britain's Memorial*, I, 53; Chesterfield to Stair, Dec. 3, 1739, John Bradshaw, ed., *Letters of Philip Dormer Stanhope, Earl of Chesterfield* (London, 1913), II, 752.

tatives think it worthwhile to make it seem that their constituents had spontaneously instructed them to do what they apparently wanted to do anyhow? The very fact that they did think it worthwhile testifies to the importance they attached to public opinion. As divine right gave way to popular sovereignty, the fact that popular opinion favored or seemed to favor a particular measure became an argument for its passage. In parliamentary debate, no matter how independent the members might affirm themselves to be, instructions obviously carried weight.

At the same time, instructions organized from above became themselves a mode of shaping public opinion in favor of measures that a faction or party within the government favored. We have noted the hortatory tone in which they were cast. When representatives formulated instructions to themselves, they hoped to persuade not only the constituents whom they asked to adopt them and not only the other legislators to whom they quoted them, but a wider public as well. Publication of instructions in the newspapers may have been more significant than the flourishing of them before a House of Commons that knew only too well how they had come into existence. And the collection and publication in book form of a whole set of instructions, all calling for the same measures, indicates that the intended audience was not merely the House of Commons.

Instructions thus embody the same ambiguities as the election of representatives and of representation itself. They looked like dictates from the sovereign people to their designated governors, and in some measure they were. But they could be as much a way for governors to shape the will of the people as for the people to shape the policies of government.

The same was true of another institution borrowed from the days when authority rested in the hands of God's lieutenant: the right of subjects to petition their government. The very word "petition" carries the implication of subjection. A petition is a request, a prayer, a supplication from an inferior to a superior. But by the end of the seventeenth century the shift from divine right to popular sovereignty had endowed the word with new connotations, implications, and ambiguities.

When the king first summoned representatives to his Parliament, they frequently carried with them petitions from individuals or groups in their locality for presentation to him. And while sitting they sometimes formulated petitions of their own, requesting relief from grievances affecting the whole realm. Already when petitions began to be recorded in the fourteenth century, they were distinguished as "singuleres" or "communes," which we may translate by the later designations of private and public.[39] Petitions were public or private "bills," for the word "bill" in the legal language of the day (Law French) was synonymous with petition. A bill or petition was a "supplicatory address," which might be discussed and approved by Parliament before it was presented to the king for approval or rejection.[40] If the king signed it, it became an act of Parliament.

By the seventeenth century, when representatives had become a regular part of government, they continued to carry private petitions from their constituents and to approve them as private bills before presenting them to the king. Most public bills now originated within the government in Parliament itself or in the king's Privy Council. Occasionally, however, the members of the House of Commons in their character as subjects still addressed the king themselves in petitions for favors or for redress of grievances in the name of the whole kingdom. Such petitions were by this time somehow distinguished from bills, which had lost their supplicatory character. But the Commons began in the first decades of the seventeenth century to remove the supplicatory character from some petitions: they distinguished between petitions of grace, sought as favors, and petitions of right, which, without enacting laws, declared what the law was. A petition of right was not quite a request and definitely not a supplication. Rather than asking a favor of the king, it told him what he must and must not do to his subjects. When subjects (as the House of Commons claimed to be) could petition God's lieutenant in these tones, the word "petition" had assumed the ambiguities that were to follow it into the era of popular sovereignty.[41]

In the 1640s, as soon as Parliament began to affirm its superiority (as representatives of the people) to the king, its petitions gave way to remonstrances; and Parliament itself became the recipient of public petitions, formulated by every partisan group in England, telling Parliament what it must and must not do. The practice of addressing

[39]Doris Rayner, "The Forms and Machinery of the 'Commune Petition' in the Fourteenth Century," *English Historical Review* 56 (1941), 198–233, 549–70.

[40]"Bill," J. A. H. Murray, *A New English Dictionary* (Oxford, 1888–1928), II, 860–61.

[41]Elizabeth R. Foster, "Petitions and the Petition of Right," *Journal of British Studies* 14 (1974), 21–45; Edward Coke, *The Fourth Part of the Institutes* (London, 1797), 11.

petitions to Parliament had begun as early as the fourteenth century, but these were truly supplications intended as much for the king as for Parliament. Now Parliament was itself addressed in the new assertive tones it had assumed in addressing the king. Petitions to Parliament were presented, like instructions, as the voice of the sovereign people, oddly supplicatory but at the same time demanding.[42]

The representatives of the people, as we have seen, were not always happy to receive these messages, which were sometimes brought to Westminster by crowds that appeared menacing and were perhaps intended to. The larger the number of signatures on a petition and the larger the number of presenters, the larger the claims that could be made for it as the voice of the people—and the more embarrassing it became for the people's representatives to reject it.

When Charles II returned to the throne, a new Parliament took the opportunity to enact a statute forbidding any petition by more than twenty persons "for Alteration of Matters established by Law in Church or State," unless it was approved by at least three justices of the peace or by a grand jury.[43] Later Charles made his own views clear when a host of petitions asked him to summon the Parliament he had prorogued in the Exclusion Crisis of 1679. In a proclamation he declared such petitions to be seditious, a charge deeply resented by those who had formulated and signed them.[44] When Charles finally allowed Parliament to meet, the Whig majority passed a resolution affirming the right to petition, a right reaffirmed in the Declaration of Rights of 1689.[45]

The right to petition seems a strange sort of right under a government based on popular sovereignty. Why does anyone need a right to pray, beg, or supplicate, especially if the power thus implored is supposed to be inferior to the supplicants? Yet Parliament continued to be uneasy about petitions. While affirming the right to petition, it refrained from repealing the statute of 1661 restraining petitions, and it occasionally punished petitioners, even those who abided by the limitations imposed in the statute. In 1701, when a seemingly humble

[42]Rayner, "Forms and Machinery," 213ff; Pearl, *London and the Puritan Revolution*, 210–36.

[43]13 Charles II, c.5. (1661). *The Statutes at Large From the First Year of King James the First to the Tenth Year of King William the Third* (London, 1763), III, 208–9.

[44]Robert Steele, ed., *A Bibliography of Royal Proclamations of the Tudor and Stuart Sovereigns* (Oxford, 1910), no. 3703.

[45]Grey, *Debates*, VII, 370–72, Oct. 27, 1680.

petition from the county of Kent requested Parliament to supply the king with funds he had asked for, the House of Commons imprisoned the members who presented it and declared it "scandalous, tending to destroy the constitution of parliaments, and to subvert the established government of these realms." This overreaction brought a storm of protest, but an underlying hostility to petitions on public policy continued to characterize parliamentary reaction to them.[46]

The reason is not far to seek. Petitioners were in a sense rivals of representatives, claiming to speak the voice of the people but unrestricted by the qualifications placed on voting and uninhibited by the responsibilities of being part of the government. Petitions were a little too literally the voice of the people. The members of the House of Commons displayed their uneasiness with them not only in such fits of hostility as their imprisonment of the Kentish petitioners but in the rule they apparently adopted around 1693 of refusing to hear any petitions having to do with current taxation.[47]

The original function of representatives had been closely tied to taxation. Representatives were there to consent for the people to whatever taxes they thought their constituents could bear. They carried full power, *plena potestas*,[48] and they did not want advice from petitioners. When petitions against taxation appeared and any member spoke in favor of hearing them, he would be told that "every man, and every body of men, had their representative in that House, who certainly would represent their case to the House, if any particular hardship was to be put upon them by any bill then before the House."[49] When the colony of Rhode Island petitioned against the duty Parliament laid on molasses in 1733 one member suggested that the petition should be heard, because Rhode Island was not represented. But other members quickly extended the fiction overseas: "as our colonies are all a part of the people of Great Britain, they are generally represented

[46]Emden, *People and Constitution*, 74–81; Peter Fraser, "Public Petitioning and Parliament before 1832," *History* 46 (1961), 195–211. On the Kentish petition see especially Lord John Somers, *Jura Populi Anglicani: or the Subjects' Right of Petitioning* (London, 1701); and Daniel Defoe, *Legion's Humble Address to the Lords* [London, 1702].

[47]I have not been able to find a record of the adoption of this rule at the time, but it was referred to in parliamentary debate in 1842 as adopted in 1693. *Hansard's Parliamentary Debates: Third Series, Commencing with the Accession of William IV* 62 (1842), 9.

[48]See Chapter 2, note 1.

[49]*Parliamentary History* 9, 5–6.

in this House as well as the rest of the people are." Therefore there was no need to hear petitions from them.[50]

Precisely because petitions could be embarrassing to a government that rested on popular sovereignty, they became a favorite weapon in contests among the few for control of the government. Some petitions, like some instructions, originated in the grass roots as spontaneous expressions of popular demands. But others, like many instructions, came from the top down, from parties within the government contending against each other and seeking public support in the contest. As soon as Parliament challenged the king in the name of the people in the 1640s, factions within Parliament challenged each other with petitions purporting to show that the people wanted what a faction said they wanted. Members of Parliament drew up petitions and passed them about for signatures, circulating them from house to house, posting them in taverns and shops, and holding public meetings for the express purpose of getting signatures.[51] The practice was so notorious that Samuel Butler satirized it in *Hudibras:*

> The Parliament drew up petitions
> to itself, and sent them, like commissions,
> to well-affected persons, down
> in every city and great town,
> with pow'r to levy horse and men,
> only to bring them back again.[52]

When the Exclusion Crisis divided the House of Commons into Whigs and Tories, the Whigs, led by Shaftesbury, organized the deluge of petitions that asked the king to summon his prorogued Parliament. Tories were quick to compare this tactic to the petitions of the 1640s, charging that the Whig petitions were "drawn by their Clubs and Cabals in London, or some say onely transcribed from an old 41 Copy and then sent down by trusty men who had five Shillings *per Centum*, for procuring hands."[53] But the Tories were not above making their own appeal to the public by organizing popular "addresses" to the king, which "abhorred" the petitions and declared support for

[50]Ibid., Vol. 8, 1264.

[51]Pearl, *London and the Puritan Revolution*, 210–36; David Underdown, *Pride's Purge* (London, 1971), 93–95, 117, 178.

[52]Quoted in William M. Lamont, *Godly Rule: Politics and Religion, 1603–60* (London, 1969), 95.

[53]E. Bohun, *The Third and Last Part of the Address to the Free-men and Free-holders of the Nation* (London, 1683), 7–9.

established authority in what it was doing.[54] Thereafter, throughout the eighteenth century, any concerted petitioning campaign by the opposition party in Parliament was likely to be met by loyal addresses opposing the measure, a process that was later imitated in the United States.

Petitions remained a tempting way not only to claim public support but to gain it. When the House of Commons refused to accept John Wilkes as a member in 1769, he and his followers made good use of petitions in expanding his popular following. In rejecting Wilkes the Commons had all but repudiated their capacity as subjects and assumed an arbitrary governmental authority. Well-publicized petitions from Middlesex made the most of this, and ten years later Christopher Wyvill used a petition from Yorkshire to launch the most extensive campaign for reform of parliamentary representation before 1832.[55]

Members of Parliament, when they were not organizing petitions themselves, continued to be irritated by them. They knew how easy it was to gather the signatures. As Horace Walpole complained at the time of the Wilkes affair, "It is impossible but some mob may be assembled everywhere to sign a petition, and then such petition is called the sense of the county."[56] The irascible Samuel Johnson supplied more detail:

The progress of a petition is well known. An ejected placeman goes down to his county or his borough, tells his friends of his inability to serve them, and his constituents of the corruption of the government. His friends readily understand that he who can get nothing, will have nothing to give. They agree to proclaim a meeting; meat and drink are plentifully provided; a crowd is easily brought together, and those who think that they know the reason of their meeting undertake to tell those who know it not. Ale and clamour unite their powers; the crowd, condensed and heated, begins to ferment with the leaven of sedition. All see a thousand evils, though they know not what. A speech is then made by the Cicero of the day; he says much, and suppresses more, and credit is equally given to what he tells and what he conceals. The petition is read and universally approved. Those who are sober enough to write, add their names, and the rest would sign it if they could. The petition

[54]*Vox Angliae . . . Being a Compleat Collection of all those numerous Addresses. . . .* (London, 1682).

[55]See below, note 63.

[56]W. S. Lewis et al., eds., *Horace Walpole's Correspondence* (New Haven, Conn., 1937–83), XXIII, 151.

is then handed from town to town, and from house to house, and wherever it comes the inhabitants flock together that they may see that which must be sent to the King. Names are easily collected. One man signs because he hates the papists; another because he has vowed destruction to the turnpikes; one because it will vex the parson; another because he owes his landlord nothing; one because he is rich; another because he is poor; one to show that he is not afraid; and another to show that he can write."[57]

Representatives in American assemblies seem to have been less jealous than their British counterparts of the exclusive right to speak for the people and less prone to use petitions either to educate the public or to gain leverage with their colleagues. They were also more willing to act on petitioners' requests in enacting legislation. A study of petitioning in eighteenth-century Pennsylvania finds that fifty-two percent of the acts passed between 1717 and 1775 originated in petitions, and these included a substantial number of petitions of province-wide interest.[58] A similar study of eighteenth-century Virginia reveals that the great majority of acts there similarly originated in petitions.[59] Though fewer of these seem to have concerned matters affecting the whole society, the most famous Virginia statute of all time would probably not have been passed if it had not been supported by a large number of petitions. The Virginia Statute of Religious Liberty was first drafted by Thomas Jefferson in 1779, but it was not enacted (with minor amendments) into law until 1786, after nearly eleven thousand persons had signed petitions against another bill calling for a general state tax to support religion. The petitions against the tax were not all identical, but at least thirteen of them, bearing 1,552 signatures, came to the legislature at the solicitation (and in the words) of one of its members, James Madison. Madison shepherded the Statute of Religious Liberty through the legislature after the tax bill failed.[60]

Madison was one of the most astute politicians (as well as the most astute political thinker) of the early republic; and ten years later, organizing the Republican opposition against Jay's Treaty, he again found

[57]Quoted in Henry Jepson, *The Platform* (New York and London, 1892), I, 12.

[58]Alan Tully, "Constituent-Representative Relationships in Early America," *Canadian Journal of History* 11 (1976), 139–54.

[59]Raymond C. Bailey, *Popular Influence Upon Public Policy: Petitioning in Eighteenth-century Virginia* (Westport, Conn., 1979), Chapter 3.

[60]James Madison, *Papers*, Robert A. Rutland et al., eds., (Chicago and Charlottesville, 1962–), VIII, 295–98 (editorial note).

petitions a useful weapon. His party manager, John Beckley, dispersed a petition through all the states for signatures against the treaty, "without, as yet," he confided to Madison," the smallest suspicion from our opponents."[61] Public meetings all over the country were soon sending petitions and memorials to Congress and the president denouncing the treaty. The Federalists, following the British model, responded with meetings that adopted loyal addresses supporting the treaty.

That Beckley thought it advantageous to keep his petitioning campaign a secret is not surprising. A petition that seemed to be spontaneous would carry more weight as an expression of public opinion than one which was known to have been generated in the body to which it was addressed. But probably few were deceived. By 1795 petitions had become in America as in England one of the rituals of popular government, messages in which it was often difficult to distinguish the giver from the receiver, the supplicant from the sovereign.

If petitions and instructions were often acts of ventriloquism, they nevertheless nourished the fiction of the people's capacity to speak for themselves. In doing so they renewed the invitation that popular sovereignty unavoidably extended to flesh-and-blood people outside Parliament who thought themselves qualified to do the speaking. While petitions and instructions were addressed to an acknowledged governing body, popular sovereignty taught that such bodies were inferior in power to the people themselves, that the people possessed "real majesty," as opposed to the government's lesser power of "personal majesty," that governments might make laws, but only the people could make "fundamental constitutions" to govern government. Those who presumed to speak for the people outside Parliament might thus be tempted to go beyond petitions and instructions. If they could direct their representatives in particular measures, why not go on in the language of real majesty to reform and reconstruct the government itself?

In retrospect it could be said that the Convention of 1689 in England had done just that, though the Convention itself had pointedly declined to make such a claim. By the 1760s it appeared to many Englishmen that the Convention's work needed redoing anyhow. In the retrospective view the Convention had restored the original constitution established by the people during a time to which the memory of man ran

[61]Noble E. Cunningham, Jr., *The Jeffersonians: The Formation of Party Organization, 1789–1801* (Chapel Hill, N.C., 1957), 102–3.

not. Since its restoration in 1689 corruption had again subverted the Constitution and altered the government without popular sanction. The eighteenth-century commonwealthmen who carried forward the ideas of Harrington and Sidney continually expounded the power of the people to reform or replace this degenerate government, but they organized no effective body of people in or out of Parliament to do the job. Indeed it was not until Americans led the way that English reformers began to think of such a thing.

The Americans, of course, were a special case. Located an ocean away from Parliament, they had been allowed, even enjoined, to form representative assemblies of their own. Every colony settled by Englishmen had one, and their relationship to Parliament had never been clearly established. When Parliament undertook in the 1760s and 1770s to bind the colonists with legislation contrary to their wishes, the colonists had ready-made representative bodies to challenge the credentials of an English House of Commons to speak for them. And when England dissolved the colonial assemblies, it was easy enough to resurrect them as popular congresses or conventions. Those congresses could then do what the Levellers had wanted to do and what the Convention of 1689 had not dared do: they exercised the "real majesty" of the people by creating fundamental constitutions for new governments (how they did it will occupy succeeding chapters).

Even before the Americans declared their independence, the boldness of their assemblies in challenging the supremacy of Parliament induced Englishmen to propose extra-parliamentary associations or conventions to dictate reforms in government at home. Parliament's repeated exclusion of John Wilkes, duly elected by the voters of Middlesex in 1769, prompted the formation of what appears to have been one of the earliest of such organizations. The Society for Supporters of the Bill of Rights enrolled English reformers sympathetic both to Wilkes and to the American colonists, but the membership did not extend much beyond greater London. Although Wilkes himself became a popular figure throughout the country and in the colonies as well, the Society achieved no wide popular following. As the American resistance expanded, the inadequacy of parliamentary representation for Englishmen as well as Americans drew larger numbers into the reform movement, and the American provincial and Continental congresses furnished a model for achieving reform.[62]

[62]Christie, *Myth and Reality*, 244–60; John Brewer, *Party Ideology and Popular Politics at the Accession of George III* (Cambridge, England, 1976), 163–200.

Hitherto most reformers had looked to Parliament to reform itself, and they continued to address it in petitions and instructions to that end. But as early as 1771 Obadiah Hulme suggested that extra-parliamentary associations might undertake the task if Parliament refused.[63] James Burgh took up the suggestion in 1775 in the last volume of his *Political Disquisitions*, a lengthy indictment of parliamentry corruption that achieved instant popularity in the colonies. Burgh repeated the familiar doctrine of popular sovereignty, that "the people's mere absolute, sovereign will and pleasure, is a sufficient reason for their making any alteration in their form of government." He called for "a grand national association for restoring the Constitution,"[64] and in the ensuing decades there were several attempts to form such an association. The most influential were the relatively moderate association of counties led by Christopher Wyvill, a clergyman from Yorkshire, in 1779 and the more radical Society for Constitutional Information, formed in 1780 and led by John Jebb, another clergyman and physician, and by John Cartwright, a militia officer.[65]

Although none of these associations achieved its objectives, their appeal to the public over the heads of Parliament, combined with the more successful American resistance, alerted less high-minded Englishmen to the possibilities of popular extra-parliamentary action for less laudable goals. In 1778, when Parliament without a dissenting vote repealed a few of the many disabilities that ancient statutes imposed on Catholics, the result was a rising tide of bigotry, directed and embodied in a Protestant Association, originating in London but gathering strength in Scotland and then spreading south again, with the object of denying all civil and political rights to Catholics. Its evil genius was Lord George Gordon, who sparked the riots that rocked London for a week in June 1780 and ended only after mobs had destroyed chapels, houses, and shops belonging to Roman Catholics, not to mention several of London's prisons.[66]

[63] *An Historical Essay on the English Constitution* (London, 1771), 161. Hulme, however, managed the extraordinary feat of denouncing Parliament as hopelessly corrupt, while affirming its right to tax the colonies.

[64] Burgh, *Political Disquisitions*, 278, 478.

[65] Ian Christie, "The Yorkshire Association 1780–89: A Study in Political Organization," *Myth and Reality*, 261–83; T. M. Parsinnen, "Association, Convention and Anti-parliament in British Radical Politics, 1771–1848," *English Historical Review* 88, (1973), 504–33; Eugene C. Black, *The Association: British Extraparliamentary Political Organization 1769–1793* (Cambridge, Mass., 1963), 1–130.

[66] Black, *The Association*, 131–73.

The Gordon riots discredited popular associations in England, whatever their political complexion, and the mobs of the French Revolution in the 1790s reinforced the sentiment. Although societies for parliamentary reform continued to exist, their objectives could ultimately be achieved only through acts of Parliament itself. Popular sovereignty in England continued to be parliamentary sovereignty. The most popular association of the 1790s was the "Association for the Preservation of Liberty and Property against Republicans and Levellers," formed with government support to support the government. And support of the government meant opposition to any extra-parliamentary attempts to alter it.[67] England's governing few thus directed even the most radical mode of popular action to sustain their own credibility, just as they did with petitions and instructions.

By the end of the eighteenth century popular sovereignty, originally invoked in England to justify resistance to government, had proved equally useful in securing submission to government. But in the process it had been necessary to widen, however cautiously, the political nation. The activities of the militia, of election campaigns, of gathering large numbers to sign petitions, issue instructions, and join associations, for whatever purpose, all tended to draw more and more actual people into the political process. Fiction shaped fact. Fiction nevertheless remained fiction. The ambiguities of popular sovereignty, its paradoxes and contradictions, especially as embodied in the mystery of representation, could be manipulated to shape fact in more ways than one. Americans, like their English ancestors, invoked the doctrine both to justify resistance to government and to support it. The resulting political institutions often resembled each other. But the Americans found a way that the British had rejected to balance the real majesty of the people against the personal majesty of their representatives.

[67] Ibid., 233–74.

PART THREE

The
American
Way

T
HE FICTION THAT frightened English conservatives in the seventeenth century had proved in the eighteenth to be adaptable to the needs of the governing few. Its success rested uneasily on the contradiction always present in representation: the sovereignty of the people could be exercised only through representatives who were at once the agents of particular people in particular communities and the wielders of the supreme power that *the* people mysteriously conveyed to them. The viability of the fiction depended, in part at least, on the people of particular communities feeling themselves to be a part of one people, their particular interests not incompatible with the interests of the whole as directed by the assembled wielders of power. The interests of a part can seldom be identified with those of the whole, but a people must cease to exist if the persons in whose minds it has its being, cease to consider themselves as belonging to it. And where the people dissolves so must the sovereignty exercised in their name.

What people were the people of England's American colonies? Were they a part of the people in whose name the British Parliament governed? Were they several peoples? And what authority did they convey to what government or governments? Could one people govern another? Or could a single people convey power to more than one government? The questions had lain submerged, unaddressed in the contests among the governing few that had generated the definitions of the people and their sovereignty in either England or America—

unaddressed until the contest began between the representatives of the people in the colonies and the representatives of the people in Britain. After that contest began, Americans explored the meaning and methods of popular sovereignty as though for the first time.

CHAPTER *10*

The Incautious Revolution

T HE AMERICANS' QUARREL with England began, as everyone knows, with the attempt of Parliament to levy taxes on the colonists in the Sugar Act of 1764 and the Stamp Act of 1765. Taxation in England had a special link to representation. It could still be distinguished from legislation by its closer association with the local, subject character of representatives in the House of Commons. Taxation was not so much an act in which Parliament shared in the authority of the king as it was a donation given by the agents of subjects to their sovereign. A tax originated from a request by the king to those agents in the Commons; the Commons, and the Commons alone, then gave and granted a portion of their constituents' property to the king in the form of a tax. As William Pitt the elder put it, "Taxation is no part of the governing or legislative power. The taxes are a voluntary gift and grant of the Commons alone."[1] By 1764 this may have appeared to most Englishmen as simply one of those forms from the past which had been emptied of meaning. But it was a respected form and one into which the old meaning could easily be poured back.

That is what the colonists did, with an energy and unanimity that surprised and annoyed the mother country. Taxes, they insisted, were a free gift of the people to their king, and no one could give the gift who did not possess it in the first place. Only persons authorized by those who owned property could give it away; only the representa-

[1] E. S. Morgan, ed., *Prologue to Revolution: Sources and Documents on the Stamp Act Crisis* (Chapel Hill, N.C., 1959), 136.

tives of the people and more particularly of the property owners, could consent to a tax. And the colonists had not authorized any representatives in the House of Commons to consent for them.

The first English response surprisingly acknowledged the validity of the colonial premise and unwisely turned to the irrational structure of the British House of Commons to provide a rational basis for Parliament's taxing the colonies. In a pamphlet that surprised and annoyed the Americans, Thomas Whately, a secretary in the British Treasury office, argued that Parliament could tax the colonists because they *were* represented there; and he invented a term for his argument that has been with us ever since, "virtual Representation": the colonists might not vote for representatives in the Commons but neither did most Englishmen. They were not actually but "virtually" represented. Every member of the House of Commons represented, not the constituents who chose him, but all the king's subjects, not only in Great Britain but in the colonies too.

By transatlantic extension of the notion enunciated earlier by Coke and Sidney, Whately assigned to the members of England's capriciously selected House of Commons powers of attorney to speak and act for all the king's subjects in the colonies. He did not deny the need for such powers of attorney. Indeed he went the colonists one better in their claim that only representatives could consent to taxation. The consent of English subjects, given through their representatives, was necessary, he said, not merely for taxation but for any legislation that affected them. The consent could be given, however, by virtual representatives, whom particular subjects need never have seen or heard of. Colonists in America gave their consent in the same way as the inhabitants of places like Birmingham and Sheffield in England, through members of Parliament whom they had no hand in choosing.[2]

This was stretching the fiction of representation beyond its elastic limit, and it pushed the colonists into a strenuous affirmation of the local, subject character of representation, in which they often repudiated not only Whately's view but Coke's and Sidney's too. It became a cardinal principle of Americans in the revolutionary period that the only legitimate representatives of any people, the only persons who could consent to acts of government for them, were persons whom they had personally chosen for the purpose. The point was made not only by the various colonial assemblies but also by the Stamp Act

[2] Ibid., 21–23.

Congress of 1765 and by the Continental Congress of 1774, "that the only Representatives of the People of these Colonies, are Persons chosen therein by themselves."[3] Newspapers and pamphlets resounded with the absurdity of supposing that Americans were represented by men in England whom they had never seen. A representative was supposed to be the creature of his constituents, and how could any member of Parliament be the representative of American constituents "when not one individual inhabitant ever did the least thing toward procuring such representation?" The answer was clear: "If we are not their constituents, they are not our representatives."[4]

The implication was that a representative ought not only to be directly chosen by his constituents but ought to be one of them, ought to live among them and share their local circumstances. And a representative assembly ought accordingly to be, as John Adams later put it, a portrait in miniature of the people at large: "It should think, feel, reason, and act like them."[5] Americans might acknowledge that those English towns which sent no representatives to Parliament were "virtually" represented by members from similar or neighboring towns or boroughs. Daniel Dulany, in the most popular pamphlet of the Stamp Act period, suggested that in England there might be a sort of double representation whereby the members of Parliament represented the voters and the voters represented the nonvoters. But this would make sense only where geography bound men together. No English constituency could be metaphorically extended to include colonies three thousand miles away.[6] And bolder voices deplored the degeneration that had overtaken representation in England itself. Originally representatives in Parliament were expected to be resident property owners of the counties or boroughs that chose them. There had been, it was said, a "personal knowledge and intercourse" between the member and his constituents: "Both representatives and electors were, like jurors, from the *vicinage*." If this geographical bond had ceased to exist in England, it ought not to have.[7]

[3] Ibid., 63, and 47–62 *passim; Journals of the Continental Congress*, W. C. Ford, ed. (Washington, D.C., 1904–37), I, 63–73.

[4] Ibid., 75–76.

[5] John Adams, *Papers*, Robert J. Taylor et al., eds. (Cambridge, Mass., 1977–), IV, 87.

[6] Morgan, *Prologue to Revolution*, 77–85.

[7] Peter Force, ed., *American Archives*, fourth series (Washington, D.C., 1837–53), 1453. Cf. John Adams, *Papers*, I, 168–69.

It was not that the colonists themselves wished to be represented in Parliament. Indeed they could not be, precisely because their "local circumstances" forbade it: distance would defeat the purpose and meaning of representation. An American sent to Parliament would be too out of touch with his constituents. He would lose "that fellow-feeling which forms the firmest barrier of liberty." Absence from home would "weaken his connections, and lessen his interest. . . . having little expectation of being re-chosen at a future election, he might be remiss in the duty he owed his constituents."[8] In other words, he might sacrifice his character as a local subject to his character as a participant in government.

That was what the members of the British House of Commons seemed to have done, in spite of Whately's insistence on their representative character. When they passed the Stamp Act they did it, they said, as "part of the Supreme unlimited power of the Nation."[9] When they repealed it, they accompanied the repeal with a Declaratory Act affirming their power to legislate for the colonies in all cases whatsoever. In this, it would seem, the Commons had abandoned all pretense of maintaining their subject character as representatives, virtual or actual, of any constituency, whether English or American. It might be admitted that the king held some sort of inherent governmental authority over the colonies, but the powers of the Commons, the Americans argued, had to come from the people who chose them. A colonist could therefore pose the question: "when an aspiring member of the House of Commons confidently declares that he has a power to bind our trade, and restrain our manufactures, I should be glad to know whether he derived this power from the honest freemen his constituents. . . . From his constituents he could receive no more power than they *naturally possessed*."[10] It was even implied (in what amounted to a repudiation of all representative authority) that representatives had no powers beyond carrying to the government the consent or dissent of the subjects in their particular communities to whatever the government might wish to do: "Every representative in Parliament is not a representative for the whole nation, but only for the particular place for which he has been chosen. . . . no member can represent

[8] *Newport Mercury*, July 21, 1766.

[9] Morgan, *Prologue to Revolution*, 30.

[10] William Hicks, *The Nature and Extent of Parliamentary Power Considered* (Philadelphia, 1768), 15.

any but those by whom he hath been elected. . . . the electors of *London* cannot confer or give any right to their members to lay a tax on Westminster. . . ."[11]

It was actually, of course, in the very nature of representation, as it had developed both in England and in the colonies, that the electors of a single constituency did confer on their member a right to impose both taxes and legislation on the whole community. The member elected from Maidstone or Kent, from London or Westminster, became, in the magic of representative government, a legislator for Great Britain. Did he also become a legislator for America? That was what the colonists denied. In doing so, in rejecting the extension of virtual representation beyond the shores of Great Britain, they were affirming, without at first being fully aware of what they were doing, that the American colonies were different national communities from the one that was represented in Parliament. From this unstated premise they argued at first only that the representatives of British constituencies had no right to tax the colonies. But from here, as Parliament continued to assert its authority in all cases whatsoever, they were led inexorably to the conclusion that British representatives had no authority over them in any case whatsoever. The farsighted had reached such a conclusion by the late 1760s. By 1774 it became the official position of a Continental Congress.[12]

To deny that Great Britain and the colonies formed a single community was not to deny all connections between them. There remained their subjection to a common king. The immediate objective of the colonial argument was to eliminate the share in the king's imperial government that had been assumed by the House of Commons in England, and thereby to place British representatives on an equal footing with those who sat in the various colonial assemblies. Each would have authority, under the king, over its own community. The effect

[11] John Joachim Zubly, *An Humble Enquiry into the Nature of the Dependency of the American Colonies upon the Parliament of Great Britain* ([Charleston, S.C.], 1769), 17.

[12] *Journals of the Continental Congress*, I, 63–73. Benjamin Franklin seems to have been one of the first to reach this position, though he was discreet about advancing his views. V. W. Crane, "Benjamin Franklin and the Stamp Act," Colonial Society of Massachusetts *Publications* 32 (1937), 56–77; L. W. Labaree, ed., *The Papers of Benjamin Franklin* (New Haven, Conn., 1959–), XIV, 66–69, 105–6, 110–11. The classic statements of the view are in James Wilson, *Considerations on the Nature and Extent of the Legislative Authority of the British Parliament* (Philadelphia, 1774); John Adams, "Novanglus," *Papers*, II, 216–387; and Thomas Jefferson, *A Summary View of the Rights of British America* (Williamsburg, Va., 1774).

of the argument, however, was not only to place the colonial representatives and their English counterparts on an equal plane, but also to emphasize the subject character of both in relation to the king. There was perhaps more than a coincidental resemblance between the colonial posture and that of the English House of Commons in the 1620s. The colonists were engaged in cutting other subjects (namely the eighteenth-century House of Commons) down to size, in much the same way that the Commons in the 1620s had sought to bring down the king's favorites by exalting the king. The irony of American rebels exalting the king was not lost on the English. The Americans, they said, were reactionary rebels, who would destroy popular liberty by restoring to the king powers that Parliament had taken from him. But the Americans were unmoved by the accusation: they claimed for their own representative assemblies within their own jurisdictions whatever rightful powers the House of Commons had acquired in England. They insisted to the end on their constitutional subjection to a king who unfortunately had been led captive by a venal ministry and a corrupted House of Commons, a House of Commons which had assumed powers not properly belonging to subjects.

In the end, of course, it was American representatives in provincial congresses and the Continental Congress, who threw off the mantle of subjects and assumed all authority to themselves, just as Parliament had done in the 1640s. But as they went about setting up new independent governments, they were conditioned by their previous insistence on representation as the voice of subjects (or citizens?) of particular local communities. Throughout their previous existence the representatives in most colonial assemblies had had to deal with a governmental authority that issued from abroad. That very fact had preserved among them, even before the quarrel with England began, a stronger sense of the local, subject character of representation than could be sustained among the men who sat at Westminster and who demonstrated so imperious a view of themselves in the measures that antagonized the colonies. In the course of the dozen years of resisting those measures the colonists insisted, again and again, that a representative derived his only legitimacy, his only authenticity, his only being from his attachment to and identification with his particular constituents. As the representatives of the thirteen colonies "in General Congress assembled" declared their several constituencies to be free and independent states and the people of the United States to be "separate and equal" to every other people, they could scarcely turn their backs on the view of representation that had impelled them to the separation. But that view, so crucial for crushing the pretensions of representatives from a distant nation, posed problems when American representatives eliminated every other authority and assumed all the powers of government to themselves.

The representatives who seized power in the Revolution were not generally the members of the legally constituted assemblies under the old royal governments. Royal governors saw to it that such assemblies were not in session when the ultimate confrontation with British authority took place. But the new assemblies, summoned by revolutionary committees, were elected in the old manner, though somewhat enlarged in membership. And they resumed the habitual posture of their predecessors toward executive authority. In their first meetings they drafted constitutions that provided for an executive, for they grudgingly recognized that they needed an executive of some kind. But they took care to make him their own creature, giving him no veto power or any other powers that might inhibit their own. The new governments would be run by representatives, and by representatives of the American kind, representatives who knew their places as agents of the people who chose them.

The men who made the Revolution were not so provincial as to believe that the agent of a town or county, closely tied to his constituents, was necessarily well qualified to make laws and policy for a larger society of which his town or county formed a part. But in the contest with Parliament they had not been obliged to confront this inescapable contradiction of representation. After 1776 it emerged as the central problem of a new nation committed both to the sovereignty of the people and to a predominantly local view of representation. The problem was, as it had always been, to get spokesmen of particular communities, without losing their local identities and local attachments, to act wisely and well for the people of a whole state. Although a representative must speak for his particular community, the laws which he shared in making received their sanction now, not from the king or from any English authority, but from the collective body of the people. All the more reason, then, that he should be guided by their collective interest, rather than the interest of his particular constituency.

The difficulty of reconciling the two perspectives was compounded by the union the colonies had already achieved before they declared independence, a union which required that representatives think in terms of a whole continent. But the problem presented itself initially and forcefully in the formation of governments for the several states. It was hard enough to make the representative, say of Hanover County, think in terms of Virginia, let alone of the whole United States.

Although there could be no ideal way to solve the problem, a middle way might have been to give a large vision to representatives in the new governments by electing them from large constituencies. It seemed reasonable that the larger the district a man represented, the closer he would come to embracing the common interest of the whole state. The ultimate possibility would be to have all representatives elected at large, each voter voting for as many candidates as there were representatives in the whole assembly. But this would destroy altogether the local, subject character of representation that Americans had been insisting on. The middle way of large constituencies would at least reduce local prejudice and would also reduce the ever-present danger of corruption: it was harder to corrupt a large district than a small one. Moreover, large districts were less prone to manipulation by demagogues and factious combinations seeking private benefits. The people of Lexington, Massachusetts, considering (and rejecting) a proposed state constitution that gave a representative to every town in the state, warned of the danger that in the choice of representatives "small Towns may become an easy Prey to the corrupt influence of designing Men."[13] The English example was to be cited again and again in this connection: it was through the small borough constituencies that a corrupt ministry had been able to dominate the House of Commons.[14] And even without corruption, it seemed likely that the representatives of small districts would be more disposed than those from large districts "to act upon the private narrow Views and Interests of their particular Constituents to the prejudice of the publick Welfare and the Injury of other parts of the Community."[15]

Another way to solve the problem might have been to refine local prejudice out of a house of representatives by a succession of elections. Thus the New Hampshire provincial congress proposed a constitu-

[13] Oscar and Mary Handlin, *The Popular Sources of Political Authority: Documents on the Massachusetts Constitution of 1780* (Cambridge, Mass., 1966), 317.

[14] Ibid., 342.

[15] Ibid., 735.

tion in 1781 that provided for the towns in each county annually to elect delegates to a county convention which would then choose from among themselves a much smaller number to sit as the house of representatives in the legislature. This would mean, the congress acknowledged, that no town would have a representative of its own, but so much the better: "Those interested views, that party spirit, and zeal for rivalry, which too often takes place in towns on such occasions, will be hereby in a great measure destroyed; and the people will be under a necessity of acting upon higher and better principles." But the people of New Hampshire did not choose to be under that necessity. Each town wanted its own representative chosen directly by its own voters.[16] And so did communities in other states, whether towns, parishes, or counties. No state adopted a system of indirect election for representatives, because such a system would have betrayed the conception of representation that the colonists had insisted on throughout the quarrel with England. And for the same reason no state adopted the other alternative of large constituencies. Instead they did the opposite: they reduced the size of constituencies, established new ones, and more than doubled the total number of representatives sitting in the various assemblies.[17] In addition, most states required that a representative be a resident of his constituency, and several specified that his constituents should have a right to instruct him.[18] The new representative assemblies, which took the lion's share of power in the new governments, would thus be even more prone to local influence, local prejudice, and local corruption than their predecessors.

And so in fact they were. Before the quarrel with England began, it had been common for communities to elect their most successful, most prominent men to represent them in the colonial assemblies. With the multiplication of constituencies and the increase in size of the assemblies went an enlargement of the kinds of men considered suitable to sit in them. The colonists had been contending that a rep-

---

[16] Nathaniel Bouton, ed., *Town Papers: Documents and Records relating to Towns in New Hampshire*, IX (Concord, N.H., 1875), 849.

[17] Jackson T. Main, *The Sovereign States, 1775–1783* (New York, 1973), 202; Gordon Wood, *The Creation of the American Republic* (Chapel Hill, N.C., 1969), 167.

[18] Of the eleven original states that adopted constitutions in the revolutionary period (Connecticut and Rhode Island continued their old governments defined by royal charters), all except New York and South Carolina required representatives to be residents of the district they represented. Massachusetts, New Hampshire, Pennsylvania, and North Carolina specified the right to instruct.

resentative ought to think, feel, and act like his constituents. Now they began to practice what they preached by electing more ordinary men, men who did not talk in the highfalutin language of lawyers, merchants, and big landowners, men more like themselves, who knew about the problems of running a small farm and keeping the tax collectors off your back.[19]

With such men sitting in the houses of representatives and calling the tune in government, some other way would have to be found to get into government people who could see beyond the fields and woods of their own neighborhoods, men who could counteract the incompetence and local dependency of representatives and look after the interest of the whole state in the larger world. And the way of doing it did not at first seem far to seek. If Harrington's solution was unacceptable, the principle behind it still made sense, namely to divide the subject character of representation from the ruling character in two separate bodies. A representative assembly might be allowed (contrary to Harrington) to formulate laws, but let there be another, smaller body, composed of men with larger vision and cooler heads. Let it be endowed with coordinate powers, an upper house that could revise or reject what the lower house of representatives proposed and that could also initiate legislation to be revised, rejected, or accepted by the lower house. John Adams took the lead in urging such a system on his countrymen in 1776,[20] and all but two (Pennsylvania and Georgia) of the thirteen states took his advice and provided for a bicameral legislature, in which the upper house was supposed to embody a greater degree of wisdom and a wider, more "liberal" outlook than the lower house.

The immediate model for such a scheme was not Harrington's, nor was it Parliament with its House of Lords, but the colonial legislatures, in all but one of which (Pennsylvania) the governor's appointed council had served as an upper house. The colonists, of course, had no titled aristocracy to make up a house of lords; and as the revolutionary enthusiasm for equality developed, Americans were sure that they did not want one. In their Articles of Confederation of 1781 they prohibited the United States and all its member states from creating titles of nobility (a prohibition that was continued in the Constitution of 1787). Americans liked now to think of themselves as a society without rank. Yet they had always distinguished the "better sort" among

[19] Main, *The Sovereign States*, 203 5.
[20] "Thoughts on Government," *Papers*, IV, 73–93.

them from the "middling sort" and from the "poorer sort." Benjamin
Rush, the Philadelphia physician, who was a passionate republican,
nevertheless thought that there were "natural distinctions of rank in
Pennsylvania, as certain and general as the artificial distinctions of
men in Europe."[21] In any society, it was believed, different natural
capacities and abilities would mark out some men for distinction. It
was these natural aristocrats, as they came to be called, who were
likely to be free of the narrow, local views to be found in a house of
representatives. It was they whom their compatriots must place in the
upper houses of their legislatures, and so bring to government the
stability and wisdom that hereditary aristocracy so poorly supplied
through the House of Lords in England.

The question was how to identify this aristocracy of talent and
merit, and how to convey to it the authority that flowed now from the
whole people. The voters could not be expected to know who the
mute inglorious Miltons among themselves might be. They would
have to be content with men who stood out from the crowd. And
what made a man stand out most conspicuously was wealth. In a society where official ranks did not exist and large economic opportunities
did exist, it was mainly property that commanded respect and deference, as a sign of ability and energy if for no other reason.

So, at least, thought those who had it. They had been the better
sort in colonial society, the sort to whom others deferred, the sort
from whom the royal governors had picked their councils. They had
no trouble identifying themselves as the natural aristocracy of the
country. Though some of them had remained loyal to the king in the
Revolution and so were out of the running, others took leading roles
in the Continental Congress and the Continental army as well as in
the provisional governments that succeeded the collapse of royal
authority. While they subscribed to republican ideals and abhorred
the very idea of hereditary aristocracy, they did think that they had
more at stake in the success of the new governments than other men,
and they did think that they knew better than other men what the
people, rightly informed, would want (namely what they, already
rightly informed, would want).

If natural aristocracy and broad vision could be identified by the
ownership of large amounts of property, then one way to place natural

[21] Benjamin Rush, *Observations upon the Present State of the Government of Pennsylvania*
(Philadelphia, 1777), 9.

aristocrats in the upper house would be by requiring such ownership
on the part of the candidates or voters for that branch. Although this
posed the danger of tying the senate to a class in the same way that
representatives were tied to a locality, that was precisely what many
not very revolutionary revolutionaries thought proper. Several states
tried the expedient, but except in Maryland the amounts of property
required were not sufficient to insure the result; and in many states
people were unwilling to allow that wealth was an adequate index of
merit anyhow or that large property entitled anyone to special power
and authority.

Another way to select natural aristocrats, however defined, would
have been to choose the upper house through indirect elections of the
kind unsuccessfully proposed for the lower house in New Hampshire,
but only Maryland adopted this method (along with Maryland's stiff
property requirements). The middle way remained: to choose the upper
house from large constituencies. Although no state was willing to try
it for the lower house, most of them tried it for the upper. In all the
states whose new constitutions provided for an upper house or senate,
it had a smaller number of members than the lower house, each member representing a correspondingly larger number of voters. The precise arrangements for achieving this effect, some of them quite complex,
varied from state to state, but generally without producing senators
who could be readily recognized as of the better sort.[22]

Only Connecticut and Rhode Island, operating under their old
royal charters, elected an upper house from the whole state at large.
In Rhode Island a long-standing de facto custom of assigning senatorial seats by county defeated any aristocratic and generalizing tendencies of at-large voting.[23] The Connecticut system, on the other hand,
offered what was in many ways the least unhappy solution to the
whole problem of representation. At a primary election held annually
in September, the freemen of each Connecticut town assembled and
named twenty persons as candidates for the upper house, which consisted of twelve persons. Any freeman could nominate or be nominated. The town votes were then sorted out, and the twenty persons
with the highest totals through the state were placed in nomination.
From them the freemen, again assembled in town meetings the fol-

[22] Jackson T. Main, *The Upper House in Revolutionary America* (Madison, Wis., 1967),
passim.

[23] David S. Lovejoy, *Rhode Island Politics and the American Revolution 1760–1776* (Providence, R.I., 1958), 15.

lowing month, voted for twelve. Under this procedure it was rare for a man not to be renominated and reelected every year as long as he chose to serve, but it was easy to eliminate the unworthy and to recognize new talent and achievement.[24]

An enthusiast for the Connecticut system later explained how it put the right men into the upper house. People, he argued, were of two kinds, those with large views and sound judgment (natural aristocrats) and those biased by local interests and prejudice. The first kind, always a small minority, were scattered thinly through any state. In a local election (as for representatives) none of them would be likely to prevail, precisely because they were not tied to local views, but in a state-wide election the votes cast by people of their kind would outweigh those of candidates whose merits lay only in local popularity. Local candidates would gain only local votes, while men of larger views would be more widely known, even though their local following might be small.[25]

That such was the case in Connecticut was evident, in fact, from the conduct of the voters. At the town meetings where the upper house was chosen, each town also elected its representatives, and the voting for them came first. The freemen turned out in substantial numbers for it, but it was notorious that after they had chosen their two representatives and the time came to vote for the twelve members of the upper house, most of the freemen departed. The candidates were unknown to them personally, and it made no difference to them which were chosen. The voters who remained at the meetings to make choice of their senators were the bigger men of a town, men whose business extended through the state or beyond it, men whose interests went beyond the local level. They naturally chose the right kind of people, their kind.[26] The Connecticut system thus achieved something of the effect that Harrington had sought. It did so by sacrificing the local, subject character of representatives in the upper house, but still derived the upper house from popular choice: there was nothing

[24] Robert J. Taylor, *Colonial Connecticut: A History* (Millwood, N.Y., 1979), 32–38.

[25] [William Pitt Beers?], *An Address to the Legislature and People of the State of Connecticut* (New Haven, Conn., 1791), 17–21.

[26] [Zephaniah Swift?], *The Security of the Rights of Citizens in the State of Connecticut Considered* (Hartford, 1792), 46–48, 83–84. Cf. Benjamin Gale to———, Feb. 7, 1787. Collection of R. Morris, Santa Monica, California. "Not one quarter of our Freemen who vote for Deputies, do vote for assistants, i.e., unless some popular commotion excites them, and for this very reason: they say they know not the men."

to prevent all freemen from participating in the choice if they wished
to. The Maryland system too produced an upper house confined to
natural aristocrats, though it removed them much farther from popular choice.

But Connecticut and Maryland were unusual. In general the state
senates were too much like the lower houses to serve the purposes
intended for them. Though the constituencies were larger they were
apparently not large enough. The members were too narrow in outlook, too attached to local interests, too subject to corrupt or partisan
influences. They were, it might be said, too representative. So, at
least, it seemed to the natural aristocrats of the country, and so it also
has appeared to subsequent historians, even those whose sympathies
might have dictated otherwise. In a remarkable series of empirical
studies Jackson Turner Main has demonstrated that the members of
the upper houses of the new state legislatures, while somewhat freer
of local attachments than the members of the lower houses, were much
less well-to-do than the members of the old colonial councils and tended
to divide over particular issues in the same way as the lower houses.
In both houses of the new state legislatures the members split into
opposing parties or factions which Main has designated significantly
as "cosmopolitan" and "localist."[27]

The cosmopolitans were distinguished not only by a broader outlook—what at the time was generally called "liberal"—but also by
greater wealth, by residence on the coast or on a navigable river, and
by commercial connections. Most of them would probably have recognized themselves and been recognized by others as natural aristocrats. The localists, on the other hand, tended to come from interior
regions engaged in subsistence farming and to be considerably less
well off. If the cosmopolitans had all found their way to the upper
houses and the localists to the lower, the legislatures might have functioned as intended.[28] But scattered through the two houses they were
frequently overpowered by the localists. As a result, the state assemblies, unchecked now by royal governors and their upper-class councils, acted in ways that alarmed many of the leaders of the Revolution.
They passed laws in haste and repealed them in haste. They passed
laws violating the treaty with Great Britain, delaying or scaling down

[27] Main, *Upper House*, Main, *Sovereign States*, and Main, *Political Parties before the Constitution* (Chapel Hill, N.C., 1973).

[28] This is not Professor Main's point but an observation based on the results of his
analysis of voting blocs.

the payment of public and private debts, issuing paper money as legal tender, refusing to pay their states' quotas of national expenses, raising their own salaries and lowering those of other government officers. The upper houses dragged their feet a little on these measures but not enough to matter.

In Virginia, George Mason, who drafted the state's Bill of Rights and much of the state constitution of 1776, was wholly disillusioned with the results by 1783. Writing to a friend, he lamented that "Frequent Interferences with private Property and Contracts, retrospective Laws destructive of all public Faith, as well as Confidence between Man and Man, and flagrant Violations of the Constitution must disgust the best and wisest part of the Community, occasion a great Depravity of Manners, bring the Legislature into Contempt, and finally produce Anarchy and public Convulsion."[29] Another Virginian, Archibald Stuart, made the same sort of complaint to Thomas Jefferson two years later and added, "We are able to draw but little aid from the Senate. That Body continues to be contemptible in point of Capacity. They have not sufficient confidence in themselves to Oppose the voice of the delegates upon any Occasion."[30] (The Virginia lower house was known as the House of Delegates.)

Stuart was preaching to the converted, for Jefferson himself had long been urging a revision of the Virginia constitution in order to achieve a more effective senate. He would have grouped the counties of the state into larger districts and then have the voters choose an electoral college for each district to make the final choice of its senators, a system comparable again to the unsuccessful proposal for the New Hampshire House of Representatives.[31] Jefferson's friend James Madison thought that even such a system fell short of the mark, because it did not sufficiently escape the "spirit of *locality*." It was too closely attached to counties, and the senators would therefore be too likely "to lose sight of the aggregate interests of the community and even to sacrifice them to the interests or prejudices of their respective constituents." Even if a measure was well calculated to satisfy the particular interests of every county or district, it would not necessarily be a good thing for the whole state. Madison thought the best way to make sen-

[29] George Mason, *The Papers of George Mason, 1725–1792*, R. A. Rutland, ed., (Chapel Hill, N.C., 1970) II, 768.

[30] Thomas Jefferson, *The Papers of Thomas Jefferson*, Julian Boyd et al., eds., (Princeton, N.J. 1950–), VIII, 645.

[31] Ibid., VI, 296 (1783).

ators direct themselves to the interest of the state as a whole was "by making them the choice of the whole Society, each citizen voting for every Senator,"[32] in other words, election at large as in Connecticut. Madison was already thinking of size as the only way to supply wisdom and virtue to representative government.

But neither Madison nor Jefferson got very far toward revamping the Virginia constitution. And the performance of the Virginia state legislature in the 1780s was typical. Even Maryland was threatened by a runaway house of representatives, bent on relieving debtors by inflationary schemes that seemed to threaten the security of property.[33] The situation was particularly distressing to men for whom the Revolution had brought an outlook on the world that reached not merely beyond their home town or county but beyond their home state. There were many such men who had fought in the Continental army or served in the Continental Congress or who carried on business on a continental scale. They were men who thought, as Alexander Hamilton put it, continentally. As they cast about for ways to curb their short-sighted state legislatures, they thought not only about the peril posed to republican principles by these bodies but also about the increasing "imbecility," that is, the impotence, of the Congress and the impending collapse of the union over which it presided. For cosmopolitans, for the continentally minded, the union had come to embody those feelings to which we attach such inadequate words as nationalism and patriotism. And at the same time it embodied some of the revolutionary hopes of a future in which hereditary monarchy and aristocracy would give way throughout the world to republican liberty, to government where the people were sovereign. But it was the people's representatives who now threatened to destroy the union and to disgrace the whole idea of popular sovereignty.

Americans were discovering, as the English had discovered in the preceding century, that the sovereignty of the people could pose threats to the very values it was ostensibly designed to protect. The difficulties the Americans encountered were not quite the same as those that had disillusioned many English publicists in the 1640s and 1650s. Americans were not troubled by a revolutionary army whose officers claimed to speak the voice of the people more authentically than the

[32] Ibid., VI, 308–9.
[33] Madison, *Papers*, IX, 95.

people's elected representatives. The only attempt of that kind was quickly quashed by the commander in chief. Nor were Americans subjected to representatives who clung to power and refused to face an election. American troubles nevertheless came, as in England, from the misuse by representatives of powers assumed in the name of the people. In dealing with the problem Americans had the benefit of English experience, though they sometimes were not fully aware that they were treading paths marked out (though not trodden) by their English predecessors.

The American reaction to the problems posed by representative government was not to restore monarchy, as the English had done in 1660, though a few talked wildly of taking this course. Instead, the Americans reacted by rethinking the sovereignty of the people, not to repudiate it but to turn it to the purposes that its accompanying fictions were already serving. Though it originated as a tool of opposition to government, it could be used to subdue the unthinking many to the thoughtful few, to curb the local prejudice of representatives and give a more cosmopolitan composition to their assemblies.

How this could be done had begun to occupy thinking Americans as soon as independence eliminated external authority, but the apparent folly of the state assemblies in the 1780s dramatized and clarified the problem and made its solution more and more urgent. The problem, it now appeared, was twofold: first, in the name of the people, to set limits on the actions of the people's representatives, and secondly, if possible, to broaden the vision of the representatives themselves, without destroying the local, subject character that made them representative. Ultimately the two problems and their solutions were entwined, but they materialized separately.

The first solution had already been worked out, but not implemented, during the English Revolution. The Levellers, even while calling for a more representative Parliament, had sought a way for the people to limit their representatives. They had called for "an Agreement of the people, begun and ended amongst the people," to be a fundamental constitution superior to parliamentary statutes. Although the Levellers failed, the exercise of popular sovereignty in England led others like Vane and Lawson to make the same distinction between the constituent power of the people and the legislative power of the government. It was left for John Locke to refine the distinction and give it classic form in his *Second Treatise of Civil Government*.

Locke's contemporaries were slow to grasp the profoundly conservative implications of his argument. In 1689 the men who engineered England's Glorious Revolution were not taking any chances on summoning the people, whoever they might be, to action. After it became clear that the social order had survived intact, they were willing to use Locke's *Treatise of Government* as a possible explanation of what had happened, but it was not an explanation that found any place in English law. The English people never, even fictionally, exercised their constituent power outside Parliament. They acted only through their representatives in the House of Commons.

Nor, in fact, had Locke told them how they could act otherwise. Neither Lawson nor Locke was clear about just how the people, already embodied in a society (however that may have been achieved), could go about forming a government. They preferred to think of it as having already happened in the unrecorded past. Even the Levellers were vague about how their Agreement of the People was to be agreed to. (How did the people authorize the drafting of it? Who would sign it? What about those who refused to sign? What if a majority refused to sign?) But this is only to say that the sovereignty of the people, like the divine right of kings, and like representation itself, is a fiction that cannot survive too close examination or too literal application. It requires that we believe not only in the existence of something we call the people but also in the capacity of that something to make decisions and to act apart from the elected representatives of particular localities. Once we adopt these fictions, the exercise of a constituent power by the people becomes a useful conception for making representative government work.

When the Americans declared independence and went about setting up new governments, the conception was there for them to use, but it was some time before they found an acceptable way to apply it. There is no evidence that they were familiar with the writings of the Levellers, where they would have found the most explicit discussions of it; but they were familiar with Locke, and in the course of the quarrel with England they had developed at nearly all levels of their society, a degree of political sophistication and experience that enabled them to translate abstractions into practice, or, to put it another way, to give a plausible factual basis to the fictions of popular sovereignty.

Americans seem to have recognized from the beginning that a constitution ought to be different in kind from ordinary legislation. When the provincial congresses that took control of government in 1775 and 1776 undertook to draft and adopt constitutions for their respective states, they tried to give special popular sanction to their constitution making, if only by claiming in a preamble that they were empowered by the people and that the constitution they produced was to be supreme as an expression of the will of the people. Voices were raised at once to point out that calling it supreme would not make it so and that a congress which was acting as a government was not the right body to act for the people in determining what the limits or the form of their government should be. A constitution ought to bear some sort of direct popular authorization that would place it beyond the power of government to change. But in the face of wartime crises it seemed unwise to press the objection.[34]

The problem may have seemed less crucial in the early years of the Revolution because of the ease with which the people had seemingly been able to act apart from their governments. When the extralegal Continental Congress formed the Association against trade with Britain in 1774, people all through the colonies had joined in local committees to enforce it in a visible display of popular action.[35] A year or two later in every state the government authorized by the king had given way to government authorized by the people, with a minimum of disorder. The representative assemblies of the old governments had been replaced by congresses elected in the same manner, often with a wider suffrage and larger membership; and these congresses simply assumed all the powers of government in the name of the people.[36] To English radicals, as we have seen, Americans seemed to be demonstrating that the people could act apart from their government whenever government betrayed its trust.

Americans continued to show a readiness for direct action, not simply to challenge existing government but to supplement it. Even before the Revolution it was not uncommon for crowds, organized and unorganized, to assemble for the purpose of implementing policies that government was slow in effecting. With the coming of independence, local communities formed committees to suppress Tories in their midst and sometimes gathered to curb profiteers who tried to fatten on wartime shortages. When the objective was larger than local they did not hesitate to organize statewide or even interstate conven-

---

[34] Willi Paul Adams, *The First American Constitutions* (Chapel Hill, N.C., 1980), 63–98.

[35] David Ammerman, *In the Common Cause: American Response to the Coercive Acts of 1774* (Charlottesville, Va., 1974).

[36] Adams, *First American Constitutions*, 27–48; Main, *Sovereign States*, 123–42.

tions, with or without government backing, to address the problem. Numerous such conventions were held in the 1770s in an attempt to control the prices of necessaries. The persons who attended were not self-appointed volunteers but elected delegates.[37]

How they were elected and whom they represented is not altogether clear, but it was only a small step from elected conventions aimed at supplementing government to elected conventions exercising the people's constituent power to define and limit government, in the manner longed for by the Levellers and made respectable by John Locke.

Massachusetts was the first to take the step. The state had proceeded under a provisional government based on its old royal charter until 1777, when the General Court, after seeking specific authorization from the voters, drafted a constitution and submitted it to the towns for a vote by all adult males. The result was an overwhelming rejection. A number of towns had already objected in principle to a constitution drafted by a governing body, and others repeated the objection in rejecting the proposed constitution. In 1779 accordingly there was held, for the first time in independent America and perhaps in the world, a convention popularly elected for the exclusive purpose of drafting a constitution to be submitted to the people for ratification, with a provision that a two-thirds majority of the whole people (not simply a majority of towns) would be required to put it in effect.[38]

Town meetings discussed the document clause by clause, accepting some articles, rejecting others, and suggesting various amendments. Although there was no two-thirds majority of the whole people for many provisions, the convention, which reconvened to count the returns, ignored the suggestions, interpreted revisions as acceptances, and declared the constitution adopted. In spite of this dubious final procedure, the Masssachusetts constitution could be said, with more plausibility than any other, to be an act of the sovereign people. As such, it gave to the other branches of government a popular authori-

---

[37] The most thorough study of these conventions is Barbara Clark Smith, "The Politics of Price Control in Revolutionary Massachusetts 1774–1780," (Ph.D. dissertation, Yale University, 1983). See also Wood, *Creation of the American Republic*, 306–43. On the relation of crowd action to civil authority see Pauline Maier, *From Resistance to Revolution* (New York, 1972), 3–26; and John Phillip Reid, *In a Defiant Stance* (University Park, Pa., 1977) and *In Defiance of the Law* (Chapel Hill, N.C. 1981), *passim.*

[38] Handlins, *Popular Sources*, 383–472; Robert J. Taylor, ed., *Massachusetts, Colony to Commonwealth* (Chapel Hill, N.C., 1961).

zation that would help them to stand up against the representative branch in any contest, and it gave to the representatives themselves a new relationship to the people as a whole.

That such was the intention of the convention or of the people who chose it may perhaps be doubted (though it was certainly the intention of John Adams, the principal author of the document). But the returns of the various towns do show a widespread concern to overcome the local limitations of representative government. In spite of the recent denunciations of virtual representation, a number of towns argued for a provision that representatives be paid by the state rather than by their constituents, "because they are Representatives not meerly of this or that particular Town (which would suppose them to have the interest of that Town only to provide for) But of the whole Body of the People . . . and we would have them, by the mode of support and Payment as well as other things, divest themselves of Party and Prejudice and seek and pursue the grand interest of the whole."[39] That such arguments may have been prompted by a desire to lessen local expenses subtracts only a little from the appeal to the interests of the people as a whole.

The new constitution did not give the elected governor of Massachusetts an absolute veto over legislation, which John Adams had wanted. But one town's argument for such a power reveals again the concern for checking the local attachments of representatives. The people of Wells, in the Maine district of Massachusetts, could have given Algernon Sidney some lessons in the pitfalls of representative government. "We can not but think," they wrote,

it would be extremely dangerous and impolitick to trust an incontroulable Power of legislation in the Hands of those who are only the Representatives of particular and smaller Districts of the Commonwealth: who may often be disposed to act upon the private narrow Views and Interests of their particular Constituents to the prejudice of the publick Welfare and the Injury of other parts of the Community—When we consider that the several Members of the Legislative Body are to be chosen only by particular Districts as their special Representatives and may not improbably be often chosen for the very purpose of serving and promoting such Views and Designs of their Constituents as would be injurious to other parts of the State.

On these grounds, the "common Representative of the people," that is, the governor, ought to "have his Hand at full Liberty and may be

[39] Handlins, *Popular Sources*, 539.

empowered to act effectually and with strong Arm for the Protection of all and every part of his Constituents as there may be occasion."[40]

On the face of it, the view of a governor as a representative of the whole people, like the idea of a constitutional convention independent of and superior to government, would appear to be an affirmation of popular power. And the Massachusetts townsmen were outspoken in asserting the superiority of the people to all their officers of government, who were to be viewed always as the servants of those who employed them. In the years that followed, such assertions became common throughout the states, as constitutional conventions became the accepted way of placing the people above their government.

How early the opposite, conservative implications of the idea became apparent is not clear. In 1787 Noah Webster, one of the most outspoken conservatives of his time, had still not grasped the fact that conservatism in America would have to build on popular sovereignty. In his *American Magazine* he gave the lie to the fiction, but in doing so unwittingly disclosed its usefulness. The people, he argued, could not be superior to their representatives, because the people could act by themselves only in small local groups. They could not run a government. The most they could do was to elect representatives and submit to them. Therefore to assign a representative convention a higher power than a representative legislative assembly was ridiculous and self-defeating. It was to bind the freshly elected representatives to the decisions of other representatives elected earlier, perhaps many years earlier, when conditions were quite different from what they later became.[41]

But that, ultimately, was the point of the fiction, to prevent representatives from doing whatever pleased them or their constituents at the moment. A constitution superior to ordinary legislation could insure a strong position in government to the executive and the judiciary as well as the legislature, by making them all representatives of popular sovereignty and guaranteeing to them all a share in the power that supposedly emanated from the people. The doctrine of judicial review had only been adumbrated in 1788, but it was inescapable once a written constitution was made supreme over legislation by pretending it to be the act of the sovereign people. If a house of representatives passed legislation that violated the provisions of the people's

---

[40] Ibid., 735–36.
[41] *The American Magazine*, Dec. 1787–Oct. 1788, pp. 75–80, 137–45.

constitution and the upper house did not reject it, a proper governor could veto it, and if his veto was overridden, the courts could decline to enforce it, indeed would have to decline since they could not otherwise enforce the superior law embodied in the constitution.

To be sure, there were constitutions and constitutions. A constitutional convention might place all power in a representative assembly. But in the 1780s belief in the separation of powers was widespread. For centuries Englishmen had bragged about their mixed government, in which executive, legislative, and judiciary powers were allegedly balanced against each other. What had supposedly gone wrong and precipitated the American revolt was the dominance, through corruption, of the executive branch over the legislative branch. Most of the first American constitutions, drafted by provincial congresses, had paid lip service to the separation of powers, even while giving the lion's share to the representative assemblies. The Massachusetts constitution, on the other hand, gave real power to the senate and to the governor and independence to the judiciary. If Massachusetts was a fair sample, constitutional conventions would prove more reliable than representative assemblies in doling out the people's power. It stood to reason that a body which would itself dissolve and have no future share in government would be more impartial in dividing authority than an assembly which was itself the legislative branch of government.

The great advantage of a constitutional convention, combined with popular ratification, was that it embodied the sovereignty of the whole people in the government and not simply in the locally elected representative branch. If a convention assigned adequate authority to the other branches and secured popular sanction for it, the local biases and shortsightedness of representatives would be checked by officers who were not tied to local constituents and who felt a larger responsibility to the whole. But by 1787 Massachusetts and New Hampshire were the only states with a constitution thus made and ratified. Whether other states would follow the example remained in doubt, and even if they did, the representative branch might remain too strong for the other branches.

The whole question was tied to the union of the states. The dominance of representatives in the state governments meant their dominance over the Continental Congress, to which they chose the delegates. The status of the Congress and its relationship to the sovereignty of the people had been ambiguous from the beginning, and the ambiguity had remained in the Articles of Confederation of 1781 which defined the union. Although independence had determined that Americans were not part of the people of Great Britain, it had not determined whether they were one people or many, or whether the sovereignty of the people, say, of Virginia was exhausted in the creation of an independent government for Virginia. If Americans were in any sense one people, did that people enjoy a sovereignty too? And if so, who were their representatives?

It was in answers to these questions, worked out gradually in the decade and a half after 1774 (though not finally answered until 1864) that Americans discovered a new and more effective way of bending the sovereignty of the people to overcome the deficiencies of locally oriented representation.

CHAPTER *11*

Inventing an American People

WHEN THE FIRST Continental Congress met in 1774, no one present was quite sure what it was. The members had been chosen in a variety of ways, by regular colonial assemblies, by extralegal provincial congress, by committees of correspondence. In one way or another each of the members thought of himself as representing the colony he came from, but it was not clear just how. Some of them thought the Congress was a kind of debating group capable only of offering recommendations, others regarded it not quite as a governing body but as perhaps the beginning of one. Without trying to determine the question, they adopted an "association" to stop trade with Great Britain, but they belied the voluntary implication of the title by arranging for the creation of local committees to enforce it on individuals throughout what was to be the union, an act that looked very governmental.[1]

By the time the second Continental Congress declared that "these United Colonies are, and of right ought to be Free and Independent States" the Congress was itself acting like the government of a single free and independent state. It was waging war, it was in the process of contracting an alliance, it had opened the trade of the colonies to the world, and it would eventually conclude the peace, all the things that the Declaration specified as hallmarks of a free and independent state.

But with the creation of the state governments and the drafting

[1] Edmund C. Burnett, *The Continental Congress* (New York, 1941, 1964), 3–59; Jack N. Rakove, *The Beginnings of National Politics* (New York, 1979), 3–62.

and later adoption of the Articles of Confederation, the boldness of
the Congress began to fade. The Articles assigned it large powers,
powers that would ordinarily belong to a government. Besides making
war, concluding peace, and contracting alliances, Congress could regulate the value of coinage, establish a post office, borrow money, build
a navy, and so on, But almost the only way that Congress could act
was through the state governments. It could borrow money, but it
could not levy taxes. It could make treaties, but it could not enforce
the terms of them. It could pass resolutions but not make laws. It was
a government with assigned powers but no power. And its anomalous
position reflected a doubt as to whether its members could be considered representatives of the people, or if so, of what people, the
peoples of the separate states or the people of the nation.

According to the practice observed as soon as the states threw off
royal authority, the members of Congress, with two exceptions, were
chosen by the state legislatures (in Rhode Island and Connecticut they
were chosen at large by the voters). If they were representatives, what
were they representatives of? An honest answer, in Patrick Henry's
phrase, was that they were mere "representatives of representatives."[2]
By the standards Americans had insisted on in objecting to British
taxation, the members of Congress were not truly representatives at
all but envoys of the several state governments. And the Articles of
Confederation acknowledged as much by not allowing them authority
to tax or to make or enforce laws.

What Congress did have were the qualities desired for the upper
house of a republican legislature: it had been indirectly elected by the
people through the state legislatures, and its members were generally
the kind of people who would be considered natural aristocrats in
their respective states. But Congress could not serve the functions of
an upper house for the nation as a whole or for the individual states.
It did not have a national house of representatives directly elected by
the people to convey their consent to any measures it proposed. Instead
it had in effect thirteen houses of representatives or more properly
twenty-four (Pennsylvania and Georgia had no senate). Any one of
the twenty-four could refuse to carry out its proposals, resolutions,
ordinances, or whatever it chose to call its actions. And yet Congress
did not have a corresponding negative on the actions taken by the
states.

[2] Paul H. Smith et al., eds., *Letters of Delegates to Congress 1774–1789*, I, 111.

While the pressures of war lasted, the state assemblies generally concurred in what Congress asked of them. But even before the war ended, the defiance or noncompliance of individual states against congressional actions had become commonplace. The state houses of representatives, dominated by localists, seemed bent on demonstrating that true representatives could not extend their vision beyond the narrow confines of their narrow constituencies. And Congress was no more a match for them than their state senates.

To the continentally minded men who contemplated this situation with increasing dismay, the most formidable obstacle in the way of remedy was the very conception of representation that made remedy necessary. If Americans had generally considered representation compatible with indirection election, they might have accepted Congress as a representative body and might therefore have been willing to grant it the powers of a representative body, particularly the power to tax. Continentally minded reformers began proposing such a grant almost as soon as Congress came into existence, arguing that the members were indeed representatives of the people.[3] On two occasions their arguments almost prevailed: they almost succeeded in gaining for Congress a very limited power to tax, power to levy a five percent duty on imports into any of the United States. But every scheme of this kind before 1787 foundered in the end on the reluctance of Americans to trust governmental powers to any body not subject to the veto of their locally elected representatives. If members of Congress were representatives, they were virtual representatives; or they were a mere executive council, and everybody knew that executives must not be allowed to levy taxes without the explicit consent of actual representatives. To endow Congress with powers to tax, it was said, would be to give it the kind of powers that Charles I had claimed in the famous ship money cases of the 1630s and that Parliament, in the grip of a corrupt executive, had claimed in the 1760s and 1770s.[4]

Before 1787 no one seems to have suggested that the answer was

[3] For example, George Washington: "For Heavens sake who are Congress? are they not the Creatures of the People, amenable to them for their conduct, and dependent from day to day on their breath? Where then can be the danger of giving them such Powers as are adequate to the great ends of government . . .?" to William Gordon, July 8, 1783, *Writings*, John C. Fitzpatrick, ed. (Washington, D.C., 1931–44), XXVII, 49–52; E. S. Morgan, *The Genius of George Washington* (New York, 1980), 75. Cf. "Connecticut Farmer" in *American Mercury*, Sept. 18, 1786.

[4] Rakove, *Beginnings*, 383–84; Herbert J. Storing, ed., *The Complete Anti-Federalist* (Chicago, 1981), II, 284; III, 59.

to create a popularly elected national house of representatives. Perhaps no one suggested it because the prevalence of the local, subject view of representation seemed to rule out such a possibility. It was an accepted maxim of political thought at the time that republican government was confined by its very nature to small states. Montesquieu, who had expressed this view most influentially, had based it on the experience of the city states of antiquity, which had not made use of representation.[5] But the idea nevertheless seemed compelling to Americans, who confined representation by its very nature to small communities. A national representative assembly on the scale employed for the state assemblies would be much too large to function as a single body. And it would be as impracticable for the people of all the various towns and counties of the country to be represented in it as it would have been for them to be represented in Parliament. This argument does not seem to have been made before 1787, but as soon as a national house of representatives was proposed, it was, as we shall see. That no one proposed such a thing before 1787 was probably owing in part to an awareness of the reaction it would bring.

It was the seeming desperateness of the situation that led to the proposal in 1787. In Rhode Island the legislature had made its worthless paper money a legal tender in payment of debts, and gleeful debtors pursued their creditors to pay them off. In Massachusetts the farmers in the western counties, despite the fact that the state constitution gave them more than their fair share of representation in the legislature, had risen in arms, closed the courts, and seized a United States arsenal. Similar risings had been narrowly averted in New Hampshire and Connecticut.[6] Although the rebels had all finally been dispersed, it was said that the new Massachusetts legislature, senate and house alike, was filled with their supporters. There they could be expected to pursue their aims, which one member of Congress depicted hysterically as "the abolition of debts public and private, a division of property and a new government founded on principles of fraud and iniquity, or reconnexion with Great Britain."[7] In Virginia too the western counties clamored for more paper money, and mobs closed the courts and burned courthouses and prisons.[8]

[5] The argument is in Chapter 16 of the eighth book of De L'Espirit des Lois.
[6] New Haven Gazette and Connecticut Magazine, Oct. 5, 1786; Christopher Collier, Roger Sherman's Connecticut: Yankee Politics and the American Revolution (Middletown, Conn., 1971), 208–10, 280.
[7] Henry Lee to James Madison, Oct. 19, 1786, Madison, Papers, IX, 144.
[8] Ibid., IX, 145n; X, 155, 161–65.

The situation may not have been as desperate as it seemed, but it looked to many like the fulfillment of the predictions of civil war that conservatives had made in 1776. John Marshall, the future chief justice, thought that without the creation of an effective national government, nothing could prevent "Anarchy first, and civil convulsions afterwards."[9] Another Virginian, James Madison, thought that the reputation of republican government had been dealt "inexpressible injury," and observed that leading minds were exhibiting an alarming "propensity toward Monarchy."[10]

It was Madison who came up with the remedy that ultimately prevailed, the United States Constitution, though it did not take quite the form that he initially hoped for, as he and his contemporaries groped their way toward it at the great Constitutional Convention of 1787. That convention, which Madison was instrumental in bringing about, did not conform to the ideal prescription for simulating an exercise of constituent power by the people, for the members were chosen by the state legislatures, not directly by popular vote. But even before the convention met, Madison recognized that it could achieve the objectives he had in mind for it only by appealing to a popular sovereignty not hitherto fully recognized, to the people of the United States as a whole. They alone could be thought to stand superior to the people of any single state. And what Madison had most directly in view was to overcome the deficiencies of the locally oriented representatives who sat in the state legislatures. To that end he envisioned a genuine national government, resting for its authority, not on the state governments and not even on the peoples of the several states considered separately, but on an American people, a people who constituted a separate and superior entity, capable of conveying to a national government an authority that would necessarily impinge on the authority of the state governments.

The full implications of what he was going to propose were not at first apparent even to Madison himself. As the English House of Commons in the 1640s had invented a sovereign people to overcome a sovereign king, Madison was inventing a sovereign American people to overcome the sovereign states. It was not one of those inventions for which the world was unprepared, but an invention crying out for realization. The Revolution had created a fund of national feeling and

[9] Ibid., X, 135.
[10] Ibid., IX, 295.

a whole class of men who had committed their lives and fortunes to a common cause that seemed to be dissolving in victory. To create a national government resting on the whole people of the nation was perhaps the obvious solution, and since 1780 a constitutional convention had been the obvious way of achieving it. But the kind of government that could challenge and overcome the deficiencies of the state governments was not immediately apparent. It would not do to create a national government with the same deficiencies, filled with locally oriented representatives tied to their local constituencies. At the same time it would not do to create a national government without the popular backing to stand up to the state governments.

Madison had been thinking about these twin dangers for some time before the convention met, and he was consequently able to take the lead in the attempt to steer between them. What he had recognized, before others did, was that the first danger was more apparent than real, that a national government by its very nature would not be subject to the faults exhibited by the states.

It is well known that Madison had been reading David Hume's "Idea of a Perfect Commonwealth," Hume's attempt to improve on Harrington's *Oceana*. Hume's scheme of government was almost as bewildering as Harrington's, with a pyramidal succession of governing bodies. What caught Madison's eye was its rejection of the popular assumption that republican government was suited only to small countries. On the contrary, Hume maintained, a large republic was preferable to a small, because in it "there is compass and room enough to refine the democracy, from the lower people, who may be admitted into the first elections or first concoction of the commonwealth, to the higher magistrates, who direct all the movements. At the same time, the parts are so distant and remote that 'tis very difficult, either by intrigue, prejudice, or passion, to hurry them into any measures against the public interest."[11]

Madison seized on Hume's insight. The trouble with the representative assemblies of the states was that the states were too small. In each of them groups with special interests were able to form popular

[11] Hume, *Essays and Treatises* (London, 1758), 280. On Madison's debt to Hume see Douglass Adair, " 'That Politics May be Reduced to a Science,' David Hume, James Madison, and the Tenth Federalist," *Huntington Library Quarterly* 20 (1957), 343–60; Garry Wills, *Explaining America: The Federalist* (New York, 1981); and E. S. Morgan, "Safety in Numbers: Madison, Hume, and the Tenth Federalist," *Huntington Library Quarterly* 49 (1986), 95–112.

majorities to carry out measures that were unfair to other groups. In particular, debtor groups were able to oppress creditors. In Virginia one religious denomination had been able to oppress the others until Madison himself had helped lead a successful campaign to end the oppression.[12] In a government extending over the whole United States, tyrannies of the majority would be much less likely, because majorities would not be so easily put together. The multiplicity and diversity of interests in so large a territory would protect minorities, just as the multiplicity of religious sects in many states already prevented any one sect from gaining the majority needed to oppress the others.[13]

Size was the key. Not only would it inhibit the formation of majorities, but it would make available a large pool of talent on which to draw for government office. As he considered the benefits of size, it occurred to Madison that even the Continental Congress had exhibited some of them. If it had had a veto over state legislation, which he thought essential for any new national government, it would have prevented most of the evils the country was plagued with. "There has not been any moment since the peace," he wrote to Washington, "at which the representatives of the union would have given an assent to paper money or any other measure of a kindred nature."[14]

Madison had calculated the benefits of size well before the Philadelphia convention met, in drawing up a catalogue of the "Vices of the Political System of the United States," vices that lay in the actions of the state governments.[15] What he had not considered as carefully was the means for giving a national government the strength that the state governments drew from the credibility of their claim to popular sovereignty. He was insistent that without a veto over state legislation a national government could not succeed,[16] but he had not quite rec-

---

[12] On Madison's role in the passage of the Virginia Statute of Religious Freedom, see his "Memorial and remonstrance against Religious Assessments" and the fine accompanying headnote by the editors in *Papers*, VIII, 295–306.

[13] Madison stated his argument for a large republic first in a paper on "The Vices of the Political System of the United States," in the spring of 1787 (*Papers*, IX, 355–57). He expounded it later at the Constitutional Convention on June 6 and in a letter to Jefferson, 24 Oct. 1787 (*Papers*, X, 32–34, 212–14) and in Nos. 10 and 51 of *The Federalist* (Jacob Cooke, ed., Middletown, Conn, 1961), 63–65, 351–53.

[14] Apr. 16, 1787, *Papers*, IX, 384.

[15] *Papers*, IX, 345–58.

[16] Madison made this point before the convention in letters to Thomas Jefferson, Mar. 19, 1787, to Edmund Randolph, Apr. 8, and George Washington, Apr. 16. *Papers*, IX, 318, 370, 383. He argued for it in the convention, June 8, July 17, *Papers*, X,

ognized that with or without a veto, it would not succeed unless it too could make a credible claim to represent the will of the new people he was calling into existence.

While Madison saw from the outset that a new national government would require ratification by popular conventions rather than by the state governments, he did not at first grasp the need for the regular renewal of the government's popular authority in direct popular elections. Hume's scheme had called for indirect election of all government officers at the national level, and in America the difficulty with the state legislatures came from the local attachments of the directly elected representatives. Indirect elections freed the Continental Congress from some of those attachments. Indirect elections were the commonly prescribed (but not adopted) cure for overcoming local bias in the state legislatures. What Madison at first failed to recognize (as indeed Hume had failed) was that if size was the key, direct elections on a national scale might be as safe as indirect ones and would at the same time give the national government the access to popular sovereignty that the state representatives boasted. Indirect elections would leave the national government with an inferior claim.

In his first thoughts about the form of the new government, expressed in letters to Washington and to Edmund Randolph, Madison had called for a house of representatives elected either directly or by the state legislatures.[17] He had not deemed direct election essential even for the representative branch. By the time the convention met, he had begun to see the light. The so-called Virginia Plan, with which Edmund Randolph startled the convention at its opening, was presumably drafted mainly by Madison, in collaboration with the other members of the Virginia delegation. In it he proposed a national government complete with executive, upper house, and judiciary—that was the most startling thing to members who had come prepared only to increase the powers of the existing Congress—and in that government he called for a popularly elected house of representatives. The other branches would be indirectly elected, the executive by the lower house and the senate also by the lower house, out of candidates nominated by the state legislatures. The composition of the lower house

41–43, 102–103; Max Farrand, ed., *The Records of the Federal Convention of 1787* (New Haven, Conn., 1911, 1937), I, 164–65; II, 27–28. And on Oct. 24, 1787, he explained to Jefferson after the convention why he thought the Constitution would fail without the federal negative on state laws. *Papers*, X, 209–14.

[17] *Papers*, IX, 370–84.

would thus be decisive, and Madison was now firmly committed to popular election for it.[18].

The Virginia Plan became the basis for discussion throughout the convention. The other members readily accepted the idea of a national government, at least tentatively, but they were much more reluctant to consider popular elections. One of the first things they took up was the election of the house of representatives, and it was at this point that various members uttered their now famous remarks about the dangers of democracy. They feared that direct elections would produce a national house of representatives with the same defects as the state assemblies. Roger Sherman of Connecticut averred that "The people . . . (immediately) should have as little to do as may be about the Government. They want information and are constantly liable to be misled."[19] Others members echoed the sentiment. But Madison now insisted that popular election of this branch was "essential to every plan of free government."[20] Though he did not say so, it was essential also to placing the national government above the states.

In the interval since the drafting of his catalogue of the political vices of the United States, Madison had evidently been thinking both about popular sovereignty and about his theory of the extended republic. In answer to the expressed fears of the other delegates about a popularly elected house, Madison now expounded the theory and held it up as "the only defence against the inconveniencies of democracy consistent with the democratic form of Government."[21] Madison may have been less confident about the validity of his own theory than he sounded, but he had finally grasped the fact that a national government with sufficient authority to challenge the state governments had to be visibly a representative government. Given the commitment of Americans to the conception of representation that had guided both their quarrel with England and their creation of state governments, they would never accept a national government that did not at least appear to provide for the same kind of representation.

Madison may have been instructed in this matter by his colleague George Mason, for it was Mason who gave the most effective answer to the proponents of indirect elections. In the existing Congress, Mason

---

[18] *Papers*, X, 12–18.

[19] Farrand, *Records* I, 48.

[20] Ibid., I, 49; *Papers*, X, 19.

[21] Farrand, *Records*, I, 134–36; *Papers*, X, 32–34.

explained, states were represented, not people, and the acts of Congress operated, insofar as they operated at all, on the states. But "the case will be changed," he said, "in the new plan of Government." The new government would operate directly on the people—that was what would make it truly a government. "The people will be represented; they ought therefore to choose the Representatives." And he went on to give the standard American meaning to representation: "The requisites in actual representation are that the Representatives should sympathize with their constituents; should think, as they think and feel as they feel; and that for these purposes should even be residents among them."[22] Later in the convention when William Paterson of New Jersey had brought forward his alternative plan of giving real powers to the existing Congress, Mason again explained why any such scheme must be unacceptable. The people had already shown their unwillingness to give real power to Congress, and rightly so because the existing Congress was not truly representative. The people would endow a national legislature with authority only if it contained their own representatives.[23]

Before the convention ended Mason would have doubts about the representative character of the government that the new Constitution provided, but he had articulated the premise on which a national government had to be built. If Madison had not seen the point before, he saw it now, and so did James Wilson and Gouverneur Morris, Madison's principal allies at the convention. Throughout the meeting they did everything possible, going beyond Mason in this respect, to rest the government directly on the people. If the national government was to have the strength to counteract the state legislatures, it would have to draw its strength where they drew theirs, from the people. Dilution of the popular base through indirect elections would be a source of weakness. Thus Wilson said, "He was for raising the federal pyramid to a considerable altitude, and for that reason wished to give it as broad a basis as possible."[24] And Madison argued "that the great fabric to be raised would be more stable and durable if it should rest on the solid foundation of the people themselves, than if it should stand merely on the pillars of the Legislatures."[25]

[22] Farrand, *Records*, I, 133–34.
[23] Ibid., I, 338–40.
[24] Ibid., I, 49.
[25] Ibid., I, 50; *Papers*, X, 19.

As the convention wore on, Madison and his friends became more and more leery of letting the national government depend in any way on the state legislatures. Where he had originally proposed indirect election of senate and executive, he shifted to favoring direct popular election here too, and he carried the most ardent nationalists in the convention with him.[26] His confidence in popular elections was not the product of any new assessment of popular wisdom. Madison's suspicion of the popularly elected state assemblies did not diminish. What he had fastened on was safety in numbers, safety in size, not merely the size of the United States as a whole, but the size of the particular constituencies in national elections. The constituencies for popular elections in the new government would have to be so large that they were bound to escape the evils accompanying direct elections in the states. While other delegates worried that popular elections would bring all the evils of the state governments to the national one, Madison became more and more convinced that size alone was crucial.

Whether Wilson and Morris reached the same conclusion on their own or were persuaded by Madison, they were ready to expound the same view almost from the beginning: "There is no danger," Wilson insisted, "of improper elections if made by *large* districts. Bad elections proceed from the smallness of the districts which give an opportunity to bad men to intrigue themselves into office."[27] And he applied this reasoning to senatorial as well as congressional elections. A popularly elected senate from large districts "would be most likely to obtain men of intelligence and uprightness."[28] Wilson and Morris also joined Madison at the end in arguing for popular election of the president on the same grounds. In Morris's words, "An election by the people at large throughout so great an extent of country could not be influenced, by those little combinations and those momentary lies which often decide popular elections within a narrow sphere."[29]

Madison and his friends did not get as broad a popular base for the government as they wanted. A familiar political combination of left and right defeated direct election for senate and executive: supporters of the existing state governments who feared so strong a national

[26] Farrand, *Records*, I, 154; II, 56–57, 109–111; *Papers*, X, 39–40, 107–8, 115–17.
[27] Farrand, *Records*, I, 133. Italics in original.
[28] Ibid., I, 154.
[29] Ibid., II, 54–56.

government combined with those who wanted to curb the state governments but feared that direct popular elections would open the national government to the same weaknesses as the states. Sometimes the same contradictory motives appeared in a single person, as in the three who refused to sign the constitution: George Mason, Edmund Randolph, and Elbridge Gerry.

But Madison had at least succeeded in securing direct election of the house of representatives. Although he himself thought the final result inadequate, mainly because it gave the national government no veto over state legislation, the provision for the house of representatives gave the government a plausible claim to the sanction of popular sovereignty on a national scale. At the same time the size of the constituencies guaranteed, if Madison's reasoning was correct, that the national legislature would be far less subject to the local limitations of representation than that of any previous republican government.

Once the convention agreed upon a national government and once the members had settled on direct election of the house, they became so occupied with other details that they scarcely considered the crucial question of the size of the house and its constituencies. The subject could appropriately have been debated, but was not, in conjunction with the long deadlock that ended in the so-called "great compromise," which produced equal representation of states in the senate and representation proportioned to population in the house. There was never any doubt that representation in the house would be proportioned to the size of the different states, either by property or by population. Debate centered on the mode of fixing the proportions. After it was agreed to key representation to population, with slaves counting as three-fifths, no one seems to have worried much about how large or small the house should be and how large or small correspondingly the constituencies of the members. There is no record of anyone suggesting a maximum size for a constituency, the only question was to set a minimum size.

This was fixed early on at forty thousand persons, along with a guesswork assignment of members (to last until the first census) to produce an initial house of sixty-five. A few attempts were made to reduce the forty-thousand minimum, but all were voted down until at the last minute Washington, in his only speech at the convention, suggested that forty thousand was too large. With his backing the convention instantly and unanimously reduced the minimum figure to thirty thousand. In other words, there must be at least thirty thousand constituents per representative. There was still nothing to prevent the Congress itself from prescribing a much larger number.[30]

The figure of thirty thousand had been talked about in the early days of the union when the Continental Congress was attempting unsuccessfully to find a basis for proportional representation, and the figure of sixty-five for the first house was apparently calculated to give the national legislature, including the twenty-six senators, the same size (ninety-one) as the Articles of Confederation allotted at a maximum to the Continental Congress.[31] Perhaps because the figures were familiar, no one worried about them. But the Continental Congress had not been a house of representatives, and it is a little surprising that no one in the convention raised the alarm over so small a representative body. It was a smaller house of representatives for the whole nation than most of the separate governments enjoyed,[32] and the constituencies were correspondingly enormous by any previous standard. For a country much larger than Great Britain in territory and with a rapidly growing population, already more than half the size of Britain's, it was less than one-eighth the size of the British House of Commons. In conjunction with the small senate and the indirect election or appointment of all government officers outside the house, it produced a government that looked decidedly aristocratic.

Madison himself had thought that sixty-five was too small a size for the house and had suggested doubling that number.[33] But he knew that he could afford that much of an increase without imperiling the virtues of size. What Madison may not have recognized, in his contempt for the state governments, was that national representatives with constituencies or 30,000, 40,000, or even more would not look much like representatives at all to those who had marched to the slogan of no taxation without representation.

Madison was not trying to put one over on the public. He was a champion of popular rights and of republican, representative government. It was his commitment to that kind of government that moved him. The state governments, he was convinced, were failing to fulfill the functions of government, failing to protect property rights and

---

[30] Ibid., II, 644. Cf. Ibid., III, 358.

[31] The figure of thirty thousand was discussed as early as June 1776. See *Conn. Courant*, June 10, 1776.

[32] Only Delaware and New Jersey had representative assemblies with fewer than sixty-five members in 1787.

[33] Farrand, *Records*, I, 568–69; *Papers*, X, 97–98.

other rights of individuals and minorities. To him, as to many others, the Philadelphia convention had seemed like a last chance for Americans to demonstrate that republican government could work. Indeed he thought it "more than probable"[34] that the fate of republican government throughout the world might depend on the success of the convention in overcoming the defects exhibited in the thirteen republics that made up the United States.

It is difficult at this time to capture the sense felt by Madison and others like him that a United States government would be contending with forces that might prove too much for it. The state governments drew their strength from the very local attachments that the national government was designed to overcome. Representatives from the large constituencies of the national government might themselves be free of such attachments, but for that reason they would lack local support in any showdown with the state assemblies.[35] Writing to Jefferson as the convention drew to a close, Madison offered the gloomy prediction that the Constitution he had done so much to shape, even if adopted, would "neither effectually answer its national object nor prevent the local mischiefs which every where excite disgusts against the state governments." The state governments with their local mischiefs would prove too strong for it.[36]

Madison's fears were genuine and not without foundation. The future of republican government did hang in the balance but in more ways than Madison yet recognized. The kind of government that he wanted and that a successful national government would bring seemed to many of his contemporaries to be more aristocratic than republican, and aristocracy had become a pejorative term in America. If he had succeeded in gaining popular election for the executive and senate,

---

[34] Farrand, *Records*, I, 423; *Papers*, X, 77.

[35] One Antifederalist ("Brutus") argued that the national government would require a standing army, because the people would not know their magistrates well enough to obey them out of confidence in them. Merrill Jensen, et al., eds., *Documentary History of the Ratification of the Constitution* (Madison, Wis., 1976–   ), XIII, 417–20. Madison thought that this argument "strikes at the foundation." *Papers*, X, 199. When other Antifederalists argued that the national government would be too powerful, Madison and Hamilton pointed out in *The Federalist* that local attachments would produce the opposite effect. *Papers*, X, 428–32, 439–40; *Federalist* 106, 308–14, 316–19.

[36] 6 Sept., 1787, *Papers*, X, 163–65. Madison explained the reasons for his pessimism more fully in a letter of 24 Oct., ibid., X, 205–19.

some of the aristocratic appearance might have been eliminated, for much of the initial popular criticism focussed on these branches. But it could not escape notice that the representative branch too would be aristocratic by virtue of the large size of its constituencies.

That, of course, was the beauty of national representation, as Madison and his friends saw it; the large constituencies would guarantee the election of the right kind of people. But the right kind for Madison was the wrong kind for those who saw representation as the means by which the local feelings and circumstances of ordinary people found expression in government. It was bad enough that a distant executive and senate would now preside over a government that reached into their daily lives; what made the innovation alarming was that the national house of representatives would be composed of the same kind of people as the executive and senatorial branches. It would not be able to fulfill the functions that Americans expected of representation.

The state legislatures consented, many of them reluctantly, to call for the elections of the popular state conventions prescribed for ratifying or rejecting the Constitution. And in every state the arguments for and against acceptance were rehearsed in the press as well as in the conventions themselves. The Constitution had no sooner been published than newspaper critics began to point out that the national house of representatives would be too small "to communicate the requisite information of the wants, local circumstances and sentiments of so extensive an empire."[37]

At the Pennsylvania ratifying convention, the first to be held, John Smilie, of Fayette County in the far western part of the state, pointed out that the senate was appropriately intended to represent the natural aristocracy of the country, but that the size of the house of representatives made inevitable that it too would represent only the natural aristocracy. The districts, he said, would be so large that ordinary people would not be acquainted with the candidates and would not even bother to attend the elections, that "only the tools of government will attend." It was no comfort to him to have James Wilson explain that "the larger the district of election the better the representation," that "It is only in remote corners of a government, that little demagogues arise," that "Nothing but real weight of character can give a

---

[37] Jensen, *Documentary History of Ratification*, II, 165; see also ibid., II, 212, 440.

man influence over a large district." Smilie was, after all, himself from a remote corner and in Wilson's eyes doubtless lacked real weight of character.[38]

In subsequent conventions in the other states the delegates rang the changes on these arguments. In Massachusetts, when the Antifederalists (those opposed to the Constitution) objected to the two-year term for representatives as too long, Theodore Sedgwick argued that it would take more than a year for a man to "divest himself of local concerns" and gain a "general knowledge of such extensive and weighty matters" as the national house would deal with.[39] Again, this divestiture of local concerns was precisely what the Antifederalists did not want from a representative, as William Heath tried to explain to Sedgwick:

It is a novel idea, that representatives should be chosen for a considerable time, in order that they may learn their duty. The representative is one who appears in behalf of, and acts for, others; he ought, therefore, to be fully acquainted with the feelings, circumstances, and interests of the persons whom he represents: and this is learnt among them, not at a distant court.[40]

In New York Melancton Smith offered the most extensive analysis of the deficiencies of the national house. The members, he said, ought to "resemble those they represent. They should be a true picture of the people, possess a knowledge of their circumstances and their wants, sympathize in all their distresses, and be disposed to seek their true interests." Since they were supposed to represent all the people, Smith conceded that they should include persons of extensive education and information, but they should also include ordinary persons, especially farmers, middling people, the substantial yeomanry of the country, who "are more temperate, of better morals, and less ambition than the great." Such people, he believed, would never find their way into the house of representatives as proposed. The numbers of the house were so small that the office would be "highly elevated and distinguished." The members would live in a style that ordinary people could not support. And in the large districts of 30,000 or 40,000 persons "There will be scarcely a chance of their [the voters'] uniting in any other but some great man, unless in some popular demagogue,

---

[38] Ibid., II, 465–66, 489.

[39] Jonathan Elliot, ed., *The Debates in the Several State Conventions, on the Adoption of the Federal Constitution* (Philadelphia, 1863 91), II, 4.

[40] Ibid., II, 13. But Heath in the end voted for ratification.

who will probably be destitute of principle. A substantial yeoman, of sense and discernment, will hardly ever be chosen." What Smith wanted was not to exclude the natural aristocrats but to balance them "with a sufficient number of the middling class to control them." The house ought to "combine the abilities and honesty of the community, a proper degree of information, and a disposition to pursue the public good." This could not be done in so small a house as the Constitution provided.[41]

In Virginia George Mason was less conciliatory than Smith. Mason had stood up for a popularly elected house of representatives at Philadelphia but later decided that national representatives, however elected, could not fulfill the functions Americans expected of representatives. He refused to sign the Constitution and joined Patrick Henry to oppose its adoption in Virginia. Using the same words he had employed at Philadelphia in support of the house, he now repeated the usual aphorism (first uttered by John Adams in 1776) that representatives "ought to mix with the people, think as they think, feel as they feel,— ought to be perfectly amenable to them, and thoroughly acquainted with their interest and condition." It would be impossible, he concluded, to have a national house of representatives with small enough constituencies to fit the description. To do so would result in a house so large that it "would be too expensive and unwieldy." It was in the very nature of the national government that it could not be truly representative, and it was therefore dangerous to assign such large powers to it as the Constitution proposed.[42] Patrick Henry supported this view. Representation in the national government, he said, would be merely nominal. It would be the same virtual representation that England had offered the colonies.[43] And in South Carolina Rawlins Lowndes, another old revolutionary patriot, felt the same way. Representation in the national government, he said, "would be merely virtual, similar to what we were allowed in England. . . . We were then told that we were represented in Parliament: and this would, in the event, prove just such another."[44]

The Federalists, in answering these charges, maintained that the kind of representation the Antifederalists wanted was already ade-

[41] Ibid., II, 243–51.
[42] Ibid., III, 29–34.
[43] Ibid., III, 320–24.
[44] Ibid., IV, 288.

quately provided in the state governments. They made a point of insisting, as Madison firmly believed, that there was no danger of the national government swallowing up the states, precisely because the people would be more attached to their familiar, local representatives in the state legislatures than they would be to their more remote national representatives.[45] But for this very reason the Antifederalists could argue that the national representatives ought not to have powers of taxation except when the states failed to comply with requisitions. If Congress had the power to tax without reference to the state assemblies, Mason argued, "the taxes will be laid by those who have no fellow-feeling or acquaintance with the people." The colonists had rejected taxation by virtual representatives, and independent Americans should do no less.[46]

The Antifederalists were playing on a chord that had resounded throughout the country since 1765. Representative government on a national scale deprived representation of the meaning that Americans had always attached to it. But in attacking the proposed Constitution, the Antifederalists found themselves in the position of attacking popular sovereignty and of defending the independent authority of the state governments and of the existing Continental Congress. The awkwardness of their position had become apparent at the outset, when the Pennsylvania assembly took up the question of calling the state ratifying convention. The Federalists, having obtained a copy of the Constitution before it was formally communicated to the states by Congress, pressed at once for a ratifying convention. Samuel Findley, who was to be Pennsylvania's most effective opponent of the Constitution, at once insisted that the state could not act until Congress recommended it, because the state was bound by the Articles of Confederation. He was answered at once that the Constitution was to be an act of the sovereign people, who had every right to change their government whenever they pleased: "What have the Congress and the

[45] The point was made in the New York ratifying convention by Alexander Hamilton and in the Virginia convention by Wilson Cary Nicholas, ibid., II, 304–5, 354–55; III, 18.

[46] Ibid., III, 29–34. This was probably the most pervasive Antifederalist objection to the Constitution. See ibid., II, 73, 217, 331; III, 56–57, 167, 320; IV, 76; Storing, *Complete Anti-Federalist*, II, 17–18, 112, 119, 142, 233–36, 239–43, 265–69, 275–78, 284, 336–38, 380–82; III, 41–42, 133, 158–59; IV, 27–28, 77; V, 89–91, 141–42, 192–94.

legislatures to do with the proposed Constitution? Nothing, sir, they are but the mere vehicles to convey the information to the people."[47]

The Antifederalists were forced by this line of argument to maintain that the people of the several states had left the state of nature and had by compacts delegated their powers to the state governments and to Congress and could not retrieve them at will. The Federalists could then pose as champions of the people's superiority to their governments. The power of the people, they said, was "paramount to every constitution, inalienable in its nature, and indefinite in its extent." "How comes it," they asked, "that these state governments dictate to their superiors, to the majesty of the people?"[48] They could even deny that government rested on any compact, because the people's power could not be limited by compacts. "The truth is," James Wilson proclaimed, "that in our governments, the supreme, absolute, and uncontrollable power *remains* in the people. As our constitutions are superior to our legislatures; so the people are superior to our constitutions."[49]

Not only did the Federalists enjoy the advantage of supporting an uncontrolled constituent power in the people, they also could show a much more direct participation of the people in the proposed government than in the existing Congress. The wisdom now became apparent of the strategy pursued by Madison and Wilson at the convention in arguing for direct popular elections. Though they had not succeeded in securing them for senate and executive, popular elections for the house of representatives, despite the large constituencies, gave to the new national government a popular base that was missing in the Continental Congress. While the Antifederalists had to defend the adequacy of an indirectly elected Congress, the Federalists could point out that "THE PEOPLE of the United States are not as such represented in the present Congress; and considered even as the component parts of the several states, they are not represented in proportion to their numbers and importance."[50]

When the Antifederalists complained that the convention had exceeded its powers, the answer was the same. Patrick Henry made the mistake of demanding what right the convention had to speak in

[47] Jensen, *Documentary History of Ratification*, II, 81–85, 89.

[48] Ibid., II, 349, 449.

[49] Ibid., II, 361.

[50] Ibid., II, 474.

the preamble of "We the people," instead of "We the states."[51] The answer was easy: the convention spoke of "We the people" because it recognized the superiority of the people to the states.

The Antifederalists were not prepared to challenge Madison's crucial invention: they did not deny that there could be an American people as opposed to the peoples of the several states. But the Federalists' insistence on the new fiction did lead the Antifederalists to a healthy insistence on the ultimate fictitiousness of popular sovereignty itself. It might be the best fiction on which to rest government, a fiction that no one wished at this point to challenge, but it had to be recognized as a fiction. In the interests of sanity and self-preservation the people who submitted to a government of their own supposed creation had to remember that government is always something other than the actual people who are governed by it, that governors and governed cannot be in fact identical. The many should therefore take safeguards against the few who wield the powers of government in their name. The Constitution provided some of those safeguards but not enough against those who would be wielding the powers of a national government in the name of a supreme American people, a people even less capable of speaking for themselves than the people of the several states. Most of the state constitutions had recognized the fictional quality of popular sovereignty by Bills of Rights, in which the people barred their governments from impinging on various rights reserved to themselves. In the new federal Constitution such a reservation was conspicuously missing.

The omission was in part simply an oversight on the part of the Philadelphia convention. The members had been preoccupied with curbing the runaway state governments and with giving strength to the national government rather than setting limits on it. By the time the subject was brought up, everyone was impatient to go home. But the omission was also a result of many members taking their own fiction too literally or of not thinking through the implications that earlier thinkers had disclosed in the fiction.

The failure was even more pronounced in Federalist defenses of the finished Constitution. A Bill of Rights, the Federalists maintained, was a proper accompaniment of the old fiction of the divine right of kings: it was a concession by a supreme king to his subjects.

---

[51] Elliot, *Debates*, III, 22.

But if subjects and rulers were the same, if government was by the people, it was a contradiction in terms for them to make concessions to themselves. As one Federalist put it, "Why then should the people by a bill of rights convey or grant to *themselves* what was their own inherent and natural right?"[52] Benjamin Rush was beside himself with the very idea of such a contradiction:

> Would it not be absurd to frame a formal declaration that our natural rights are acquired from ourselves, and would it not be a more ridiculous solecism to say, that they are the gift of those rulers whom we have created, and who are invested by us with every power they possess? Sir, I consider it as an honor to the late Convention that this system has not been disgraced with a bill of rights; though I mean not to blame or reflect upon those states which have encumbered their constitutions with that idle and superfluous instrument.[53]

Conversely, since it was "We the People" who conveyed specific powers to the national government, Federalists could argue that the whole Constitution was "nothing more than a bill of rights—a declaration of the people in what manner they choose to be governed."[54] According to James Wilson, the "single sentence in the Preamble is tantamount to a volume and contains the essence of all the bills of rights that have been or can be devised."[55]

There was some basis in historical fact for the Federalist argument. Magna Carta, the Petition of Right of 1628, and even the Bill of Rights of 1689 had been wrung from reluctant monarchs who may have regarded them as concessions. But the men who drafted them regarded them as statements of right, with the implication that the king who violated them ceased, in doing so, to be God's lieutenant, or that he broke some sort of contract with his subjects. With the advent of popular sovereignty, as the Federalists argued the case, neither concession nor contract was possible because people and government were one and the same. But the evil consequences of so literal an application of the fiction had become clear long before 1787. If Magna Carta and the Petition of Right and the Bill of Rights stated what was

---

[52] Jensen, *Documentary History* II, 421.

[53] Ibid., II, 434.

[54] Ibid., II, 387.

[55] Ibid., II, 383–84.

right, violation of them would be as wrong by the people or their government as by a king.

As in so many ways the Royalists and the Levellers of the 1640s had been the first to probe the fictional qualities of popular sovereignty and to insist on limits to what the people's representatives could of right do. The Royalists had insisted that the people could not convey powers they did not have; and the Levellers, while admitting that the people had many powers to convey, had singled out at least one that they did not have and so could not convey, namely the power to prescribe religious belief and practice. Subsequent thinkers had pondered the question of natural rights inherent in the individual, some of which were conveyed to government while others were inalienable or reserved. Even within the dimensions of the fiction, the idea remained of a contract, first among individuals to form a community and then between that community and the persons whom it designated to govern. What the Antifederalists now insisted on, in demanding a national Bill of Rights, was that the Constitution spell out all the terms of such a contract. Unless it included specific prohibitions to protect reserved or inalienable rights, there would be no way either for individuals or for the community to hold the governing body to respect them. " 'You have exceeded the powers of your office, you have oppressed us' will be the language of the suffering citizens. The answer of the government will be short: 'We have not exceeded our power; you have no test by which you can prove it.' "[56]

The Antifederalists were right. Government and people could not be the same. Though there might be no effective way for the people to act except through their representative governors, the fiction itself assumed the possibility of such action; the Federalists themselves assumed it in treating the Constitution as the act of the people. James Wilson assumed it in arguing that the people, through the Constitution, simply endowed their governors as trustees, whose powers they could withdraw or alter at will. Whether governors were trustees or contractors, it was proper that the terms of the trust or contract should state what the government could not do as well as what it could do. And the Antifederalists were quick to point out that the Constitution did place several prohibitions on the federal government (in article 1, section 9). Why not then all the prohibitions that were usual in a Bill

[56] Ibid., II, 392; Storing, *Complete Anti-Federalist*, II, 372–77; V, 9–16.

of Rights?[57] In the end Madison himself undertook to draft a Bill of Rights and shepherded it through the House of Representatives as the first ten amendments to the Constitution.

Madison was quite willing to make such a concession, however anomalous he may have thought it in theory,[58] for with the adoption of the Constitution his crucial invention of a sovereign American people found realization. How ready Americans were for it may be seen in the almost immediate acceptance of the new national government as a legitimate expression of popular authority. It was only a year or two before the policies of the government became the subject of intense controversy, with Madison himself leading the opposition. But the opposition addressed the policies themselves, not the validity of representative government on a national scale.

The acceptance of national representation is the more remarkable because what initiated the opposition was Alexander Hamilton's fiscal program, which had the effect of requiring the national government to engage in heavier taxation than many, perhaps most, Americans thought necessary. Taxation was the function of government most closely linked to representation, and the Antifederalists in the ratifying conventions of state after state had objected to giving it to a government where local representation was so lacking.[59] But in the lengthy congressional debates of 1790 and in the newspaper and pamphlet attacks on the Hamiltonian program and on the taxation it would require, there was scarcely a mention of the deficiencies of national representation. The most strenuous opposition was to the national assumption of the state debts, but it was mainly addressed to the inequities in the way assumption would affect the different states, not to the fact that state representatives were better qualified than national representatives to levy the necessary taxes.[60]

The question of representation did come up when Congress con-

[57] Jensen, *Documentary History* II, 391–92; Storing, *Complete Anti-Federalist*, II, 323–30; VI, 11.

[58] To Jefferson, 17 Oct. 1788, *Papers*, XI, 297–300.

[59] See above note 46.

[60] The only significant exception to this statement I have found is in *The Freeman's Journal or the North American Intelligencer*, Feb. 3, 1790, in which an unsigned article opposed assumption on the ground that the states were better qualified than the national government to levy taxes, because, knowing local circumstances, they could do it "in such a way as that the people shall feel it less, and be better able to bear it."

sidered the apportionment of it. Since the Constitution set only a minimum size for constituencies, there was considerable discussion—repeated after every decennial census—of the advantage of the smallest possible electoral districts in order that representatives be familiar with their constituents and conversely of the advantage of large districts in bringing men of stature and ability into the government. But in these discussions there was no suggestion that the minimum size fixed by the constitution was too large for representation to work at all.[61] Madison's scheme stuck.

And he was stuck with it. In the attack on Hamilton's program he and his friend Jefferson focussed on its aristocratic tendencies, the tendencies that Antifederalists had predicted in the extension of representative government over so large a territory as the United States. The question of aristocracy, of the few governing the many, had lain beneath representation from the beginning. In a sense, representation had always been a fiction designed to secure popular consent to a governing aristocracy. Neither Madison nor Jefferson, despite their subscription to the developing creed of human equality, had ever been against the natural aristocracy which the Antifederalists had feared would control the national government. It was right and good that the people of any district, of whatever size, should choose men of demonstrated merit and position to govern. But Hamilton's program seemed designed not to secure consent to this natural aristocracy but to create a new and unnatural one, an aristocracy of speculators and financiers.

In the eyes of Madison and Jefferson and most other devotees of republican government this was to invert the proper order of things, as it had been inverted (in the eyes of England's Country party) in eighteenth-century England. In thinking about the advantages of a large republic for overcoming the deficiencies of representation, Madison had avoided the question of aristocracy. He had invented a sovereign people, but he had assumed an existing social structure in which the people would know and recognize and defer to their natural leaders. But except during the revolutionary war, Americans had experienced and granted this deference, as they had experienced representation, only on a local level. The aristocracy that Hamilton was creating was on a national level, an aristocracy beholden to the national government. The success of his program posed a challenge

---

[61] *Annals of Congress,* I, 719–28; II, 173–210, 243–51, 254–74, 331–36, 403–18, 473–83, 540–50; VII, 325–404.

and raised a question: What sort of aristocracy was natural in an extended republic?

Or, put another way, how ought political leadership to operate on a national level? How were the sovereign people of the United States to be led? Was there to be an unnamed national aristocracy as there had been unnamed local aristocracies? Was there a difference between aristocracy and leadership?

From Deference to Leadership

UME MARVELLED at the ease with which the few were able to
govern the many and attributed it to opinion. We have
examined some of the opinions that sustained government
in the seventeenth and eighteenth centuries, but we have
only touched obliquely on one that accompanied the others, a fiction
whose glaring contrast to fact has made it a potent instrument of change.
The idea of equality, that human beings are all in some way equal to
one another—that they are created equal or will be equal or ought to
be—is older than popular sovereignty. It lies at the heart of most religions, offering consolation in another world for the indignities suffered in this. It was present, as we have seen, in the political fiction
that preceded sovereignty of the people: though the king was exalted
by divine right as God's lieutenant, all others must be equal in their
subjection to him. With the coming of popular sovereignty the idea of
equality assumed a larger, if unintended and at first latent, significance. It was an essential ingredient in the new configuration of fictions, but its implications were scarcely dreamed of by those who first
invoked it.

When the members of Parliament, in their quarrel with the king,
substituted popular sovereignty for divine right, it was to bring the
king too down to a level where they could contend with him as equal
recipients of a primeval power. The sovereignty of the people assumed
the existence of a state of nature in which there were no kings but all
men were equal in whatever powers nature or nature's God conferred
on men. The Parliamentarians had no intention of suggesting that all

remained equal, but rather that they had willingly given up their natural, inherent, divinely conferred powers (or most of them) to a government in which Parliament shared authority with the king. As the
quarrel progressed, Parliament claimed a larger and larger share of
that authority and then claimed it all, the members of the House of
Commons exalting themselves as they had once exalted the king.

The gentlemen saw no contradiction in thus elevating themselves
on a popular foundation. The equality associated with popular sovereignty was supposed to have existed as fact in a time too remote to
have left a record. Current inequalities could thus be explained as the
product of subsequent transactions, also unrecorded, beginning with
the original surrender of political powers and privileges by the many
to the few. But popular sovereignty, like other political fictions, found
expression most often in disputes among the few over the possession
of the powers and privileges allegedly surrendered. When such disputes grew heated, one side or the other was likely to argue that powers surrendered could be recalled (at least from one's opponents), that
the people of today could undo what was done by the people of yesterday. The fiction required that the people be supposed capable of
acting as they had acted in the "original contract." If that was the case,
it had also to be supposed that they could act now too, as equals.

It was a necessary but disconcerting supposition to those who called
on popular sovereignty only to promote their own superiority. In the
disputes of the 1640s in England the Royalists were quick to seize
upon it in order to embarrass their opponents. If the House of Commons claimed powers from the people, the Royalists argued, then they
would have to show that *all* the people, every man, woman and child,
had participated in granting it. The Royalists knew well enough that
the members of the House of Commons would not relish submitting
themselves to such an improbable donation. Even in the Convention
of 1689 that conferred the crown on William, Tories argued against
any alteration in the form of government unless women, children, and
men unqualified to vote for Parliament joined regular voters in dele-
gating powers to the members. The Tories could safely urge the need
of such a delegation because they knew it would be not only unacceptable to their opponents but impossible to achieve. The argument,
moreover, was successful, as we have seen, in that the Convention
picked its way through the verbiage of popular sovereignty with great
care to avoid any implication that they were returning to a state of
nature, in which it would have to be presumed that people were equal.

Popular sovereignty would have have held no charm for its inventors if the equality it implied had required the literal application that the Royalists and Tories suggested. Nor did the Americans who launched the quarrel with England anticipate or advocate anything quite that literal. But the prospect of returning to a state of nature was not as alarming to them as it had been to the English Parliament, and the very nature of their contest with the mother country emphasized the egalitarian implications of popular sovereignty. In the initial stage of the contest they asked for nothing more than the rights of Englishmen. They were Englishmen and equal to the king's subjects in England. What they objected to was that they were not being treated as equals, not taxed only by consent of their representatives, not tried by juries of their neighbors in cases where they would have been if resident in England. "Britons," the Boston town meeting declared, "have been as free on one side of the Atlantic as on the other." They were now, said John Adams, "degraded below the rank of an Englishman" by laws that constituted "A Repeal of Magna Charta, as far as America is concerned."[1]

As the quarrel progressed, it became apparent that Americans could retain the rights of Englishmen only by casting off the authority both of England's Parliament and of England's king. And to do so they must recur to the fundamental principles of popular sovereignty. They must recur, if not to a state of nature, in which all must be equal, at least to the condition prevailing immediately after the state of nature, that is, to the community or society that a contract among individuals supposedly produced just prior to their creation of government.

If the members of such a society without government were not equal, they would have to have been pretty close to it. When Jefferson in the Declaration of Independence described as self-evident the process by which people created governments, he did not emphasize whatever inequalities might already have come into existence among them: they were all created equal. From Jefferson's later writing it is apparent that he did not think the Declaration returned Americans to a state of nature, and thus of complete equality;[2] and most of the governments they constructed immediately after the Declaration in fact followed the old boundaries that had defined the jurisdiction of

[1] David S. Lovejoy, "Rights Imply Equality: The Case Against Admiralty Jurisdiction in America 1764–1776," *William and Mary Quarterly* 16 (1959), 459–84. Quotations at pp. 473, 481.

[2] Jefferson discussed the question at some length in a letter to Edmund Randolph, Feb. 15, 1783, *Papers*, Boyd ed., VI, 247–48.

the several colonial governments, thus implying the continuation of the old communities with their existing social structures. But it was not wholly illogical for the people, say, who lived on the northern reaches of the Connecticut River, and who did not wish to submit to the government of the independent state of New Hampshire, to argue that they, at least, were in a state of nature and propose to form a distinct society with its own government, equal to that of New Hampshire or any other state.[3] If Americans did not all think themselves to be in a state of nature most of them probably did think they were only a step removed from it and from the equality that went with it.

More significant for the future was the choice of governments that the various state communities, (acting through elected provincial congresses that looked very much like the old colonial assemblies) made for themselves. Although there was nothing in the Declaration of Independence that condemned monarchy as such, no state seriously considered establishing a monarchical government. There never seems to have been any question that an independent America would be a republic or a series of republics. The ideas of the seventeenth-century English republicans had retained a popularity there that they did not enjoy in England. Americans revered Harrington and Sidney as much as John Hampden, and they remembered and adopted Harrington's insistence both that a general equality of property was necessary to republican government and that republican government was the only form suited to a society where such an equality prevailed. As they looked about them it seemed not only that they had just such a situation but that they ought to preserve it. "We may as well think," one Connecticut politician proclaimed, "to repeal the great laws of attraction and gravitation, as to think of continuing a popular government without a good degree of equality among the people as to their property."[4] And nearly everyone agreed that a popular, that is, republican, government was the right kind for Americans.

Republican government did not necessarily mean a government in which one person was considered as capable of governing as another. Although Harrington would have forbidden the accumulation of huge estates, whose owners would threaten the stability of his republic, he was no enemy to aristocracy. His government would have left the

[3] Thad W. Tate, "The Social Contract in America, 1774–1787: Revolutionary Theory as a Conservative Instrument," *William and Mary Quarterly,* 22 (1965), 375–91.

[4] E. S. Morgan, *The Gentle Puritan: A Life of Ezra Stiles* (New Haven, Conn., 1962; New York, 1982), 344.

formulation of all legislation to a senate composed of what Americans called the better sort. And the architects of the new American republics and of the greater republic created in 1789 still expected the voters to choose the better sort to govern them. They reckoned without the transformations that had occurred in American society from the founding of the colonies by seventeenth-century Englishmen to the conclusion of a revolutionary war. By 1789, although Americans still spoke of a better sort, what constituted membership in it and what the privileges and prerogatives of membership might be had become increasingly uncertain, especially in the preceding decades.

Popular sovereignty had been successfully directed for more than a century to support the beneficiaries of England's social hierarchy and of America's attenuated version of it. But there was nothing in the doctrine itself or in the accompanying paraphernalia of elections, instructions, petitions, and associations to require the assignment of popular powers to one set of men or women rather than another. While making it possible for the few to govern the many, popular sovereignty offered, in itself, no prescription for restricting membership in the few to the sort of people who had traditionally expected it. In England such a restriction proved easy to maintain, because long-term habits of deference and the reinforcement of them in reaction to the turmoil of the 1640s and 1650s tended to suppress the egalitarian implications of popular sovereignty. Even during the interregnum, despite the proliferation of levelling proposals, the continuing concentration of wealth and of the economic and social advantages conveyed by wealth dampened aspirations for political office by persons who lacked those advantages. But in American the concentration was much less marked and the advantages correspondingly fewer. In America, much sooner than in England and even before the Revolution, the implications of equality carried by popular sovereignty began to reform, that is, to make fundamental changes in, social and political life. And the first great reformation was the separation of political preeminence from social status. Even in America the separation took place only gradually, but we can observe its beginnings in a variety of circumstances and phenomena before, during, and after the Revolution, that drained the meaning from talk of the better sort and disappointed the expectations of James Madison and his friends at Philadelphia.

The most important circumstance fostering the division of political authority from social rank was the uncertain and amorphous character of social rank itself. The social distance separating the "better sort" from the "lower sort" in America had always seemed less than their respective economic circumstances would have suggested because of the prevalence of a Protestant ethic that frowned on conspicuous consumption and paid homage to the dignity of work. The rich and the poor tended to look and act more alike than they did in England. In the southern colonies, where the Protestant ethic was less in evidence (though by no means absent), and where the economic gulf between rich and poor was probably wider than elsewhere, the presence of an underclass of black slaves brought wealthy planter and poor farmer together in a common pride in being both white and free.[5] In America, moreover, the comparatively easy access to land tended to blur the social distinctions that in England depended heavily on land ownership. The possession of large landed estates was the hallmark of social superiority and influence in England. In America land was so abundant and available that it lost much of its social significance. Mere wealth became correspondingly more significant, but American wealth, embodied in credit and personal possessions (or even in land held for speculation), was apt to be here today and gone tomorrow, along with the social prestige attached to it. By the same token, the accumulation of wealth could be more rapid, economic opportunity greater, and admission to the ranks of the better sort more open.[6]

The revolutionary war served to heighten the transitory character of great fortunes and of the social prestige attached to them. In the northern colonies wealth had been concentrated among merchants, and they had gained it mainly by trading within the patterns allowed by the British government.[7] With the coming of the war and the subsequent closing of British imperial ports to American vessels, most American merchants had to make their way in an unfamiliar world where the old rules offered no guidance. Older mercantile firms were often unable to work out new and profitable trade routes, and their places were taken by newer, upstart houses with less to lose and with

[5] I have discussed this relationship in *American Slavery American Freedom: The Ordeal of Colonial Virginia* (New York, 197), 293–387. On the Protestant ethic in the South see "The Puritan Ethic and the American Revolution," *William and Mary Quarterly* 24 (1967), 3–43, and C. Vann Woodward, "The Southern Ethic in a Puritan World," ibid., 25 (1968), 343–70.

[6] Jackson T. Main, *The Social Structure of Revolutionary America* (Princeton, N.J., 1965).

[7] There may have been smuggling, but it is highly probable that most trade was conducted within the limits allowed by the British Navigation Acts.

more daring.[8] In the southern colonies (where great planters were also often merchants) the war shut off British markets for tobacco, the principal American export, and before new ones could be found, many plantations lay in ruins.[9]

As the war closed familiar sources of profit and opened new ones, the economic strain of fighting it upset the distribution of wealth in another way. War has always been the most expensive undertaking that a government can engage in. Few governments have been able to support it on a pay-as-you-go-basis. The new American governments came into existence already engaged in war, a war they had undertaken in order to protect their property from British attempts to tax them. They were consequently reluctant to alienate their supporters by levying much larger taxes than Britain had ever proposed. And although they created a Continental Congress and a Continental army to conduct the war, they carefully refrained from giving the Congress any power to tax at all. In lieu of taxation, Americans borrowed a little from the French, but mostly they borrowed from themselves in a manner that virtually guaranteed economic turmoil. Not only the state governments but the Continental Congress too paid their bills by printing money.[10]

For a brief period the paper was accepted at face value, but by 1781 Continental currency was discounted at a rate of more than 100 to 1.[11] The inflation was fed not only by reluctance to tax but by wartime shortages. The war diverted a substantial portion of the work force from producing food or manufactures to service in the militia or the Continental army. The army itself was swallowing up a huge portion of available supplies, as an army always does. Imports from England had of course been cut off, and France was unable to supply the commodities or the credit to take their place. As a result the supply of all goods fell far short of the demand.

Runaway inflation, in which money loses virtually all its value, is

[8] Robert A. East, *Business Enterprise in the American Revolutionary Era* (New York, 1938), 213–38, argues that the number of the older houses that failed during the war has been exaggerated but acknowledges the rise of a "small but vigorous set of newcomers."

[9] Myra L. Rich, "The Experimental Years: Virginia 1781–1789" (Ph.D. dissertation, Yale University, 1966).

[10] E. James Ferguson, *The Power of the Purse: A History of Public Finance, 1776–1790* (Chapel Hill, N.C., 1961); Clarence L. Ver Steeg, *Robert Morris: Revolutionary Financier* (Philadelphia, 1954).

[11] Ferguson, *Power of the Purse*, 32.

a drastic, speedy, and capricious way of redistributing wealth, a concealed mode of taxation that can bankrupt some and enrich others. The precise effects are difficult to calculate, and no one has calculated them for the inflation of this period. But no calculation is needed to ascertain that it greatly accelerated the rapid transfers of wealth already so characteristic of American society.

Wealth remained a prime qualification for entry into the better sort, and the time lag between its acquisition and the arrival of the prestige that adhered to it was probably shortened. But in the turbulent American world social prestige was itself becoming more volatile and the better sort a more uncertain category. As the outlines of it became more blurred, the presumption that political authority should be conferred on its members was correspondingly weakened.

The vulnerability of the presumption was made more apparent in two phenomena experienced by eighteenth-century Americans, the one in the church, the other in the military. Traditionally both the ministry of the church and the command of the military fell to the better sort. By the end of the century Americans had witnessed the exercise of both ecclesiastical and military office by persons whose social credentials seemed to be irrelevant. A look at these two phenomena, though it will take us backward in time, may illuminate the way in which social rank was also losing its political prerogatives.

The ecclesiastical development is most readily observed in New England, where the churches had operated from the beginning as independent spiritual republics. Each church gathered itself from the "visible saints" of a neighborhood, who covenanted together in a kind of social contract, agreeing to "walk together" in the worship of God. Having thus become a church, they chose a minister or ministers to instruct them and to conduct their services. Although chosen in this popular manner, the minister was held to receive his powers from God himself. His position was a revered one and mere piety was not considered a sufficient qualification for holding it.[12] A minister had to be learned, with an erudition not to be found outside the ranks of college graduates, and college graduates, almost by definition, belonged to the better sort. As in the state, office itself conveyed authority, but

[12] The discussion in this and the succeeding paragraphs is based on works too numerous to cite, including especially those by Perry Miller, David Hall, and Robert Middlekauff.

the recipient was expected to bolster that authority by his own social position.

New Englanders were proud of their churches, which they believed to conform more closely than any others to those described in the New Testament. But they had neglected a crucial element. They composed their churches of persons who had already experienced the "conversion" which assured them of their predestined election to eternal salvation. New England ministers preached to the converted, helping them to grow in a faith already possessed. The first churches did not lack for a supply of converts, but the original members had experienced their conversion in England, where church membership was not merely open to all but required of all who did not forfeit it by palpable and open wickedness. As the number of visible saints made in England grew old and died off, their children did not experience conversion in sufficient numbers to supply the churches of New England with members. The result was a chronic ecclesiastical crisis that by the opening of the eighteenth century was altering the character not only of the churches but of the ministerial office and the persons who held it. Everyone lamented the seeming decline in piety that threatened to leave the churches without converted members, and more and more ministers bent their efforts toward winning converts, with sermons addressed as much to the emotions as the reason.

With the arrival of the English preacher, George Whitefield, in 1740, the evangelical impulse reached high tide. Whitefield toured the colonies from Georgia to New England, perfecting the emotional appeal of his sermons as he went, dramatizing the torments of the damned and the bliss of the saved. Under the impact of his preaching thousands were converted in a contagion of ecstasy, known to historians as the Great Awakening. And he was followed by a horde of imitators, both self-appointed prophets and ordained ministers who deserted their own congregations to bring the message of salvation to those who had missed it in the ministrations of their own chosen pastors.[13]

Where the local minister welcomed the itinerants and perhaps altered his own preaching to conform to the new mode, he might be rewarded by a revitalized church. Where he opposed the itinerant as a religious fraud and demagogue, as was often the case, he might find his church

[13] No general history of the Great Awakening is yet available, but see Edwin L. Gaustad, *The Great Awakening in New England* (New York, 1957); C. C. Goen, *Revivalism and Separatism in New England* (New Haven, Conn., 1962); David S. Lovejoy, *Religious Enthusiasm in the New World* (New York, 1985), 178–214.

split in two. If the recently awakened "New Lights" constituted a majority, they could dismiss him, and he would be left to gather those faithful to him into a new church. If the New Lights were a minority, they might secede to form a new church themselves. In either case there were likely to be two churches where one stood before, competing with each other for members and for the taxes that New England governments collected in support of the church.

The competition, moreover, was not confined to the congregational churches that the founders of New England had designed. Long before the Great Awakening, New England had been invaded by Quakers, among whom self-appointed itinerant evangelists were numerous. New England Congregationalism had itself spawned a number of Baptist churches, whose strict standards of membership appealed to New Lights. And even the Anglican Church had been competing successfully for members in New England, ever since the rector and several tutors of Yale College had converted themselves to Anglicanism in 1722. With that stunning event the Anglican Society for Propagation of the Gospel had turned its efforts from the Indians to the Puritans. Those efforts bore fruit when the ecclesiastical quarrels arising from the Great Awakening induced many former Congregationalists to say a plague on both your houses and join the Church of England.

The multiplication of denominations in New England left the Congregationalists still a majority, but the minority of other sects was large enough, combined with pressure from England, to persuade New England governments to alter the tax laws that supported only the Congregational church. Hitherto all the families in a New England town had been taxed for the benefit of the Congregational minister, whether they were members of his church or not. Now anyone could shift his payments to a Protestant church of his own choice (provided such a church was locally available). Thus a crucial economic advantage not previously available accrued to a church whose minister's preaching attracted members; and the evangelical orientation of the ministry, of whatever denomination or theological persuasion, gained an economic incentive.

The outcome of these developments was an unacknowledged popularity contest among ministers and a profound change in the character of religious leadership. No longer did the minister's position depend so heavily on his erudition. No longer did his congregation look to him primarily for instruction in theology. What counted now was his ability to affect people. If they could be affected by instruction, well and good, but what mattered was his ability to move them, and that ability might have little to do with his learning or with the social status that went with it.

This is not to say that the New Lights or others who fell into the new mood were overtly anti-intellectual. Jonathan Edwards, the great defender of the Awakening, was himself as learned as any New England minister had ever been and the most creative theologian America has produced. But the net effect of the Awakening and of Edwards's own theology was to give to reason and intellect a lesser role in religion than had hitherto been the case. It was not a Jonathan Edwards but a George Whitefield who enjoyed the greatest success in the Awakening, and Whitefield was no theologian and no thinker. Whitefield was simply the first of a long line of religious leaders—minister is not quite the right word for Whitefield or for Charles Finney or Dwight Moody or Billy Sunday or Billy Graham—who were distinguished mainly by their personal charisma, by their ability to win the passionate adulation of large numbers of people. Whitefield was the first American religious hero, a kind of substitute saint for Protestants. And his success made him a model for ministers to emulate.

With the rise of religious heroes like Whitefield, the old insignia of authority and social status attached to the ministry began to fall away. The willingness to defer to a learned minister was weakened when learning ceased to be the most important qualification for a minister. And the minister's status in the community seemed less important when so many persons had experienced the greatest inspiration of their lives under the ministrations of an itinerant who had no standing in the community at all. Many of the itinerants had no standing in any community, coming as many did from the ranks of farmers and artisans. A minister who could play the role of religious hero might enjoy more respect, more prestige—one may even say more authority—than the old-fashioned one had gained from his office and from the deference owing to his social position. But it was a different kind of respect, a different kind of prestige, a different kind of authority.

With the new style of religious leadership went a new attitude and new expectations among those who followed, a shift in the political mood of congregations. Before the Great Awakening it had been only the most daring who ventured to leave the pastor of the local Congregational church for the unfamiliar attractions of the Quakers or Baptists or Anglicans. But when a large portion of a congregation underwent the excitement of conversion, they came out of it with a determination to cling to what they had gained. If that required dismissing their pastor or forming a new church of their own, so be it. They were certain that they were acting in a holy cause, and once they had ousted or deserted one minister and chosen another, they might continue to take a more active role than hitherto in running the church. In New England churches the congregations had always been sovereign, with power to choose and dismiss ministers. They were now much more ready to exercise their powers. They had been, in an ecclesiastical sense, politicized.

What happened in New England was only more dramatic than in the other colonies. In most of them the multiplication of denominations had proceeded, not by heresies and divisions within a single church, but by immigration of peoples with varying ethnic and religious backgrounds: Scots-Irish Presbyterians, German Lutherans and Mennonites, Dutch Reformed, English Catholics, Anglicans, and Methodists. In some colonies the Anglicans enjoyed a favored status, like the Congregationalists in New England, but in most of them no denomination enjoyed a majority, and all competed both for communicants and for government support. In all of them too the character of the ministry was undergoing the same transformation under the pressure of the evangelically oriented preachers of the newer sects, who generally lacked the social standing of the Anglican establishment.

The effect of the Revolution on these developments, both in New England and elsewhere, was to intensify them. Wherever the Anglican Church enjoyed tax advantages, it lost them. Although Congregationalists continued to enjoy a somewhat privileged status in Connecticut until 1818 and in Massachusetts until 1833, elsewhere all denominations were left to compete for members on an equal footing. Support of the church was left to the voluntary contributions that a minister was able to elicit from his followers. Social prestige may have contributed in many cases to a man's ability to win followers, but it was that ability, whatever its source, that counted. Social status and ecclesiastical office were effectually separated if not quite divorced.

How the separation may have contributed to a similar separation in the political world is difficult to assess. The withdrawal of state support for religion was itself a matter of heated political controversy

in many states, and it seems altogether likely that the general willingness to leave religion to a competition among religious leaders had a
symbiotic relationship to what was happening at a somewhat slower
pace in politics. The decline of social status as a force in ecclesiastical
polity seems to have preceded, and may have contributed to, its decline
in civil polity. But the action of state governments in separating religion from politics was in itself a blow at the privileges customarily
connected with social status. The lesson can scarcely have been lost
on aspiring politicians whose social position would previously have
stifled expectations of high political office.

Whatever the impact of the religious example, the Revolution
brought with it a war effort in which, as in most wars, military leadership departed from its customary peacetime congruence with social
rank, and its departure dealt another blow to the political deference
accorded the better sort. Military and social rank have always been
closely related. The locus classicus usually cited to illustrate the dedication of the Elizabethan world to a social hierarchy is the speech by
Ulysses in Shakespeare's *Troilus and Cressida*.

> Take but degree away,
> Untune that string,
> And hark, what discord follows.

The context of the speech is often forgotten. Ulysses was not
speaking, directly at least, about the social hierarchy. He was affirming the importance of military rank in a situation where military leadership, based on talent, was departing from official rank.

Rank is essential to the military, and in peacetime social and military rank can bolster each other. In the American world of the eighteenth century the two were closer than they have since become. We
have seen how rank in the colonial militia was synchronized with local
political and social prestige. Commissions as officers went only to
gentlemen or noblemen in England, only to the better sort in America. At the beginning of the revolutionary war enlisted men might
refuse to serve under an officer who was not their social superior,[14]
and Washington, moved by similar considerations, disciplined officers
for fraternizing with their troops in the Continental army.[15] But in
war the survival and safety of the state depends on talents that do not

[14] *Archives of Maryland* (Baltimore, 1892), XI, 350–51.

[15] Washington, *Writings*, Fitzpatrick, ed., X, 434, 473; XIII, 7, 22; XII, 212.

necessarily coincide with the qualities accorded deference in the social situations of peacetime.

In peacetime the militia might serve as a school of social subordination, but when it came to actual warfare, neither the teachers nor the lessons they taught were thought sufficient for winning battles. When England went to war, whether in the seventeenth or the eighteenth century, it was with professional soldiers. They were commanded by gentlemen, but in order to win it was generally necessary to jump talented officers above their previous social and military superiors. In the colonies the militia might engage in an occasional foray against the Indians under its regular officers, but when it came to sustained warfare, the militia gave way to separate volunteer or drafted companies commanded by officers whose militia rank had seldom been high. The colonels at the top of the militia generally remained peaceable. They left the fighting to newly fledged officers who had more taste and talent for it but less social standing.[16]

By the end of a winning war the structure of military command had been wrenched some distance from the social structure. Degree had not been untuned, but social and military degree were in discord. The effect on the social and political structure after the return of peace could vary. Men who had won high office in the war might be able to translate military prestige into social prestige and political power—or they might not. After the French and Indian War of 1754–63, the longest sustained conflict engaged in by the colonies before the Revolution, the Connecticut men who had achieved high military rank were not generally able to move into comparable social and political positions in Connecticut society.[17] Massachusetts military officers seem to have fared better.[18]

The military leaders who emerged from the revolutionary war faced a more complex situation than their predecessors in previous wars. The republican ideology that had blossomed in the Revolution accorded no high place to the professional soldier and generated a curious distrust of the army that had made the republic possible. The officers who joined in the postwar Society of the Cincinnati in order to preserve their wartime comradeship found themselves under fire as aspi-

[16] Harold Selesky, "Military Leadership in an American Colonial Society: Connecticut 1635–1785." (Ph.D. dissertation, Yale University, 1984).

[17] Ibid.

[18] Fred Anderson, *A People's Army: Massachusetts Soldiers and Society in the Seven Years' War* (Chapel Hill, N.C., 1984).

rants to aristocracy. And as national feeling gave way to local politics
in the 1780s, the former officers were among those who clung to a
continental viewpoint, at odds with the trend exhibited in the state
governments. The situation was complicated too by Washington himself, a national hero more revered than any other before or since, but
one who rebuffed every attempt of his officers to reach for political
power, either for themselves or for him.[19]

The military leaders of the Revolution did not, then, move automatically into a place at the top of a social hierarchy. They had been
drawn from the better sort and they returned to civil life with additional claims to that place. Frequently they retained the titles they
had earned in war—captain, colonel, major, general. But the republican ambivalence toward the military robbed the titles of the larger
significance they had carried in some colonial societies and still carried
in European society. The storm that Patrick Henry confronted when
he proposed to appoint former Continental officers to the highest ranks
of the Virginia militia suggests how great the discord was in Virginia
between social and military distinction.

At the same time the fact that men of lesser social rank had won
the highest military commands offered eloquent testimony that the
talents necessary for military leadership did not coincide with social
dignity. It had already become evident that the talents making for
religious leadership could be found outside the better sort. And
Americans had just established independent republican governments
in defiance of an imperial power operated by men whom they would
have acknowledged to be of a still better sort than any of them. In this
atmosphere it required no great imagination to reach the conclusion
that political talent might bear as little relation to social distinction as
military or religious talent.

It was an idea embedded in popular sovereignty and prevented
from emerging earlier only by strenuous efforts to discourage it. Anyone observing the election contests of the eighteenth century could
scarcely escape it. Leadership in those contests had been confined to
the better sort, especially in England, because only the better sort
could afford the expense. But contests among the elite brought out
talents that went beyond the hiring of thugs and the buying of votes.

[19]Charles Royster, *A Revolutionary People at War: The Continental Army and American
Character, 1775–1783* (Chapel Hill, N.C., 1979); F. Wayne Carp, *To Starve the
Army at Pleasure: Continental Army Administration and American Political Culture, 1775–
1783* (Chapel Hill, N.C., 1984); Richard H. Kohn, *Eagle and Sword: The Federalists
and the Creation of Military Establishment in America, 1783–1802* (New York, 1975).

And the available voting statistics suggest the future awaiting those who could exercise such talents to the full.

What the available statistics show is that the few who governed the many in the eighteenth century, despite the strenuous election campaigns we have noticed, remained mere amateurs in the art of mobilizing voters. Whether in large constituencies or small, whether in England or America, it would seem that candidates on either side enlisted only a fraction of the possible voters. For example, in the English country of Northamptonshire in 1702, 4,517 persons voted; in 1705, 4,876 persons voted, but only 2,875 voted in both elections. At Mitchell, a small Cornwall borough, 40 persons voted in 1705 and 36 in 1713, but only 18 in both elections.[20]

In the colonies, where the potential electorate probably exceeded that of England by the last quarter of the eighteenth century, the same phenomenon occurred. In a few hotly contested elections a large proportion of the qualified voters went to the polls, but usually not much more than half appeared. In Rhode Island in the 1760s, for example, where political factions contended more hotly than in most other colonies, attendance at the polls varied from 38 percent to 52 percent of the qualified voters.[21] And in the colonies too the people who voted in one election might be considerably different from those who voted in the next one. In the New York City elections of 1768 and 1769 a total of 2,234 persons voted in the two elections, but 37 percent of those who voted in 1768 failed to vote in 1769, and 25 percent of those who voted in 1769 had not voted in 1768.[22] In Halifax County, Virginia, in precisely the same years, of the 545 people who voted in the two elections, only 214 voted in both years.[23] Similarly in Burlington, New Jersey, in elections held in 1783 and 1787, a total of 502 persons voted, but only 96 voted in both elections.[24]

The volatility of voters can perhaps be appreciated more readily

[20] W. A. Speck, *Tory and Whig: The Struggle in the Contituencies, 1701–1715* (London, 1970), 19–20.

[21] David S. Lovejoy, *Rhode Island Politics and the American Revolution* (Providence, 1958), 17.

[22] Roger Champagne, "Liberty Boys and Mechanics of New York City," *Labor History* 8 (1967), 129.

[23] R. E. and B. K. Brown, *Virginia 1705–1786: Democracy or Aristocracy?* (East Lansing, Mich., 1964), 161.

[24] The poll list for 1783 is in A M Papers 1715, State Library, Trenton, N.J. That for 1787 is in H. C. Chinn, "An Early New Jersey Poll List," *Pennsylvania Magazine of History and Biography* 44 (1920), 77–81.

from an election in 1757 for Boston's four representatives in the Massachusetts assembly. On the morning of the tenth of May 528 votes were cast, and the polls closed at noon. Upon counting the ballots, the selectmen found that only three candidates had received the necessary majority. They therefore announced that the polls would again be open for an hour at three o'clock that afternoon to choose the fourth representative. In the next three hours aspiring candidates for the position rounded up 754 voters, an increase of nearly 43 percent over the total morning turnout.[25]

The figures point to a large reservoir of voters, available in these constituencies to any candidate who was able to bring them to the polls. In a given election it would have been possible to collect a majority of votes from persons who had not voted at all in the preceding election. The ability to collect votes doubtless continued to depend on a great variety of personal characteristics. Social prestige, service to the community, religion, race, sex, and a host of unnamed attributes affected a candidate's appeal, as they still do. But the process had begun that eventuated in the situation described by Robert Dahl in present-day American society, where inequalities tend to be "noncumulative," where social prestige, wealth, and political power do not necessarily coincide.[26] In such a situation political talent, however constituted, comes into its own, and politicians organize political parties to give it expression and take command of government.

That possibility, lurking in popular sovereignty from the beginning, had been the nightmare of the social and political elite who invented the doctrine and used it to advantage in their contests with the king and with one another. Hence the continual eighteenth-century denunciations of faction, as an organization designed to capture votes and power for its members. Faction was a political candidate's word for what his opponents were doing, and it implied not only a devotion to private rather than public interests but also an overuse of political art. It implied, indeed, that one's opponents were politicians, with the prejorative connotations that the word has always carried. They were not members of the better sort preparing to serve the public interest in a kind of noblesse oblige. Rather they were practitioners of political skill divorced from the dedication to public interest that the better sort—and only the better sort—were supposed and expected to exhibit.

[25] *A Report of the Record Commissioners of the City of Boston Containing the Boston Town Records, 1742 to 1757* (Boston, 1885), 304–5.

[26] *Who Governs? Democracy and Power in an American City* (New Haven, Conn., 1961).

When Madison and his colleagues at Philadelphia in 1787 invented an American people and gave them a government, it was with a view to overcoming the factions and the politicians in the state governments. The size of the new nation, Madison believed, would make it difficult for the locally oriented politicians of the states to assemble a majority faction. Control of government would then return to the public-spirited members of the better sort who alone would have the national renown to win elections in a continental contest, without regard to the talents that lesser men might devote to winning votes.

Madison did not take into account the development of political skills and aspirations that the exercise of popular sovereignty had fostered in the revolutionary generation. Neither he nor anyone else at the time anticipated that the national government would be operated by national political parties. Nor did he anticipate that he himself would take the lead in organizing the first one. Madison, of course, did not think of his Republicans as a party in the old sense: they were public-spirited citizens of the better sort—organized to save the national government from the machinations of factious politicians who had somehow taken possession of it, contrary to his expectations. But the separation of politics from social status was already well advanced in Madison's own organization and would become more so. The future lay with the politicians, with those who could organize political parties and draw on the reservoir of voters awaiting their talents.

The idea of a better sort, if not the phrase, has not wholly disappeared from the American scene nor is it likely to; and the word "politician" has continued to designate someone who manipulates the political process in a way that members of the better sort, however defined, are not supposed to. But seen in a larger context the rise of the politician and of the political parties he created was part of a restructuring of society that had been proceeding ever since the House of Commons first called up the sovereignty of the people. From the beginning the egalitarian implications of the doctrine had rested uneasily beneath the deference that the better sort expected from the rest of the population, a deference that was supposed to place the better sort "naturally" in positions of authority in the church and the armed forces as well as in the state. Political deference died a slow death, but every contest in which the few appealed to the many dealt it a blow. By the end of the eighteenth century in America and somewhat later in England, something that we call "leadership" was taking its place in the ordering of society.

The word "leader" is old, but "leader*ship*" was a term that no one seems to have felt a need for as long as the qualities it designates remained an adjunct of social superiority. The decline of deference and the emergence of leadership signalled the beginnings not only of a new rhetoric but of a new mode of social relations and a new way of determining who should stand among the few to govern the many. It signalled not only the rise of the professional politician and the religious hero but the vulnerability of any institution that denied the equality in which men and women had been created.

From its inception in the England of the 1640s the sovereignty of the people had been filled with surprises for those who invoked it. It was a more dynamic fiction than the one it replaced, more capable of serving as a goal to be sought, never attainable, always receding, but approachable and worth approaching. It has continually challenged the governing few to reform the facts of political and social existence to fit the aspirations it fosters. The presumption that social rank should convey a title to political authority was only the first casualty in its reformations, and we have not yet seen the last. The fiction endures. The challenge persists.

Index